The Virtue Ethics of Levi Gersonides

Alexander Green

The Virtue Ethics of Levi Gersonides

palgrave
macmillan

Alexander Green
SUNY - Buffalo
Williamsville, New York, USA

ISBN 978-3-319-82192-4   ISBN 978-3-319-40820-0   (eBook)
DOI 10.1007/978-3-319-40820-0

Cover illustration: © Agarunov Oktay-Abraham / Noun Project

Printed on acid-free paper

This Palgrave Macmillan imprint is published by Springer Nature
The registered company is Springer International Publishing AG
The registered company address is: Gewerbestrasse 11, 6330 Cham, Switzerland

Translations from Gersonides' Commentary on Genesis *are reprinted thanks to the permission of David Horwitz from David Horwitz,* Gersonides' Ethics: The To'alot Be-middot in Ralbag's Biblical Commentaries. *PhD Diss., Yeshiva University, 2006*

PREFACE

Over the last fifty years, Western ethical and political thought has received a barrage of criticism for their dependence on universal moral laws and have henceforth undergone a major shift by focusing on individual and cultural difference. Charles Taylor characterizes this transformation as a shift from a politics of universal dignity to a politics of difference.[1]

While the politics of universal dignity claims it stood for equal rights for all citizens, critics argue that underlying it lay a claim to a preference of certain rights over other rights. For example, the American Declaration of Independence famously began with the statement that "all men are created equal, that they are endowed by their Creator with certain unalienable Rights," but those rights were not equally applied to all citizens at the time of the founding of the USA. Concurrently, universalistic ethics has also faced an equally strong criticism from religious traditionalists who argue that universalism is imposing militarist secularism on the values of religious communities and have responded by making a case for their positions in the public sphere. Universalistic ethics and politics guided by rational principles have been strongly criticized since rationality has been presented as being violent, oppressive, falsifying and homogenizing. As a result, a counter movement to modern universalistic ethics arose, calling itself "virtue ethics," focused on diversity and difference, by reconstructing an ethics of character (*ethos*) out of elements of Aristotle's ethics of

The original version of this book was revised. An erratum to this book can be found at DOI 10.1007/978-3-319-40820-0_7.

virtue (*arete*) in his *Nicomachean Ethics* and its reception throughout the history of Western thought, which highlights the multiplicity of different ways of organizing the virtues in different cultures, religious traditions and epochs.[2]

One of the most prominent and influential virtue ethicists to reconstruct a virtue ethics for contemporary multicultural society is Alasdair MacIntyre. For MacIntyre, virtues develop as practices within a particular community and become known as a "tradition" as it develops its own form of rationality in dialogue with other competing traditions. MacIntyre builds a model of virtue as a form of practice that unifies a social group. He defines a practice as a coherent and complex form of socially established cooperative human activity in which one achieves the internal goods of activity.[3] MacIntyre argues that every tradition has certain common virtues that must serve as a common dominator for that tradition to survive, such as truthfulness, justice and courage.[4] Beyond that, there are too many different lists of virtues in order to have a consistent history, as different traditions prioritize different sets of virtues. MacIntyre lists a wide range of ethical thinkers and works in order to demonstrate this point: Homer, Sophocles, Aristotle, the New Testament, medieval thinkers (within Judaism, Christianity and Islam), Benjamin Franklin and Jane Austen.[5] The wide historical and cultural diversity of this list is reflected in their very different priorities of virtues: Homer prioritizes physical strength; the New Testament that of faith, hope and love; Benjamin Franklin that of cleanliness, silence and industry; and Jane Austen that of constancy and amiability.[6]

As such, the virtues of a community develop into a historical tradition through developing a tradition-based form of rationality. Every tradition is constantly seeking to determine the errors and resolve contradictions in its current configuration and strengthen itself by repairing these problems. This is attempted by seeking out other traditions that may have more efficient mechanisms and resources to diagnose these faults and adapting their solutions to one's own tradition. This at times requires translating the contentions of one's rivals into one's own language.[7] Thus, progress represents a limited advance from one's predecessors. As MacIntyre explains,[8]

> [the] past is never something to be merely discarded, but rather that the present is intelligible only as a commentary upon and response to the past in which the past, if necessary and if possible, is corrected and transcended,

yet corrected and transcended in a way that leaves the present open to being in turn corrected and transcended by yet some more adequate future point of view.[9]

This is why MacIntyre refers to tradition-based rationality as both a tradition-constituted enquiry and a tradition-constitutive enquiry, the first representing the values of the past that have shaped the tradition and the latter the freedom of members of that tradition to reevaluate those claims.[10] MacIntyre argues that a tradition of virtues and tradition-based rationality balances diversity and commonality better than the two alternative modern paradigms: the model of the ninth edition of the *Encyclopedia Britannica*, which attempts to reduce all ethics to a single comprehensive rational model striving for universal enlightenment, and Nietzsche's genealogical model in his *Genealogy of Morals* that works to undermine or subvert any consensus or truth, while secretly relying on it.[11]

This new form of virtue ethics is not simply the individual's development of certain virtues and perfection of the self within one political society (*polis*) as Aristotle presents it in the *Nicomachean Ethics*, but a dialog across history between competing practices and definitions of the virtues that allows for internal debate and conflict, while still rooted in a shared language of virtue. Similarly, one goal of MacIntyre's project is that "once the diversity of traditions has been properly characterized, a better explanation of the diversity of standpoints is available than either the Enlightenment or its heirs can provide."[12] In this sense, MacIntyre advocates virtue as the unifying basis for how a diversity of competing ethical models between different cultures can coexist and conflict simultaneously.

But MacIntyre recognizes that his project is inherently a Christian one and that there exists an independent Jewish tradition of virtue ethics.[13] Indeed, MacIntyre points to the dangers of a Christianity that does not recognize its roots in Judaism as a rival and competing tradition. He argues that "Christians need badly to listen to Jews. The attempt to speak for them, even on behalf of that unfortunate fiction, the so-called Judeo-Christian tradition, is always deplorable."[14] Therefore, he sees the need for Jewish ethics to serve as a rival tradition to Christian ethics to help Christians return to their ethical core and to correct deficiencies. At the same time, he admits that this must be done by adherents of the Jewish tradition from within their own tradition and not imposed from the outside, suggesting why he himself cannot carry out the project.[15]

Where does one look to find competing traditions of Jewish virtue ethics? The most influential works have been mainly Neoplatonic and/or Kabbalistic. Neoplatonic virtue ethics such as Ibn Gabirol's *Improvement of the Moral Qualities* and Bahya ibn Paquda's *Duties of the Heart* entail an ascetic journey of the soul away from this world toward God. Kabbalistic virtue ethics, such as Moses Cordovero's *Palm Tree of Devorah* and Moses Hayyim Luzzato's *Path of the Just*, advocate imitating and influencing the inner workings of the divine.[16] But there is also a distinctly Jewish Aristotelian tradition of virtue ethics that can be studied independent of the purely Neoplatonic and Kabbalistic works. This includes Moses Maimonides' (1138–1204, Spain/Egypt) *Eight Chapters* and *Laws of Character Traits*, Levi Gersonides' (1288–1344, Provence) biblical commentaries and Isaac 'Arama's biblical commentary *Binding of Isaac* (1420–1494, Spain/Italy).[17]

The nature of such an Aristotelian Jewish tradition of virtue ethics must contain multiple authors focused on answering certain basic questions about the nature of reality: How is God involved in the world, and how precisely do humans imitate that in virtuous action? What are the limits of intellectual contemplation, and what is the ethical outcome of reaching that limit? What are the goods that human beings strive for? What are different categories of virtues, and what is the relationship between them (e.g., physical, moral, intellectual, theological)? What role does luck play in ethics, and how is it compatible with the divine rule of the universe? Are there moral conflicts and how are they resolved? How is the cultivation of ethical virtues related to the development of political society, and which one takes priority in ordering human life? This book begins by examining MacIntyre's description of the nature of traditions of virtue in order to trace the first step in the development of a tradition of Jewish Aristotelian virtue ethics by asking how Gersonides challenged the Maimonidean model while still remaining within it.

Acknowledgments

The writing of this book is a culmination of many years of thinking about the relationship between the Bible and Western philosophy. I must thank numerous teachers at both the University of Toronto and the Hebrew University of Jerusalem who have guided me along the way.

The members of my doctoral committee at the University of Toronto—David Novak, Clifford Orwin, James Diamond and Alan Mittleman—have been supportive of this project throughout and I owe them a debt of gratitude. David Novak's wise guidance and encouragement is everything one could ask for in a doctoral supervisor. Thank you as well to my MA adviser, Warren Zev Harvey, who helped me set a course of studies in medieval Jewish philosophic thought which contributed to my eventual decision to work on Gersonides. I also appreciate his careful reading of this manuscript. In addition, I owe a debt as well to Robert Eisen, Steven Harvey and Marc Shapiro for graciously reading the manuscript and helping to sharpen its arguments. Thank you also to Rabbi Asher Turin for being willing to study together and for being my *chavruta* partner and to Libby Garshowitz for assisting me with some of the translations and transliterations. I also would like to express my appreciation to the faculty and staff in the Department for the Study of Religion at the University of Toronto, for their constant and generous assistance in arranging all the logistical details of the doctoral program. My new colleagues in the Department of Jewish Thought at the State University of New York, University at Buffalo, have provided me with an intellectually stimulating and collegial environment for me to finish editing this work for publication and I thank them for that.

I would also like to thank the following institutions and scholarships for their generous financial support of my work: the Social Sciences and Humanities Research Council of Canada (SSHRC), the Ontario Graduate Scholarship Program (OGS), the Shiff Family Graduate Student Award in Jewish Studies, the H. Albert Ellam Memorial Travel Grant, the McGuaig-Throop Bursary, the Molly Spitzer Award, the Department for the Study of Religion conference travel grant, the School of Graduate Studies conference travel grant, the Terek-Hedgy Graduate Scholarship in Jewish-Muslim Study, the Tikvah Scholarship in Jewish Thought and the Kathleen Coburn Fellowship.

In addition, I want to thank my parents who spent countless hours listening to my ideas as I developed them over the past few years. Most of all, I want to thank my wife Keren for her loving encouragement and patience, all of which gave me tremendous sustenance as I worked so hard to achieve this goal.

Notes

1. Charles Taylor, "The Politics of Recognition" in *Multiculturalism: Examining the Politics of Recognition*, ed. Amy Gutmann (Princeton: Princeton University Press, 1994).
2. Daniel Statman, "Introduction to Virtue Ethics" in *Virtue Ethics: A Critical Reader* (Edinburgh: Edinburgh University Press, 1997), 1–41 and Martha Nussbaum, "Virtue Ethics: A Misleading Category?" *The Journal of Ethics* 3, no. 3 (1999), 163–201. Scholars have debated whether virtue ethics exists as a singular philosophic movement with a cohesive foundation that unifies many different thinkers or is only a rubric to group critiques of different strands of modern ethics. While all these thinkers prioritize the cultivation of character, as Martha Nussbaum has pointed out, many thinkers in the past, who have been categorized as deontological or utilitarian thinkers, such as Immanuel Kant and Jeremy Bentham, have in fact their own theory of the virtues which works alongside their deontological model.
3. MacIntyre, *After Virtue*, 2nd ed. (Notre Dame: University of Notre Dame Press, 1984), 187.
4. Ibid., 192.
5. Ibid., 181.
6. Ibid., 180–187.

7. Ibid., 166.
8. Stern, "MacIntyre and Historicism," in *After MacIntyre: Critical Perspectives on the World of Alasdair MacIntyre*, eds. John Horton and Susan Mendus (Cambridge: Polity Press, 1994), 150, 151, 153.
9. MacIntyre, *After Virtue*, 146.
10. MacIntyre, *Whose Justice? Which Rationality?* (Notre Dame: University of Notre Dame Press, 1988) and Christopher Lutz, *Tradition in the Ethics of Alasdair MacIntyre* (Oxford: Lexington Book, 2004), 33
11. MacIntyre, *Three Rival Versions of Moral Enquiry: Encyclopaedia, Genealogy, and Tradition* (Notre Dame: University of Notre Dame Press, 1991). Specifically at p. 55 he says that "the intelligibility of genealogy requires beliefs and allegiances of a kind precluded by the genealogical stance."
12. MacIntyre, *Whose Justice? Which Rationality?*, 9.
13. Alan Mittleman argues that his new book on Jewish ethics is an attempt to reconstruct Jewish ethics along the lines of MacIntyre's described project in *A Short History of Ethics*. See Alan Mittleman, *A Short History of Jewish Ethics: Conduct and Character in the Context of Covenant* (West Sussex, 2012), 1–3.
14. MacIntyre, *Whose Justice? Which Rationality?*, 10–11.
15. In reviewing Lenn Goodman's book *On Justice*, he comments that
    Nothing is more important for our common culture than genuine dialogue between the different and often rival moral and religious traditions that contribute to it. Goodman's *On Justice* is a remarkable statement of what we all have to learn from the Jewish tradition of thought and practice. It is a book for moral philosophers, but it is also a book for everyone with moral concerns. (Alasdair MacIntyre, Review of Lenn Goodman, *On Justice: An Essay in Jewish Philosophy* [New Haven: Yale University Press, 1991] on the back cover of the book)
16. Mittleman, *A Short History*, 100–106 and 131–155 and Joseph Dan, *Jewish Mysticism and Jewish Ethics* (Seattle: University of Washington Press, 1986).
17. Here I am only dealing with the first two and I hope to write on 'Arama the latter in a future work. The ethics of Isaac 'Arama has been studied, but not analyzed in a larger comparative framework with regard to the nature of virtue ethics. See Bernard Septimus,

"Isaac Arama and *the Ethics*," in *Jews and Conversos as the Time of the Expulsion*, eds. Yom Tov Assis and Yosef Kaplan (Jerusalem: The Zalman Shazar Centre for Jewish History, 1999), 1–24; Sarah Heller-Wilensky, *The Philosophy of Isaac 'Arama in the Framework of Philonic Philosophy* (Jerusalem: Bialik Institute, 1956); and Baruch Frydman-Kohl, *Faith, Felicity and Fidelity in the Thought of Yishaq Arama*. DHL Dissertation, Jewish Theological Seminary of America, 2004.

CONTENTS

1 Introduction   1

2 Luck and the Virtues of Physical Preservation   19

3 Altruism and the Beneficent Virtues   63

4 Justice and the Practical Wisdom of the Individual   91

5 The Ethics of Divided Political Institutions: King, Priest and Prophet   123

6 Conclusion   157

Erratum to: The Virtue Ethics of Levi Gersonides   E1

Bibliography   175

Index   189

LIST OF ABBREVIATIONS

WORKS OF GERSONIDES CITED

Comm Deut   *Perush 'al ha-Torah (Commentary on the Pentateuch)*, vol.
                         v: Deuteronomy, ed. Jacob Leib Levi. Jerusalem: Mossad
                         ha-Rav Kook, 2000.

Comm Early Proph I   *Perush 'al ha-Neviim (Commentary on Joshua, Judges and
                         Samuel)*, ed. Jacob Leib Levi. Jerusalem: Mossad ha-Rav
                         Kook, 2008.

Comm Early Proph II   *Perush 'al ha-Neviim (Commentary on Kings, Chronicles,
                         Ezra and Nehemiah)*, ed. Jacob Leib Levi. Jerusalem:
                         Mossad ha-Rav Kook, 2008.

Comm Exod   *Perush 'al ha-Torah (Commentary on the Pentateuch)*,
                         vol. ii–iii, eds. Baruch Brenner and Eli Fraiman. Maale
                         Adumim: Maaliot, 1999–2000.

Comm Gen   *Perush 'al ha-Torah (Commentary on the Pentateuch)*, vol.
                         i, eds. Baruch Brenner and Eli Fraiman. Maale Adumim:
                         Maaliot, 1992.

Comm Leviticus   *Perush 'al ha-Torah (Commentary on the Pentateuch)*,
                         vol. iv–v, eds. Baruch Brenner and Eli Fraiman. Maale
                         Adumim: Maaliot, 2002, 2005.

Comm Megillot   *Perush 'al ha-Megillot (Commentary on the Five Scrolls)*,
                         ed. Jacob Leib Levi. Jerusalem: Mossad ha-Rav Kook,
                         2003.

Comm Numbers   *Perush 'al ha-Torah (Commentary on the Pentateuch)*, vol.
                         vi, eds. Baruch Brenner and Eli Fraiman. Maale Adumim:
                         Maaliot, 2008.

Comm Proverbs	*Perush 'al Mishlei* (*Commentary on Proverbs*), ed. Jacob Leib Levi. Jerusalem: Mossad ha-Rav Kook, 2015.
Comm Song of Songs	*Commentary on Song of Songs*, trans. Menachem Kellner. New Haven: Yale University Press, 1998.
DH	David Horwitz's translation of Gersonides' ethical lessons in David Horwitz, *Gersonides' Ethics: The To'alot be-Middot in Ralbag's Biblical Commentaries.* PhD Diss., Yeshiva University, 2006: 408–464.
Supercomm De Anima	*Supercommentary on Averroes' Commentary on De Anima*, ed. and trans. Stephen Jesse Mashbaum. In Stephen Jesse Mashbaum, *Chapters 9–12 of Gersonides' Super-commentary on Averroes' Epitome of the De Anima: The Internal Senses.* PhD Diss., Brandeis University, 1981: 1–184.
Supercomm De Animalibus	*Supercommentary on Averroes' Commentary on De Animalibus*, ed. Ahuva Gaziel. In Ahuva Gaziel, *The Biology of Levi Ben Gershom (Gersonides).* PhD Diss., Bar-Ilan University, 2008: 91–266.
Wars	*Wars of the Lord*, trans. Seymour Feldman. Philadelphia: Jewish Publication Society, 1984.

OTHER WORKS CITED

BT	Babylonian Talmud, ed. Isidore Epstein. London: Soncino Press, 1961.
DA	Aristotle, *De Anima*, trans. Robert Drew Hicks. New York: Barnes and Nobles Library, 2006.
EC	Moses Maimonides, "Eight Chapters," in *Ethical Writings of Maimonides*, eds. Raymond L. Weiss and Charles E. Buttersworth. New York: New York University Press, 1975: 59–104.
Guide	Moses Maimonides, *The Guide of the Perplexed*, trans. Shlomo Pines. Chicago: University of Chicago Press, 1963.
Kuzari	Judah Halevi, *The Kuzari*, trans. Henry Slonimsky. New York: Schocken Books, 1974.
LC	Moses Maimonides, "Laws Concerning Character Traits," in *Ethical Writings of Maimonides*, eds. Raymond L. Weiss and Charles E. Buttersworth. New York: New York University Press, 1975: 28–58.

Metaphysics	Aristotle, *Metaphysics*, trans. Hippocrates G. Apostle. Bloomington: Indiana University Press, 1966.
MT	Moses Maimonides, *Mishneh Torah*. Jerusalem: Mossad ha-Rav Kook, 1956–1968.
NE	*Nicomachean Ethics*, trans. Robert C. Bartlett and Susan D. Collins. Chicago: University of Chicago Press, 2011.
Politics	*Politics*, trans. Carnes Lord. Chicago: University of Chicago Press, 1984.
Republic	Plato, *Republic*, trans. Allan Bloom. New York: Basic Books, 1991.

LIST OF FIGURE

Fig. 4.1 The deliberation between conflicting goods   105

LIST OF TABLE

Table 1.1 The development of Gersonides' thought   10

CHAPTER 1

Introduction

GERSONIDES' DIALOGUE WITH MAIMONIDES ON ETHICS

One of the projects of Moses Maimonides in his philosophic and legal writings was to restructure the Jewish tradition around the core concepts of Aristotelian virtue ethics.[1] He does so in his two large works on ethics: *Eight Chapters*, an introduction to his commentary on the tractate *Avot* in the Mishnah, and *Laws of Character Traits*, a summary and reinterpretation of the ethics of the Jewish tradition in the first book, the *Book of Knowledge*, of his restatement of Jewish law, the *Mishneh Torah*.[2]

There are certain elements that make it distinctly Aristotelian. First, Maimonides adopts the Aristotelian model of the human soul (*psyche*) as the form (or "lifeforce") giving function and organization to the physical matter of the human body.[3] The soul as the form of the body's matter is neither completely separate nor completely unified with its matter. This model can be differentiated from modern materialism, which envisions the soul as purely physical, or modern dualism which draws no connection between the soul and the body, the soul thus being non-physical. In contrast, the Aristotelian soul has five parts: nutritive, sentient, imaginative, appetitive and rational. The nutritive part includes activities such as physical nutrition, reproduction and growth; the sentient part is the collecting of sensory data using the five senses; the imaginative part stores and reorganizes sensory data; the appetitive part is the source of the emotions and desires; and the rational part is concerned with obtaining knowledge.[4] Second, proper human action results from a perfection of certain

© The Author(s) 2016   1
A. Green, *The Virtue Ethics of Levi Gersonides*,
DOI 10.1007/978-3-319-40820-0_1

character traits, which are rooted in the appetitive part of the soul that deals with emotions or temperaments, but can be influenced by reason.[5] This appears to be the explanation for why Maimonides refers to the emotions or temperaments as *de'ot* in the *Mishneh Torah*, since it has the dual meaning of "character trait" and "knowledge."[6] Third, the different emotions of the soul mimic the larger structure of nature in that they can be seen as a spectrum with two extremes, and the perfected way is the mean.[7] For example, courage is the mean between being too fearful and being too rash, or moderation is the mean between taking too much pleasure for oneself and taking not enough pleasure for oneself. The mean is not a static middle position, but differs depending on when one ought, cases in which one ought, toward right people, reasons for the sake of which one ought and the manner one ought.[8] Though, Maimonides interestingly does not highlight the role of practical wisdom in deliberating the variability of the mean. Fourth, moral virtues, for Aristotle, are political virtues as they are controlled by a specific law; however, for Maimonides they are cultivated in a more perfect way by a divine law.[9] Fifth and last, the highest goal of human life and of the divine law is the pursuit of knowledge for its own sake and for any practical end. Aristotle describes the contemplative life as the highest, most continuous, most self-sufficient and most loved for its own sake, and knowing that God is the first existent is the first commandment in Maimonides' legal code and the highest human endeavor, represented through the metaphor of the Sultan's palace.[10]

This book will focus on where Gersonides differs from Maimonides on ethics. Gersonides continues these elements and the focus on the mean as the basis for ethics, but also adds two new categories of individualistic virtues, virtues of self-preservation and virtues of altruism, which transcend the political nature of moral virtues. The virtues of self-preservation arise as a response to "luck" as an unavoidable feature affecting everything in nature. For Maimonides, the ability to avoid the effects of luck is tied to one's intellectual perfection. He says that "providence watches over an individual endowed with perfect apprehension."[11] Contrastingly, Gersonides demonstrates that in order to deal with the seemingly capricious element of luck, human beings must focus on virtues in imitation of the nature of animal biology such as endeavor (*hishtadlut*), diligence (*ḥariṣut*) and cunning (*hitḥakmut*) in crafting stratagems (*taḥbulot*) aiming at physical self-preservation. This also affects certain of Gersonides' reasons for the commandments as he gives them reasons which are more explicitly connected to self-preservation than in earlier rabbinic discussions. Gersonides' argument implies that Maimonides did not go far enough and that knowledge must be applied more to virtues that directly focus on the body and not merely knowledge of the whole.

He bases his second model of ethical behavior, which is altruistic in nature, on the human imitation of God, who to his mind, created the laws of the universe for no self-interested benefit. Maimonides and Gersonides derive different lessons from God's altruism. For Maimonides, the overflow to others is an outcome of one's own perfection and thus humans imitate God loving-kindness (*ḥesed*) through necessarily leaving one's private contemplation to involve oneself in political leadership, especially in legislation where moral virtues are cultivated. Contrastingly, for Gersonides, altruism takes the form of a non-political universal and altruistic ethics whereby humans are obliged to cultivate the virtues of loving-kindness (*ḥesed*), grace (*ḥanina*) and beneficence (*haṭava*) in knowledge and action independent of the state.

These differences between Maimonides and Gersonides also are apparent with regard to the manifestations of self-preservation and altruism on the collective level. For example, Maimonides idealizes the unification of power in the prophet as philosopher–legislator, while Gersonides advocates the benefits of separate institutions parallel to these two models in the political institutions of the kingship, whose primary communal function is ensuring the physical preservation of the political community, and the priesthood, whose primary communal function is altruistically spreading knowledge to the political community. In Gersonides' model, the prophet takes on the role of challenging and correcting both institutions. This is an important point regarding Gersonides' philosophy of law, and tells us something about his constitutional thinking. Maimonides also highlights the supreme role of the divine law in minimizing or solving conflicts of values, while Gersonides brings out the greater role for a practical wisdom to deliberate these different conflicts. Gersonides recognizes the conflict between the objectives of physical preservation, achieving peace, and divine commands and he develops a hierarchy of priorities for how to reconcile these competing obligations.

The Hermeneutics of Narrative

Gersonides' decision to write on ethics and politics in the form of a biblical commentary is also not accidental. In fact, Gersonides' commentary is one of the first by an Aristotelian philosopher to provide a successive commentary on most of the Bible, excluding mainly the books named for individual prophets.[12] Prior to that, as Colette Sirat argues, Jewish Aristotelian philosophers did not see the Bible as a continuous text.[13] Indeed, it might even be suggested that his biblical commentary takes the place of writing a supercommentary on Averroes' commentary on the *Nicomachean Ethics* and the *Republic*.[14] However, he appears to be commenting on the ideas of the *Nicomachean Ethics* and the *Republic* both through Averroes' commentaries on Plato and Aristotle and through Maimonides' Al-Farabian interpretation of them.

The first element of Gersonides' biblical hermeneutics is the centrality of narrative. He begins his Introduction to *Commentary on the Torah* with a justification of the Bible teaching ethics and political philosophy through narratives:

> Had the Torah commanded us not to be angry except about what we ought to be angry, about the extent of the anger and about its place and time…and similarly with the other moral qualities and characteristics, then everyone would be in a constant state of sinning, except for a very small [meritorious] few. Moreover, it is inappropriate that such matters should be dealt with by commandments or prohibitions because this would cause people to become lenient in observing the rest of the commandments, since they would see that it is impossible for them to observe many of the Torah's commandments. Therefore, the Torah has aroused us regarding this part [on political philosophy] by its recounting to us, in their entirety, some of the stories of our ancestors well-known for their perfection concerning their behavior, to direct us to follow in their footsteps and to conduct ourselves in their ways. And along with this it [the Torah] tells us some of the reprehensible actions that were carried out, and the evil end that came about because of them so that we might avoid doing these same actions.[15]

He seems to have come to the novel but decisive conclusion that practical matters are more effectively discussed through examples of the lives and actions of individuals in a narrative form than in a scientific commentary or through the commandments of the law. There are two reasons that he is giving. The first is for the sake of imitation and the imagination: ethical lessons are best instructed through imitation of the life and actions of specific individuals and the most effective way to do so is through stories over that of rules since stories more effectively appeal to the imagination so that we can "follow in their footsteps and to conduct ourselves in their ways." The second is for the sake of simplicity and variability: they are based on a choice number of examples that if systematized in scientific treatises would have too many different cases and examples for people to follow without failure. The number of different potential cases of which the virtues could be applied is quite large and would lead to much confusion if listed. These are merely examples that do not claim to cover every single case and help train the individual in practical reasoning that can be applied to cases that are not mentioned in the narrative. Aristotle makes a similar statement at the beginning of the *Nicomachean Ethics*, in his stating how ethics is not a precise science like mathematics, but is based on conventions and opinions, and hence inevitably contains disputes and variability.[16] Contrary to appearances, or to what contemporary convention has it, Aristotle is not making a relativist argument, seeming to propose that there is no standard to weigh whether one decision is better than the other or that ethics is purely contingent to the regime or society. More likely he strategically does not want to lay out the metaphysical side of ethics this early in the argument in the *Nicomachean Ethics*, but is merely clarifying that ethics contains a much greater variability than metaphysics. But Gersonides took Aristotle' argument on the contingency of ethics much more literally and much farther than Aristotle himself did, asserting instead that the contingency of ethics is much more effective in narrative form and thus requires a form of writing that exemplifies that variability.[17] In fact, one can take Gersonides' reading a step further and intimate that, according to him, ethics should be presented in a narrative like the Hebrew Bible over reading a treatise such as the *Nicomachean Ethics* because its stories successfully present characters that exemplify in their actions the outcome of the cultivation of moral virtues.

The second feature of Gersonides' biblical hermeneutics is the project to derive useful or practical lessons (*to'alot*) from the text.[18] Gersonides argues that nature bequeaths to every object in nature a natural end, a *takhlit*, and a useful means to achieve these ends, a *to'elet*. In interpreting Proverbs 16:4, "the Lord hath made every things for His own purpose, yea, even the wicked for the day of evil," he derives from this that everything created by God is for the sake of a *takhlit* and a *to'elet*.[19] Scholars of Gersonides have been searching to find an external influence in Gersonides' Christian cultural milieu for his unique style of deriving lessons from the biblical text, but to no avail.[20] Gersonides was more likely influenced by a general trend of philosophical Jewish exegetes in Provence who derived *to'alot* as a means of showing how the Torah is a tool for different forms of perfection.[21] However, Gersonides' unique system of *to'alot* can also be seen as an internal development from within his own thought, taking on two distinct stages. *To'alot* are first most prominent in Gersonides' supercommentary on Averroes' commentary on *De Animalibus* (in Hebrew: *Sefer Ba'alei Ḥayyim*). There he shows how most of the different organs of animal creatures are constructed in such a way that allows the creature to best pursue its natural ends.[22] In doing so, he furthers Averroes' synthesis of Galen's work *De Usu Partium Coporis Humani* (*On the Usefulness of the Parts of the Body*), which in Hebrew is *To'elet ha-Evarim*, with Aristotle's biological thought. Galen emphasizes there the usefulness of all the different parts. Gersonides applies this concept of usefulness, *to'elet*, to the biblical text around the beginning of 1329 with his Commentary on Esther. There is thus an implicit parallelism between animal biology and the biblical text: like the body, every part of the biblical text is constructed to usefully guide man toward achieving their natural ends, from the highest to the lowest. With regard to the ethical lessons, Gersonides' concept of *to'alot* are practical maxims that enable one to achieve perfection. According to Gersonides, one can derive these useful maxims, which are a form of advice or recommendations, from studying human behavior in the narratives of the Hebrew Bible which suggest the best means to cultivate virtues.

The method of my project will be to trace certain common trends among Gersonides' virtue ethics, even though he purposely wrote it in a narrative and seemingly scattered fashion. While this may appear at first in contradiction to Gersonides' own designated method, I argue that his usage of similar terms in multiple locations throughout his writings is a hint for careful readers to draw the connections between his disparate ideas on ethics and politics.

Ethics in the Development of Gersonides' Thought

Gersonides begins to write on practical philosophy around 1328, before which he had little to say on it. Why the sudden shift? It is impossible to know for sure, but I argue that one can interpret the shift in Gersonides' research interests from strictly scientific matters in writing supercommentaries on Averroes' commentaries on Aristotle's scientific works, as well as the *Wars of the Lord* (1317–1325), to writing biblical commentaries (1325 onward) as a gradual shift in focus in Gersonides' thought.[23] This shift is similar to that of Socrates, as described in the Platonic dialogues as the "Socratic turn," an expression that refers to Socrates' account in Plato's *Phaedo*, which is set on the day before his execution, of how as a young man he studied natural philosophy, but at a certain point in his life dramatically shifted interest to philosophical conversations about opinions regarding moral and political matters.[24] Gersonides never explicitly announced such a transition, but it can be discerned if one takes note of the shift in genres and the changing nature of his mature writings.[25]

There are a few possible ways to explain such a turn. One possible explanation is to consider the serious impact which may have been made on Gersonides by Samuel ben Judah of Marseille's translation into Hebrew of Averroes' *Commentary* on Aristotle's *Nicomachean Ethics* and the *Republic* in the early 1320s.[26] Around that same time, in the 1320s and 1330s, the *Nicomachean Ethics* became a central text in Gersonides' surrounding Christian culture, where study of that pivotal work became a requirement for Dominicans of Provence; indeed, Gerald Odonis and Jean Buridan both published popular commentaries on the *Nicomachean Ethics*.[27] At the same time, Joseph Ibn Kaspi wrote a summary of the *Nicomachean Ethics* and *the Republic* entitled *Oblation of Silver (Terumat Kesef)* and recommended the *Nicomachean Ethics* highly for his son's education in his *Book of Admonition (Yoreh De'ah)*.[28] Since Gersonides had access to the rest of the available Hebrew translations of Averroes' and of Aristotle's works, and refers both to the *Ethics* and the *Republic* in his own works,[29] it seems highly likely he had access to them and seriously thought about them, like the rest of Aristotle's scientific or theoretical work, even though he did not write supercommentaries on the practical works.[30] Another possible explanation is that Gersonides witnessed the dangers of asceticism of Jewish philosophers studying Averroes, who withdrew interest from writing on the practical sciences, which as he had previously read Averroes had once caused him to lose interest in writing on the practical sciences.[31] Yet his study of the writings of Averroes had shown him also that practical implications, ignored by earlier Jewish Averroists, can be discerned. This new awareness resembles the conclusions that Latin Averroists came to during that period.[32] Furthermore, Gersonides worked for the Pope when the Papacy was situated at Avignon in its "Babylonian Captivity" during the 1320s, being hired to do astronomical research. The Pope was involved at the same time in a famous dispute with Emperor Louis of Bavaria, which led to the excommunication of Marsilius of Padua and William of Ockham, and which had brought Marsilius to write his *Defender of the Peace* (1324) and William of Ockham to compose his many political writings advocating a form of separation of powers. As a result, it may be that Gersonides saw it as a necessary outcome of his theoretical study to also be involved in the practical sphere, even if he may still have viewed the latter as less important than the former. While it is unclear whether Gersonides read Latin, he could not have ignored the arguments of these works due to their political relevance.[33]

Another possible reason for this ethical-political shift can be traced, I argue, to Gersonides' development of philosophical theories of astronomy and astrology.[34] I trace this to a three-part intellectual development (see map below). In the first stage of Gersonides' intellectual development, from 1317 to 1322, he focused mostly on the terrestrial sciences, with little interest in the practical sciences. Similarly, Gersonides reports his observations in his *Astronomy* dating from 1321, but does not publish anything during this time.[35] His major intellectual endeavor during this period was his commentaries on Averroes' epitomes on the first four books on natural science: *Physics, De Caelo, De Generatione et Corruptione,* and *Meteorology* written between June 1321 and January 1322. During this period, Gersonides also wrote a draft of book six of *Wars* dealing with creation. There were no biblical commentaries written during this time.

In the second stage of Gersonides' thought, from end of 1323–1328, he discovers the practical intellect rooted in animal biology and the soul in his supercommentaries on Averroes' epitomes on *De Animalibus* and *De Anima.* He applies these lessons to his writings of Books 1–4 of *Wars.* In Book 4 of *Wars,* Gersonides compares the practical intellect in animals and humans; quoting from Aristotle's biological writings, he asserts that both species aim for preservation through different means.[36] He also begins writing biblical commentaries as well during this period. During this stage in his *Commentary on Song of Songs,* Gersonides also develops a higher model of ethics based on his understanding of astronomy in which the stars are ordered for this worldly benefit. Imitating the stars, humans must act beneficently to help others achieve intellectual knowledge. In his *Commentary on Ecclesiastes,* written during the same period, he reads the work as an investigation of the different ways and ends of life achieved through studying common opinions (*endoxa*) of good and evil.[37] But Gersonides does not reference the *Nicomachean Ethics* there, perhaps implying to the reader that he has not studied it in depth yet.[38] Instead, he proposes that this work is parallel to Aristotle's *Topics* (*Niṣuaḥ*) and *Metaphysics* (*'Aḥar ha-Ṭevaʿ*).

In Gersonides' third stage of development, from the end of 1328 onward, he begins to concurrently and seriously write both biblical commentaries with ethical and political lessons, and continue his astronomical research, having performed some of his most productive experiments between 1333 and 1339.[39] Gersonides completed a first draft of the astronomical section of *Wars* (Book 5) in December 1328 after working heavily on experiments all throughout 1328.[40] I do not think the relationship between his astronomical research and the ethical and political lessons of his biblical commentaries are merely coincidental. According to Gersonides, the motions of the different celestial spheres and astral bodies contained within, as studied by astronomy and astrology, affect natural events in the world like earthquakes and especially human temperaments. Gersonides comes to accept that astrology explains the seemingly random operations and physical occurrences of all living beings, including humans, and is thus an essential part of their being that cannot be ignored and must be explored further. Ethics is thus construed by Gersonides as a necessary human response to the randomness of this reality through a new form of reading the Bible, deriving practical or useful lessons (*to'alot*) from the text, discussed later, and deriving a set of virtues that are a result of them as exemplified by biblical characters. One sees this change in Gersonides' thinking in his shift from Ecclesiastes where physical and moral perfections are separate, to Genesis where physical perfection is a central component of political philosophy in the form of the *to'alot ha-middot*, hinting to an increasingly materialistic focus to ethics. The first work to employ the *to'alot ha-middot* is his commentary on Esther, which is quite fitting due to its primary concern with human preservation.[41]

This study reads Gersonides' ethical thought through the third stage of its development in his biblical commentaries, without ignoring the earlier stages. Gersonides develops some of the pieces of his model in the earlier stages and only puts them all together in the third and final stage.

The following chart shows the development of the three stages in Gersonides' thought (Table 1.1)[42]:

ETHICS IN THE MODERN SCHOLARSHIP ON GERSONIDES

Gersonides is recognized by historians as one of the most innovative Jewish philosophers of the medieval period in metaphysics and physics, though seldom in the fields of ethics or politics.[43] In fact, he mentions ethics and politics only in sporadic sections in his magnum opus *Wars of the Lord*, relegating these topics to his *Commentary on the Torah*. One reason that he explicitly gives for this omission is that there is nothing normative and scientific to ethics, suggesting that the discipline of ethics is merely utilitarian and subordinate to more important scientific and metaphysical pursuits.[44] In recent years some scholars have rejected the conventional

Table 1.1 The development of Gersonides' thought

Supercommentaries on Averroes on Aristotle	Wars of the Lord	Biblical commentaries
1 June 1321–January 1322: Commentaries on Averroes' epitomes *Physics, De Caelo, De Generatione et Corruptione*, and *Meteorology*	1317: First draft of Book 6, on creation 1321: Draft of Book 6 completed, but not circulated 1321–1324: Preliminary versions of Books 5–6	
2 1323: Averroes' *Middle Commentaries on Porphyry's Isagoge*; on the six books of Aristotle's *Organon*; and on *De Anima* and *De Animalibus*	1325: Books 1–3 Nov 1328: Book 4, Book 5 part 1–2	Job (Dec 1325) Song of Songs (June/July 1326) Ecclesiastes (Oct 1328) Proverbs (Completed April 1338)[a]
3	Dec 1328: Book 5, part 3 Jan 1329: Book 6, part 1–2	Esther (March 1329) Ruth (May 1329) Pentateuch (1329–1338) Former Prophets (Jan 1338) Daniel (Jan–Feb 1338) Ezra, Nehemiah, Chronicles (Feb–Mar 1338)

[a]Glasner, "Development of the Genre," 11

notion that Gersonides had lacked any interest in practical concerns, and likewise they have rejected the notion that there is any essential scientific grounding to the practice which he advocated.[45] It is argued that another reason for the neglect of his ethics is that they are located in his biblical commentaries, and hence they have often been considered by scholars to be a mere popularization for the masses of his more important philosophic and theological work, *Wars of the Lord*.[46] In fact, the scholar Amos Funkenstein goes so far as describing Gersonides' biblical commentaries as "boring," "non-esoteric," and "dogmatic."[47] However, over the last few decades, scholars have begun to challenge these assumptions. Recent studies have found rich material in Gersonides' biblical commentaries that are curiously not at all present in *Wars of the Lord,* such as reflections on the ideas of chosenness and covenant (by Robert Eisen), on halakha (by Assael Ben-Or and Carmiel Cohen), on ethics (by David Horwitz), and on politics (by Esti Eisenmann).[48] And there has also been an impetus to critically edit Gersonides' commentaries such as the carefully annotated edition of Gersonides' *Commentary on the Pentateuch* by Baruch Braner, Eli Freiman, and Carmiel Cohen and even translate into English a few of Gersonides' commentaries such as A.L. Lassen's 1946 translation of Gersonides' *Commentary on Job*, Menachem Kellner's 1998 translation of Gersonides' *Commentary on Song of Songs*.

As a result, this study will challenge the longstanding scholarly consensus that Gersonides' ethics was considered unimportant by him or merely a repetition of Maimonides' ethics with slight variations, while also arguing that he develops a different approach to ethics and politics.[49]

NOTES

1. There has been much scholarship on this topic. Some central articles and books include the following: Herbert Davidson, "The Middle Way in Maimonides' Ethics," *Proceedings—American Academy for Jewish Research* 54 (1987), 31–72; Marvin Fox, "The Doctrine of the Mean in Aristotle and Maimonides: A Comparative Study," in *Interpreting Maimonides: Studies in Methodology, Metaphysics, and Moral Philosophy* (Chicago: University of Chicago Press, 1995), 93–123; Daniel Frank, "Anger as a Vice: A Maimonidean critique of Aristotle's Ethics," *History of Philosophy Quarterly* 7, no. 3 (1990), 269–281; Kenneth Seeskin, "Maimonides' Appropriation of Aristotle's ethics" in *The Reception of Aristotle's Ethics*, ed. Jon Miller (Cambridge: Cambridge University Press, 2013), 107–112; David Shatz, "Maimonides' Moral Theory" in *The Cambridge Companion to Maimonides*, ed. Kenneth Seeskin (Cambridge: Cambridge University Press, 2005), 167–192; Raymond Weiss, *Maimonides' Ethics: The Encounter of Philosophic and Religious Morality* (Chicago: University of Chicago Press, 1991). Dov Nelkin has preceded me in arguing that there is a tradition of Jewish virtue ethics within rabbinic literature. I am distinguishing the Maimonidean model from the rabbinic model in that Maimonides' model is more explicitly Aristotelian. See Dov Nelkin, *Recovering Jewish Virtue Ethics* (PhD diss., University of Virginia, 2003).

2. He adopts the ethical framework of Aristotle's *Nicomachean Ethics*, as interpreted in Al-Farabi's *Aphorisms of a Statesman* (*Fusul al-Madani*). When writing *Eight Chapters*, Maimonides did not have

access to Aristotle's text directly and relied heavily on Al-Farabi's *Aphorisms of a Statesman*. See Herbert Davidson, "Maimonides' *Shemonah Peraqim* and Alfarabi's *Fusūl al-Madani*," *Proceedings of American Academy for Jewish Research* 31 (1963), 33–50. However, it is highly possible that when writing the *Mishneh Torah* in Egypt he had seen a copy of the Arabic translation of the *Nicomachean Ethics*. See Steven Harvey, "The Sources of the Quotations from Aristotle's *Ethics* in the *Guide of the Perplexed* and the *Guide to the Guide*," *Jerusalem Studies in Jewish Thought* 14 (1998), 100–101.

3. *DA*, 27–29 (2.1).

4. *NE*, 23–25 (1.13) and *EC*, 61–64 (Chapter 1).

5. Maimonides does not explicitly refer to "practical wisdom" and there is a large scholarly debate about why. See Chap. 4, section "Practical Wisdom: Deliberation and Choice". Nonetheless, he identifies the mean with wisdom: "Every man whose character traits all lie in the mean is called a wise man…if he moves only to the mean and his humble, he is called a wise man; this is the measure of wisdom" (*LC*, 29–30 [1.4-5]).

6. Compare Mishnah Avot 4:10 to Ps. 73:11 and Jer. 3:15. Discussed in Weiss, *Maimonides' Ethics*, 89. Maimonides uses the first definition of *de'ah* in his own *MT*, *Book of Knowledge, Laws of the Foundations of the Torah* 4:8–9 to describe "intellect" or "separate intelligence." See Bernard Septimus, "What did Maimonides mean by 'madda'?" in *Meah She'arim: Studies in Medieval Jewish Spiritual Life, in Memory of Isadore Twersky*, eds. Gerald Blidstein, Ezra Fleischer and Bernard Septimus (Jerusalem: Magnes Press, 2001), 96–102.

7. *EC*, 67–68 (Chapter 4) and *LC*, 29–30 (1.4-6). Fox, "The Doctrine of the Mean," 101: "Aristotle's answer is that the mean is the way in which nature and art normally achieve their goals of proper excellence" because "nature does not itself give us specific norms or standards of behavior, nor tell us what virtuous character is, apart from its general principle that the middle way is the best…nature gives us only the form and not the content of moral life."

8. *NE*, 33–36 (2.6).

9. *NE*, 229–235 (10.9); *Guide*, 381–385 (II 40) and 510–512 (III 27).

10. *NE*, 223–226 (10.7); *MT*, *Book of Knowledge, Laws of the Foundations of the Torah* 1.1; *Guide*, 618–620 (III 51).

11. *Guide*, 624 (III 51).
12. While Gersonides' writings were popular and published consistently from the time of his writing until the present, some of the writings of the more radical philosophic biblical exegetes in Provence were lost and only recovered over the last 200 years. Two notable examples are Joseph Ibn Kaspi and Nissim of Marseilles. What differentiates Gersonides, as I will show later, from the Maimonidean tradition and from his Jewish Provençal contemporaries, is the centrality of his new interpretation within the practical realm of ethics and politics. The radical philosophic biblical exegetes marginalized practicality also in the realm of *halakha*. It is noteworthy to mention Ibn Kaspi's famous story about not remembering details in Jewish law due to his focus on metaphysics. See Joseph ibn Kaspi, *Yoreh De'ah*, ed. and trans. Israel Abrahams in *Hebrew Ethical Wills* (Philadelphia: Jewish Publication Society, 1926), 151–152.
13. Sirat, "Gersonide, la scholastique et le commentaire biblique," 2. There were Jewish Aristotelian biblical commentaries by Samuel ibn Tibbon, Moses ibn Tibbon, Levi ben Avraham, Menachem Meiri and Nissim ben Moses of Marseilles, but they were on selected biblical sections.
14. David Horwitz, *Gersonides' Ethics: The To'alot Be-middot in Ralbag's Biblical Commentaries* (PhD diss., Yeshiva University, 2006), 190. One challenge to this argument is: how do we know that Gersonides is always responding to Aristotle even when not citing him? Couldn't he have come up with these ideas without Aristotle? Could not many of them be almost "common sense?" My response is that Gersonides' entire philosophic career in physics, astronomy, logic, biology and others is centered around commenting on Averroes' interpretation of Aristotle. It would be a bit odd for him to suddenly decide when it comes to ethics and politics that Aristotle is not the center of his oeuvre, especially when he makes references to both the *Ethics* and the *Republic* in his writings.
15. *Comm Gen*, 2.
16. *NE*, 3–4 (1.3).
17. For a discussion of parallel in the medieval Christian world, see: Judson Boyce Allen, *The Ethical Poetic of Later Middle Ages* (Toronto: University of Toronto Press, 1982), 1–13.
18. Gersonides referred to the plural of *to'elet* as *to'alot*, though the first editor, Yeḥ'iel ben Shlomo Maharih (1825–1873), changed the

plural of *to'elet* to *to'aliyot*. See Menachem Kellner, "Gersonides' To'aliyyot: Sixteenth Century Italy Versus Nineteenth Century Spain" in *As A Perennial Spring: A Festschrift honoring Rabbi Dr. Norman Lamm*, ed. Bentsi Cohen (New York, 2013), 281 and 287.

19. *Comm Proverbs*, 71 (on Proverbs 16:4).
20. Gad Freudenthal, "Gersonide, Génie Solitaire", in *Les Méthodes de Travail de Gersonide et le Maniement du Savoir chez les Scolastiques*, eds. Colette Sirat, Sara Klein-Braslavy and Olga Weijers (Paris, 2003), 299–304.
21. Yechiel Tzeitkin, "'The Straight Path Our Forefathers Followed': *To'alot* Interpretation of Biblical Narratives in Provençal Exegesis," *Jewish Studies* (*Ma'adei ha-Yahadut*) 49 (2013), 103–130.
22. Ahuva Gaziel, *The Biology of Levi Ben Gershom (Gersonides)* (PhD diss., Bar-Ilan University, 2008), 72–74.
23. A list of the dates can be found in Seymour Feldman, "Introduction," in *Wars*, vol. i, 3–31, 55–60.
24. Plato, *Phaedo*, 97a–99a.
25. Ruth Glasner, "The Evolution of the Genre of the Commentary in Gersonides," *Da'at* 74–75, 185–196.
26. Lawrence V. Berman, "Greek into Hebrew: Samuel ben Judah of Marseilles: Fourteenth Century Philosopher and Translator" in *Jewish Medieval and Renaissance Studies*, ed. Alexander Altmann (Cambridge: Cambridge University Press, 1967), 289–320.
27. George Wieland, "The Reception and Interpretation of Aristotle's *Ethics*," in *The Cambridge History of Later Medieval Philosophy*, eds. Norman Kretzmann, Anthony Kenny, Jan Pinborg and Eleonore Stump (Cambridge: Cambridge University Press, 1982), 662–668. Warren Zev Harvey suggests that there may be further parallels between Gersonides and Odonis. See Warren Zev Harvey, "Gersonides, Odonis, and the Heart Analogy," in *Studies in the History of Culture and Science: a Tribute to Gad Freudenthal*, eds. Resianne Fontaine, Ruth Glasner, Reimund Leicht, and Giuseppe Veltri (Leiden: Brill, 2011), 356–359.
28. Ibn Kaspi, *Terumat Kesef* and *Yoreh De'ah*, 133 and 144. It was likewise on the curriculum of a group of Jewish intellectuals in Provence, a bit later, entitled *Shoshan Limudim*. See Lawrence V. Berman, "A Manuscript Entitled *Shoshan Limudim* and the Group of *Me'aynim* in Provence," in *Kiryat Sefer* 53 (1978), 368–372.

29. Gersonides references the *Nicomachean Ethics* (*Sefer ha-Middot*) explicitly at *Comm Gen*, 5 (in Intro), 85–86 (on Gen 2:4–3:24) and *Comm Deut*, 41 (on Deut. 6:5). Gersonides references the *Republic* (*Medina ha-Ḥashuva*) explicitly at *Wars*, vol. ii, 36 (2.2); *Wars* vol. iii, 340 (6.1.18); and *Comm Gen*, 76 (on Gen. 1:24–31). Generally when Gersonides references one of Aristotle's works, he is actually referring to the Hebrew translation of Averroes' *Commentary* on that work.

30. Cf. Steven Harvey, "The Nature and Importance of Averroes' Middle Commentary on the Ethics and the Extent of its Influence on Medieval Jewish Philosophy," in *Averroes et les Averroïsmes Juif et Latin*, ed. J.-B. Brenet (Turnhout, Belgium: Brepols, 2007), 271–272. Harvey argues that Samuel ben Judah of Marseille's translation had little impact on medieval Jewish thought. If my interpretation of Gersonides is correct, this would be evidence of the first serious impact made by Samuel ben Judah of Marseille's translation on medieval Jewish thought. Similarly with the *Republic*, it is not clear what other sources were accessible to Gersonides other than Samuel ben Judah's translation.

31. Rafael Jospe, "Rejecting Moral Virtue as the Ultimate Human End," in *Studies in Islamic and Judaic Traditions*, ed. William Brinner and Stephen Ricks (Atlanta: Scholars Press, 1986), 185–204.

32. The political Averroists criticized the Thomistic synthesis of Aristotle with Christian theology, focusing on a more practical, this-worldly and materialistic Aristotle. This appears less consistent with Averroes' unification of philosophy and power, but with the apparent crediting of Averroes with holding a separation between reason and faith. See Charles Butterworth, "What is Political Averroism?" in *Averroismus im Mittelalter und in der Renaissance*, eds. Friedrich Niewöhner and Loris Sturlese (Zurich: Spur Verlag, 1994), 239–250 and Alan Gewirth, "Philosophy and Political Thought in the Fourteenth Century," in *The Forward Movement of the Fourteenth Century*, ed. Francis Lee Utley (Columbus: Ohio State University Press, 1961), 125–164.

33. David Horwitz begins to sketch some similarities between Gersonides and Marsilius of Padua. See Horwitz, *Gersonides' Ethics*, 112–122.

34. Ruth Glasner also notes that Gersonides' intellectual activities can be divided into three periods. In the first period, Gersonides claimed

to be "a mathematician, natural scientist, and philosopher," in the second period he turned away from metaphysics and Aristotelian science, and in the third period Gersonides focused on mathematical astronomy. See Ruth Glasner, *Gersonides: A Portrait of a Fourteenth-Century Philosopher-Scientist* (Oxford: Oxford University Press, 2015), 16–18. I mostly follow Glasner in the division, though I date the division between stages slightly differently due to a focus on practical philosophy.

35. J. L. Mancha, "Levi ben Gerson's Astronomical Work: Chronology and Christian Context," *Science in Context* 10, no. 3 (1997), 474.
36. *Wars*, 176–177 (4.5).
37. Ruth Ben-Meir, *Gersonides Commentary on Ecclesiastes: Commentary and Text* (PhD diss., Hebrew University of Jerusalem, 1993).
38. Ibid., 116.
39. Ibid., and 474.
40. Mancha, "Levi ben Gerson's Astronomical Work," 490 ("Table 1: Dated and Datable Observations in Levi's *Astronomy*").
41. Collette Sirat, "Gersonide, la scholastique et le commentaire biblique," 2012 (unpublished), 12.
42. Glasner, "Development of the Genre," 1–7.
43. This facet of Gersonides' thought is absent from the major histories of medieval Jewish philosophy. See Isaac Husik, *A History of Mediaeval Jewish Philosophy* (New York: Harper and Row, 1966), 328–361; Julius Guttmann, *Philosophies of Judaism*, trans. David Silverman (New York: Schocken, 1964), 236–254; Colette Sirat, *A History of Jewish Philosophy in the Middle Ages* (Cambridge: Cambridge University Press, 1990), 282–308; and Eliezer Schweid, *The Classic Jewish Philosophers: from Saadia through the Renaissance*, trans. Leonard Levin (Leiden: Brill, 2008), 335–356.
44. *Wars*, vol i, 130 (1.4).
45. Warren Zev Harvey, "The Philosopher and Politics: Gersonides and Crescas," in *Scholars and Scholarship: The Interaction Between Judaism and Other Cultures*, ed. Leo Landman (New York: Yeshiva University Press, 1990), 53–65; Ibid, "Ethical Theories among Medieval Jewish Philosophers," in *The Oxford Handbook of Jewish Ethics and Morality* (Oxford: Oxford University Press, 2013), 95; Menachem Kellner, "Politics and Perfection: Gersonides vs. Maimonides," *Jewish Political Studies Review* 6 (1994), 49–82; and

Hava Tirosh-Samuelson, *Happiness in Pre-Modern Judaism: Virtue, Knowledge and Well-Being* (Cincinnati: Hebrew Union College Press, 2003), 349–372.

46. Guttmann, *Philosophies of Judaism*, 237. Though we do see ample references to the biblical commentaries in Charles Touati, *La Pensée Philosophique et Théologique de Gersonide* (Paris: Les Editions de Minuit, 1973).

47. Amos Funkenstein, "Gersonides' Biblical Commentary: Science, History, and Providence (or: The Importance of Being Boring)," in *Studies on Gersonides*, ed. Gad Freudenthal (Leiden: Brill, 1993), 306.

48. Robert Eisen, *Gersonides on Providence, Covenant, and the Chosen People: a Study in Medieval Jewish philosophy and Biblical Commentary* (Albany: State University of New York Press, 1995); Assael Ben-Or, *Commandments and Philosophy in Gersonides' Thought* (PhD diss., Bar-Ilan University, 2000); Carmiel Cohen, *Legal Exegesis through Peshat in Gersonides' Commentary on the Torah* (PhD diss., Hebrew University of Jerusalem, 2007); Horwitz, *Gersonides' Ethics*; and Esti Eisenmann, "Social and Political Principles in Gersonides' Thought" in *Religion and Politics in Jewish Thought: Essays in Honor of Aviezer Ravitzky*, eds. Benjamin Brown, Menachem Lorberbaum, Avinoam Rosenak and Yedidia Z. Stern (Jerusalem: Israel Democracy Institute, 2012), 319–347.

49. In this regard, my project is building on the groundbreaking studies of Eisen, Horwitz and Eisenmann.

CHAPTER 2

Luck and the Virtues of Physical Preservation

One difference between Maimonides and Gersonides on ethics is the emphasis put on the preservation of the body in the cultivation of character and action. Maimonides does not focus on this at all in his ethical works and discusses it at the end of the *Guide* as the lowest form of perfection. In contrast, Gersonides redefines the practical intellect with physical preservation as its main goal. Thus he makes virtues that strive to achieve this end a central part of his ethical lessons, such as endeavor (*hishtadlut*), diligence (*ḥariṣut*) and cunning (*hithakmut*) in crafting stratagems (*taḥbulot*), along with arts which also now serve this purpose. Humans share this practical intellect with the animal world and cannot ignore this commonality in their cultivation of virtue.

THE PRACTICAL INTELLECT AND PHYSICAL PRESERVATION

In Aristotle's division of the human soul into five parts, he further divides the rational part into two capacities: theoretical and practical. The theoretical part contemplates the necessary beings in the universe, while the practical part deliberates about the best course of action among matters that are contingent for human life.[1] Gersonides adopts this Aristotelian framework, but adds a more specific goal for the practical intellect, which is that it is the faculty that deals with all concerns of physical preservation and survival.[2] For Gersonides, this is what the Bible is referring to in "knowledge of good and evil."[3] He explains that the practical intellect uses three other parts of the human soul in guiding the process from

© The Author(s) 2016
A. Green, *The Virtue Ethics of Levi Gersonides*,
DOI 10.1007/978-3-319-40820-0_2

the sentient faculty to the imaginative faculty to the appetitive faculty.[4] The five senses observe the surrounding world, which is then used by the imaginative faculty (*koah ha-medamme*) to combine these senses to form a judgment.[5] As a result of this judgment, the imaginative faculty awakens the appetitive faculty (*koah ha-mit'orer*) to desire or reject that sensed object, leading to physical motion, such as an action.[6]

Nonhuman animals achieve physical self-preservation through bodily organs and not with the practical intellect, such as instinctual desires, skills or mental powers, which achieve the same goal without the human ability to consider multiple options for how to achieve self-preservation and deliberate about which to choose. Gersonides explains that, for animals, the practical intellect is manifest in bodily organs to protect against predators, so that some animals are endowed with horns, cloven hooves or beaks to keep them from harm, or to enable predatory animals to catch prey; there are bodily organs for protection against the environment, such as wool, feathers, scales and poison; and there are bodily organs for offensive survival, such as limbs of carnivorous animals which are necessary for killing their prey.[7] Some animals have instinctual desires built in for their survival. For example, a natural instinct of a lamb is to run away from a wolf upon seeing it, even though it does not know that the wolf will harm it, and even though it may not have previously seen a wolf. Or many birds flee from predator birds although they have never seen them previously; for example, birds know they have to migrate north in summer and south in winter, even though they do not know whether the place to which they are to migrate is beneficial for them.[8] The last disposition many animals have is a skill or mental power. For example, bees make hives for breeding and to make honey from which they are nourished when there is no food, without having a practical intellect that orders them how to use these activities.[9]

According to Gersonides, the practical intellect is necessary for human beings, who possess reason and cannot rely on a biological organ, skill or desire; instead, they must construct arts (*melakha, techné*) by perfecting their imagination. Man has practical arts because he has no bodily material for his protection, so he was given the capacity to make clothing and houses, and he has no natural organs for self-defense or for conquest over those animals he desires to eat, so he has the ability to make weapons of war and for hunting. Man cannot find proper food without labor, and hence he was given the capacity to work the earth and to prepare food.[10] Since man's matter is too fine to grow wool, fur or horns, he was therefore given a rational faculty to achieve the same purpose.[11]This is why man was given hands and feet as they are the most perfect organs for creating practical arts.[12] In commenting on "his hands are as rods of gold set with beryl,"[13] Gersonides states that "his *hands* hint at the practical intellect since the hands are the most distinctive and the most perfected of the organs for the accomplishment of all the practical arts."[14] Indeed, man can achieve the same ends that animals achieve through biological organs, skill or desire by constructing arts to fulfill the same purpose. Gersonides sees this exemplified in the story of the Garden of Eden, in which he views Eve as a metaphor for the practical intellect. In his reading of the story, Adam represents the material intellect, the physiobiological capacity for knowledge, striving for theoretical perfection and Eve the practical intellect striving for physical perseverance.[15] He interprets the line "it is not good that man should be alone"[16] as hinting to the fact that the theoretical intellect cannot exist without the active operations of the practical intellect in man. He adds that

> for by himself he would not be able to attain it [intellectual perfection], since a considerable part of his time would be required first in the preparation of his food and in performing work (of various kinds) necessary for the subsistence of his body. Therefore God, may He be blessed, consented to create a helpmate for him, namely woman.[17]

Just as Adam needs Eve to assist him in physical self-preservation, through her focus on the practical arts, the material intellect likewise needs the practical intellect.[18] Though, while one is dependent on the other, they still carry out their operations quite independently.

Gersonides' interpretation of the practical intellect as rooted in the needs of the body results in a conception of practical wisdom (*phronesis*) which, unlike Aristotle's, is not dependent on the study of the larger principles of the physical and metaphysical world. Aristotle's *Nicomachean Ethics* presents one of the strongest cases for understanding the realm of practical wisdom as neither reducible to a material art (*techné*) nor a theoretical science (*episteme*), but as falling somewhere between both. Practical wisdom is an intellectual virtue, which necessarily operates in all the moral virtues. Aristotle offers an ideal form of practical wisdom, which operates along with theoretical wisdom. Suggesting that knowledge of universals and particulars are both crucial components of practical wisdom, Aristotle states, "and prudence is not concerned with the universals alone but must also be acquainted with the particulars."[19] He also adds that "prudence is bound up with action. As a result, one ought to have [knowledge of] both [universals and particulars]."[20] In the next chapter, he goes on to describe that one may err in one's deliberations concerning either the universal or the particular, such as by thinking that all heavy water is bad to drink or that this water is heavy. At the same time, he also limits the practicability of this for most people, arguing that practical wisdom without theoretical wisdom is sometimes more effective. He develops this in his example of choosing healthier chicken. For example, an individual who knows the theoretical principle of biology knows that light meats are easily digested and healthy, but may be ignorant of the practical detail of which meats are light and thus are not going to produce health. Contrastingly, an individual who knows just the practical detail of which light meats are healthy will produce health, even if he is completely ignorant in biology.[21]

One can see an example of how Gersonides' interpretation of Aristotelian practical intellect and practical wisdom have a distinct goal and method of operation than the theoretical intellect through his reference to Aristotle's *Nicomachean Ethics* in his commentary on Genesis.[22] Gersonides quotes *Nicomachean Ethics* 1.4 (1095a15–25) as evidence that the ends of human practical decision-making are the same ones that animals have that arise from sensation, such as pleasure (*ha-ʿarev*) and pain (*bilti ʿarev*), the useful (*moʿil*) and damaging (*mazziq*), and the pleasant (*na'eh*) and disgusting (*megune*).[23] He expands this idea by saying

> It is also clear, that in these human comprehensions [of the imaginative and appetitive faculties], they are not unique to man as man, but man participates in them in some sense like any living being. And that is, comprehension of good and evil; such as knowledge of what is pleasureful and painful; the useful and the damaging; the pleasant and the disgusting—those are considered good and evil for some people; because in all these matters good and evil is defined by what people perceive. So much so that some will identify the good as pleasureful and evil its opposite, good as honor and evil is its opposite, good as victory and rulership and evil its opposite, good as noble actions and the evil its opposite, and some will perceive the good as the useful and the evil its opposite, as mentioned in the *Nicomachean Ethics* [1.5, 1095a15–25].[24]

One problem with Gersonides' use of *Nicomachean Ethics* 1.4 is that Aristotle is merely presenting the common opinions (*endoxa*) about the different ends of life, not recommending them all equally. Gersonides takes Aristotle's statement on the basic premises that humans *consider* basic goods in life and reinterprets those as examples of the instinctual ways animals make value judgments of their surrounding through the imaginative and appetitive faculties, something not unique to humans. Thus in showing how the practical intellect is closer to the imagination, which is the opposite of the theoretical intellect, he makes it more biological and hence more in common with the animal kingdom.

CHANCE (QERI) AND HUMAN AFFAIRS

One of the primary obstacles to the success of the practical intellect in achieving bodily perfection is the effects of chance in the world. Gersonides develops an astrological model of chance through reinterpreting Aristotle's definitions of chance at *Physics* 2.4-6.[25] Aristotle presents two methods of classifying chance (*tyche* and *automaton*) in nature. The first of Aristotle's definitions of chance is in relation to frequency: events happen in the majority of cases in the same way, while there are always a certain number of events that occur on rare occasions and infrequently. These infrequent events are considered chance. The second of Aristotle's definitions of chance is in relation to a goal or purpose. Events can be divided into those that have a particular goal and those that have no purpose. A chance occurrence is a result of an accidental encounter between two actions, each with its own goal that results in a new chance event.[26]

At *Wars* 2.1, Gersonides references Aristotle's discussion of chance in the *Physics*, but uses astrology as a means of explaining these chance events in the world.[27] For Gersonides, astrology is a system of explaining events in the material world that Aristotle would describe as chance. It gives rational order and system to what appears as chance both in the sense of rarity and purposelessness. Sara Klein-Braslavy argues that this is a "demonstration that astrological determinism can fit into an Aristotelian world picture."[28] One might even say that Gersonides presents a conception of nature that is more teleological than Aristotle or Maimonides in endeavoring to explain the cause and end of parts of nature that they did not conceive possible. This is evident in Gersonides' model of the Agent Intellect (*ha-sekhel ha-po'el*), which presents the architectonic plan of the universe in the mind of God, similar to the blueprint of a house in the mind of the architect.[29] Unlike Maimonides, who describes the limitations of our cognition of the supra-lunar world, Gersonides presents a much deeper (though not complete) access to understanding God and the heavenly realm.[30] Similarly, miracles are not against nature, but speed up the occurrence of events that could happen through nature's processes.[31] Gersonides frequently cites in his biblical commentary the refrain that miracles only happen when absolutely necessary and when they cannot be done through purely natural means.[32]

However, in such an ordered universe, is there a role for chance? Gersonides accepts Aristotle's category of infrequent events (such as luck) at *Wars* 2.1, but minimizes their importance in the context of predicting the future through dream, divination, and prophecy. This is to stress the importance of the rationally ordered element of events by the Agent Intellect as a more central prerequisite for predicting the future. Contrastingly, Gersonides interprets Aristotle's other category of chance events that have no purpose as a significant occurrence in biblical narrative and prophecy. He explains in *Wars* 2.2 that these "chance" events are in fact ordered by the heavenly bodies, by different means which we will categorize below. This is the case of two independent series of events, each with their own purpose, but the outcome of their coincidence could not have been predicted, where neither is the cause of the other. He gives the example of 1 Samuel 9–10 where the prophet predicts the random meeting of Saul who was looking for his donkeys and the man making a pilgrimage to the Bethel shrine, who happened to have found his donkeys. He also gives the example of 1 Kings 13 where a prophet receives a warning of his death if he turns back on his journey, which is the result of the crossing paths of the prophet turning back and a lion on his own journey who killed him for food. Both these examples confirm that Gersonides' usage of chance to describe them is the prophet's knowledge of the specific ordering of events by the stars. The question is, why describe this phenomenon as "chance" when its causes can be determined?

One solution to this problem is employed by Klein-Braslavy who suggests that Gersonides is using "chance" merely to reflect the common opinion of how this event appears to the ordinary observer. She states that in order to comprehend the true causes of what appear to the unscientifically trained observer to be chance requires an education, starting from basic appearances. She notes that

[a]ccording to Aristotle's definition of chance, their forecasts are not "chance" and such forecasts of future events must have essential causes. Hence, Gersonides concludes, the theory in which the astrologers' calculations

are based is true; all incidents that happen to individual human beings are determined and ordered by the stars, including those events we habitually include in the category of incidents caused by chance and accident.[33]

There is truth to Klein-Braslavy's position that chance is a human construct, but I argue that Gersonides maintains it for ethical and not pedagogical reasons. The science of astrology may technically be able to explain the operations of chance, but the limited progress in astronomy and astrology makes it very difficult to draw ethical conclusions from astrological observations and ascertain which stars we are affected by and how they affect us. However much Gersonides desires the proper knowledge of the stars to overcome their effects, he ends the discussion with the sober wish for conclusive answers for how to achieve these results. He states that

> [t]he reports of the astrologers confirm this fact, for they can frequently predict the thoughts and actions of men correctly. Yet it happens that they often err because of the inadequate procedures of verification characteristic of this discipline, which results from the great distance with respect to substance and space between us and these divine bodies and the difficulty of obtaining the necessary positions of these bodies by observation. For it is impossible to have the repeated observations required for the empirical principles of astrology, since the zodiac position of a heavenly body at a given time is repeated only once in a thousand years....This indicates that there is some kind of determination and order obtaining in chance events. But would that I knew how this is possible![34]

Even though, according to Gersonides, we know that the heavenly bodies guide human affairs, the zodiacal position of a heavenly body at a given time is repeated only once in a thousand years and astronomers have not been successful in tracing the movements of heavenly bodies.[35] Instead of trying to comprehend and overcome the stars, the practical intellect should focus its efforts on achieving self-preservation through developing one's physical capacities in cultivating arts and virtues to withstand the impact of the whims of fortune. This explains why in the context of *Wars* Book 2, it is more prudent for human preservation to consider these phenomenon as "chance" events, since for all practical human purposes, they have the effect of chance events.[36]

Gersonides' concept of chance is an important part of why, unlike for Aristotle, the practical intellect is focused on physical self-preservation through the construction of arts and virtues that attempt to withstand the deleterious effects of chance.[37] While the practical intellect should strive to attain physical self-preservation in light of all future possibilities, not only in cases of chance (infrequent or purposeless events), chanceful occurrences are the most difficult to predict and thus if one could control those, one could control the destiny of one's physical existence. In this regard, it is worthwhile to note the fine distinction between the position of Gersonides and the position of Aristotle on luck. Aristotle sees greater knowledge as giving one the perspective to understand the uncontrollable forces of luck, without striving to overcome them. Aristotle states that a happy person will neither ignore fortune nor succumb to it, but will instead bear it nobly.[38] Although Gersonides' astrological model of chance is based on his interpretation of Aristotle, his system has a more expansive and powerful system of luck, while also a greater emphasis on the forces needed to overcome it.

The Arts and the Virtues of Physical Preservation

Gersonides' two methods of responding to the forces of chance are the construction of human arts (*technai, melakhot*) and cultivation of virtues (*middot*), which are both described in detailed examples throughout his *Commentary on the Torah*. Though Gersonides does not explicitly reference chance in his *Commentary* when describing the content of the ethical lessons, he solidifies this link in his tangential discussion of dreams, divination and prophecy predicting chance events at *Wars* 2.2. There he admits the limitations of human knowledge of the heavenly bodies to predict and understand what humans conceive of as "chance" and thus the inability to derive a practical ethics from astrology. We do not know, he explains, how men of good fortune prosper and men of bad fortune suffer, except that it derives from the heavenly bodies.[39] As a result, he admits the existence of an "intellectual capacity that enables us both to act contrary to what has been ordered by the heavenly bodies and to correct, as far as possible the [astrally ordained] misfortunes that befall us."[40] This capacity, which he later in *Wars* refers to as the practical intellect,[41] is described here as achieved through arts and virtues.[42] One has to read his *Commentary on the Torah* to see how the workings of the practical intellect play out in specific examples.

Arts

An art or craft (*techné*) is defined by Aristotle as the method of construction and bringing into being of a physical object, such as the preparation of food, clothing, shelter and medicine.[43] The uniqueness of Gersonides' interpretation of Aristotle is that he amalgamates the arts and practical wisdom, making them two segments of the practical intellect, while Aristotle purposefully kept these two realms distinct.[44] For Aristotle, arts serve the purpose of constructing objects while practical wisdom is for the purpose of practical decision making.[45] In contrast, Gersonides unifies them under the overarching goal of human physical preservation, something Aristotle rejected as below the concerns of either craft making or the cultivation of character. For example, in comparing the different ways of life, Aristotle ranks money-making as a necessary prerequisite for virtue and knowledge, but not an essential part of the subject matter of the *Nicomachean Ethics*.[46] Maimonides, even more critical than Aristotle, saw the perfection of possessions as the lowest and most worthless perfection, describing it as "an effort with a view to something purely imaginary … a thing that has no permanence."[47] However, Gersonides regards the cultivation of crafts as the embodiment of the central goal of physical preservation; he incorporates this into his interpretation of Aristotle and Averroes' commentary on the discussion of the practical intellect in the *De Anima* 3.10.[48] Averroes had already begun this process by adding a new goal into the practical intellect, that "animals have no other faculty beside these which benefit their survival. For, since a creature's preservation lies in either avoiding [harmful] sensibilia or moving towards [favorable] sensibilia."[49] Gersonides then adds an important next step to Averroes' *Commentary* that it is the arts that are the means to achieve this end for humans. The reason for Gersonides' amalgamation of crafts into the practical intellect is that the goal of practical wisdom is no longer merely a deliberation to attain different and sometimes conflicting ends, but a rising in priority of physical preservation from a basic prerequisite to *the* central goal of the practical intellect. The necessity to "flee from harmful things and obtain advantageous things"[50] becomes a vital imperative. One reason why this is so, is that within the Aristotelian–Maimonidean framework, much of the responsibility for physical preservation is carried by the state, which serves as a basis for the individual to attain higher ends. But in Gersonides' model, the state has a much more minimal role and derives its duties of self-preservation from the collective of individuals who each possesses this duty.[51]

Gersonides elucidates the implications of these theoretical (though terse) comments through examples in his *Commentary on the Torah*. There he shows how the knowledge of these arts slowly developed through experience and random trial and error over a long period of time.[52] Tracing the empirical basis of all practical knowledge to the consequence of the sin in the Garden of Eden, Gersonides offers a unique perspective on God's punishment that "thorns also and thistles shall it bring forth to thee; and thou shalt eat the herb of the field"[53]: he interprets it as a metaphor for the fact that man will have to achieve all knowledge purely through the senses, which will lead only to difficulty, pain and mistakes.[54] In fact, Gersonides sees the process of developing different arts for human preservation as being a constant process. He posits that perfection in creation arose a long time after the six days of creation and arose with great difficulty.[55] It is also a cumulative process not achievable through one generation, but must be viewed as part of a larger historical development. Gersonides explores this point further in interpreting the Song of Songs 7:14, "new and old, which I have laid up for thee," citing it as evidence that most knowledge cannot be apprehended by any one individual alone, but is gathered and built on that which has been explored by one's predecessors.[56] In this regard, translation between languages is essential as it maintains and conveys the wisdom achieved by one's predecessors.[57] Even with cumulative scientific research over multiple generations, this pursuit has only studied a minutia of potential knowledge of the universe, stating that "we have grasped less than an iota of God's creation."[58] Furthermore, he adds that we cannot assume that what was not known by the former sages will also not be known by their successors.[59] However, Gersonides does not conceive of this scientific pursuit as limitless and does recognize that certain sciences, like medicine, have been brought to perfection or closure.[60]

Furthermore, Gersonides reads the post-Eden narrative as constructed to teach about the historical development of practical arts and the dangers in attempting this process without the proper ethical discipline. None of these arts are completely closed to further revision and experimentation, as we see in the example of the construction of cities below. The first art developed was the creation of clothing or "garments of skin" (*kutnot 'or*)[61] for the sake of protecting man from the damage of the surrounding air.[62] He explains his commentary on specific verses that "garments of skin" are

"Garments of skin"- as the translator [Onkelos] explained,[63] the intention [of referring to the garments as "garments of skin"] is that the garments already had the quality of softness and smoothness that were pleasant to wear on skin of the body. And God created these garments for them through a miracle, like what he created during the six days of creation. However, he created them [now], so that it would be necessary to wear to protect from surrounding air. If [God] would have waited until he explained the way of this art (*melakha*), time would have passed and they would have died either from the heat or the cold.[64]

Unlike the rest of the arts created by human initiative after Eden, Gersonides is obliged to explain how this one was created in Eden without human effort. Gersonides surmises that this art was created miraculously by God for man, since waiting until man discovered this art would mean that time would have passed and man would have died from cold or heat. Using a miracle as a justification seems at first to be a theological rationalization and deviation from Gersonides' philosophic description of how arts are related to the practical intellect. This can be avoided if one assumes Gersonides wants one to apply his understanding of miracles in *Wars* to his biblical commentary here. There he describes a miracle, not as breaking the rules of nature, but as increasing the speed by which natural events occur.[65] Therefore in applying this principle to Genesis 3:21, Gersonides is suggesting that the essence of the miracle was that Adam and Eve discovered clothing at an increased speed since they needed it to survive, and did not have to go through the toil of experimentation. One could pose a further question of why clothing deserves such a miracle, while other arts do not. This becomes more complicated by looking at his second explanation where he summarizes the entire parsha:

> Since it was already mentioned that Adam and his wife [Eve] learned of their disgrace because they were naked, it also was mentioned that God already brought into existence worthy clothing to wear on the skin of their body. And God brought into existence this clothing through a miracle, like he brought everything else into existence during the six days of creation. However, he created them [the clothing], so that it would be necessary to wear to protect from the surrounding air. If [God] would have waited until he explained this art (*ha-melakha*), time would have passed and they would have died either from the heat or the cold.[66]

Gersonides adds another element that was missing in the original analysis: clothing was created as a response as well to shame (*boshet*) and disgrace (*genut*).[67] How do we reconcile the first explanation of survival and the second explanation of shame? Gersonides implies that shame is an emotional mechanism, perhaps the primary human emotion to which the practical intellect responds. As something endowed by God, it contains a reactive instinct to cover the sexual organs and as a consequence man is moved to develop clothing. God's miraculous involvement in human survival is exemplified in implanting a sense of shame in humans which compels them to speedily react and develop some form of clothing.

The two practical arts that are first developed through trial and error are exemplified in Gersonides' reading of Cain and Abel whom he regards as the two first scientists to create competing arts.[68] He explains that

> Abel is the one who brought into existence this art [animal husbandry (*himṣe't mezonot*)] and Cain brought into existence the art of agriculture (*melekhet 'avodat ha-'adama*). Animal husbandry was mentioned first because it is more important than agriculture. And this is for two reasons: the first—the subject it is dealing with is a more important subject than the subject of agriculture, since animals are more important than plants; the second—you will find there is a greater output in determining the food for animals and its end than the output of agriculture and its end. This is because the animal, when it eats the food appropriate to it, will grow and bear fruit in the correct way, as long as external factors do not prevent [its growth], such as from the surrounding air and similar external factors. Whereas agriculture may be already in its perfect form, but the right product may not come, since the plant is dependent on rain and sometimes the rain does not come to the plant in the correct way.[69]

Gersonides refers to them as "great sages" (*hakhamim gedolim*).[70] According to Gersonides' reading, Cain developed the art of agriculture and Abel the art of animal husbandry.[71] Accordingly, the Bible describes Cain as a farmer and Abel as a shepherd as a metaphoric way of expressing this difference.[72] Gersonides infers that Abel discovered animal husbandry through experimentation in giving animals different amounts of food, until finding the right food.[73] Cain employed a similar method through experimentation in harvesting plants in different soils.[74] To Gersonides, the text itself subtly suggests that Abel was more successful than Cain in his research by the fact that Abel was mentioned before Cain. The ordering of the names is also interpreted by Gersonides as an indication that the end is more important with respect to animals than it is for plants.[75] Because of this difference, "God's favor" or "God's will" (*raṣon*) came to Abel and not to Cain since Cain's plants did not receive the rain they needed to produce the successful results.[76] Here Gersonides appears to be following Maimonides and the medieval philosophic tradition of inter-preting God's will as a metaphor for nature.[77] As a result of Cain's failure, he was angry, embarrassed and jealous, and killed Abel.[78] Cain's failure to integrate his perfection of the practical intellect with a development of character led to a loss of the knowledge of this art for the world and the need to wait another five generations for Cain's great-great-great grandson Jabal to rediscover it later.[79] In doing so, Jabal took animal husbandry even farther both in depth and scope, expanding the science to every animal and teaching to all, in order that the knowledge would not get lost and others would be able to benefit from it.[80]

Gersonides also points out that other important practical arts were developed by Cain's descendants. Cain's son Enoch invented the art of construction and built the first city.[81] Jubal invented the art of musical instruments.[82] Tubal-Cain invented the art of metal working designed for sharpening and creating objects of copper and iron.[83] Moreover, Noah accumulated all the arts that Cain's children had discovered and he preserved them so they would not get lost after the flood. For example, Noah had to know which foods to provide for different animals and preserve the seeds of various plants in the ark.[84] Later artisans who created the Tower of Babel did so with the intention of improving on Enoch's efforts in the art of construction. The idea to build a tall building of bricks and mortar was for the purpose of safety in order not to spread out too far in the land to search for habitable places to live where one grows plants for food. The Tower served as a focal point for human civilization, so that individuals could see the building from afar and know not to wander off into inhabitable lands.[85] He describes one of the motivations for building the Tower of Babel as

[i]t [the Tower of Babel] will protect them so that they will not go spread out throughout the world in search of suitable places to live and [go find] plants necessary for man because they will see this building from afar, because of its height, and it will protect them so they will not move a far distance away from it. Because of this, their efforts will be repaid in that everyone will be gathered in one place in the land. In addition, in building this city, it will always increase their numbers. And God already saw that gathering man in one place in the world is not fitting for the existence of the human species, since if there is a catastrophe in one part of the world, if from a noise and shifting of a wind in the belly of the world, if from a strong wind that dismantles mountains and breaks stones, if from stones of crystal, if from flood of water or other similar catastrophic reasons. If the entire human species is

in one place, they could all be lost if everything is destroyed in that one part of the world. This is why it is necessary for man to be spread out throughout the world, so that if there is a catastrophe in one part, the species will be preserved in the rest.[86]

God's decision to destroy the Tower was in order to correct their prudential reasoning: it is not better for preserving the human species to be located in one place, since all can be lost with one tragedy, such as a large wind or a flood. Therefore God is teaching them that it is in fact more practical to spread out throughout the world to preserve humanity more effectively, since if loss happens in one place, the rest will survive.

Gersonides argues that there is a miraculous element in the fact that the arts were developed in such a short time from the creation of the world.[87] What he may also be hinting is the fact that God's giving man the practical intellect allows his mind to uniquely construct arts at a quicker speed than any other animal species. Yet continuing the general pattern of the practical intellect discussed above, he does not think that this represents the perfection of the practical arts, when many practical arts have in fact been pursued by scholars in different nations in the world after the time of the Hebrew Bible. He gives the example of Galen who perfected medicine. It was not completed until his time since it requires a substantial amount of empirical information, especially knowledge from experience and dissection.[88] In light of the development of the practical arts in this area, Gersonides' reading of the ethics in the Bible must be shaped by advances.

Virtues

Both Aristotle and Maimonides present a model of ethics that is rooted in the cultivation of character (*ethos*) whose ideal state is a balance of emotional extreme states at the mean. The mean itself is not a set middle, but shifts toward the different extremes depending on the various criteria: time, location, context and so on, and practical wisdom constantly adapts the mean to the criterion factors.[89] Furthermore, luck is part of the nature of the world and should not be a major factor in ethical cultivation.[90] In Gersonides' early thought, his conception of virtue ethics is quite consistent with this model.[91] Even in his later *Commentary on the Torah*, Gersonides still interprets many biblical characters as exemplifying the traditional moral virtues as interpreted by Maimonides in *Eight Chapters*, such as courage (*gevura*), contentedness (*histapkut*) and magnificence (*nedivut*).[92] For example, Abraham is praised for his courage in leading soldiers into battle against Abimelech the four kings at Genesis 14[93] and in having the right balance of rashness and fear in confronting Abimelech.[94] Abraham is also praised in his contentedness, which is a mean between avarice and slothful indifference with respect to money in not taking booty from the four kings and satisfied with the amount of possessions after parting with Lot.[95]

However, for Gersonides, these moral virtues are much less frequent than a new set of materialistic virtues which humans share with animals (even though animals are given these virtues directly from the Agent Intellect and do not have the practical intellect to deliberate about the means). Gersonides adds a whole new layer of virtues such as *hishtadlut* (endeavor), *ḥariṣut* (diligence), and *hithakmut* (cunning) in crafting *taḥbulot* (stratagems) which are focused on creating the material strength necessary to overcome the random whims of fortune.[96] As discussed above, these random forces of the heavenly bodies do have causes and are not in truth random, but due to the human incapability to comprehend the complex causes, for practical purposes they are caused by chance. None of these virtues claims to know or change the decree of the stars with human force, but through physical and material strength one can strive to evade or withstand its impact. For example, the belief that events are influenced by the stars does not entail that *all* events are *strictly* determined by them. Someone may have decided to become a pianist because the stars gave him musical talent; however, he might have chosen to become a football player instead. Neither do these virtues contain the ideal of balancing and channeling the emotions to appropriate end as the moral virtues do. All three are physiobiological capacities rooted in the human imagination that humans can perfect to maximize physical self-preservation. Thus to fully understand Gersonides' inferences in ascribing these virtues to different characters in his biblical readings, one requires an understanding of the scientific contexts of these terms in *De Animalibus* and *De Anima*, an aspect mostly ignored in studies of Gersonides' biblical commentaries.[97]

The first and most frequently used of the physical virtues is *hishtadlut* (endeavor). This term is used in rabbinic writings to represent effort and hard work given to man to achieve God's commandments.[98] For example, "three things did Rabbi Yoḥanan say in the name of the men of Jerusalem: when you go out to battle, do not go out among the first but among the last, so that you may return among the first; and treat your Sabbath like a weekday rather than be dependent on your fellow-beings, and strive (*hishtadel*) to be on good terms with him upon whom the hour smiles."[99] Maimonides (in Ibn Tibbon's translation) uses the term, in the last few chapters in the *Guide*, to highlight the difference between endeavor toward the intellectual versus endeavor toward the practical, praising intellectual *hishtadlut* and denigrating physical *hishtadlut*. For example, in reaching the inner part of the Sultan's Palace, a metaphor for the quest toward intellectually knowing God, he suggests that "it is indispensable that they should make another effort (*yishtadel hishtadlut aheret, min sa'ah ahr ya'sa'ahu*)" to reach the most inner chamber.[100] He also uses the example of how David exhorted Solomon to "endeavor (*hishtadel, al-sa'ah*) to apprehend Him and his endeavor (*hishtadel, al-sa'ah*) to worship Him after apprehension has been achieved."[101] But Maimonides also describes *hishtadlut* with respect to the body and possessions as the two lowest forms of perfection. He is harshly critical of this form of *hishtadlut*, saying, "the endeavor (*hishtadluto, sa'ika*) and the efforts directed by man towards this kind of perfection are not but an effort with a view to something purely imaginary, to something that has no permanence."[102]

Gersonides, as a careful reader of the *Guide*, attempts to reverse Maimonides' deprecation of physical preservation and stresses the importance of this form of as an independent pursuit.[103] Gersonides adapts Maimonides' framework, but reverses his negative approach to physical preservation and instead claims it to be a moral necessity. To Gersonides, the primary perfection is thus a necessary perfection and must be focused on through an emphasis that is independent of intellectual *hishtadlut*. This is a result of a revised model of nature (*physis, ṭeva'*), which is constructed to preserve the existence of its creatures and does so with greater strength, the more complex the organism.[104] Thus Gersonides expands upon Averroes' statement that "nature endeavors (*yishtadel ha-ṭeva'*)" to bring about "the greatest possible perfection."[105] Nature's *hishtadlut* is in giving superior organs for superior beings to preserve (*shemira*) their existence more effectively within the hierarchy of nature. It also does so through "retroactively finding utility for appendages caused unintentionally by the necessity of matter," such as hair, horns and hooves, in which nature takes advantage of their existence and endows with a useful purpose, protection.[106]

Nature senses the material needs of animals and reconstructs the existing parts of animals in a way that most effectively preserves their being, and the more so depending on the nobility of their rank. Humans have the ability to imitate nature's *hishtadlut* through the practical intellect. As Warren Zev Harvey has shown, "nature endeavors (*yishtadel ha-ṭeva'*)" is not found in Aristotle, but is a modification of Averroes, especially as it manifests in biology.[107] While Aristotle presents a model of physical matter that is teleologically neutral, Averroes' conception of physical matter is cultivated for very clear goals, which is then strengthened by Gersonides in his interpretation. For example, in Gersonides' *Commentary on Song of Songs* 3:3, he interprets the line "the watchmen (*shomerim*) that go about the city found me," noting that the watchmen are a metaphor for the senses (*ḥushim*), which were put in the animal body to protect it from injury and direct it to appropriate ends.[108] Similarly, in describing the imagination as the faculty that follows the senses through combination and separation, Gersonides adds the example of an animal that moves to seek food, a primary necessity of physical preservation.[109] Thus already from Gersonides' earlier scientific writings, one can detect a discernible shift. First, he gives sensation and imagination a clearer goal in preservation (*shemira*) and second, he suggests that nature endeavors (*hishtadel*) to give man the ability to perfect his practical intellect for preservation (*shemira*), though he does not yet see man imitating nature's *hishtadlut* as a human virtue or human ethical *hishtadlut* as rooted in the practical intellect.

In his biblical commentaries from 1329 onward, beginning with Esther, Gersonides develops *hishtadlut* as a practical virtue, shown through the actions of biblical characters.[110] One of its central goals is the striving of good people to successfully obtain goods that are part of the natural biological cycle, such as having and maintaining the health of children, safeguarding the well-being of one's family, and ensuring proper burial. Producing offspring is a central imperative of *hishtadlut*. Gersonides interprets Abraham's statement to God about his lack of offspring as fulfilling the natural imperative that it is "appropriate for man to *hishtadel* to produce offspring to perpetuate the species."[111] Thus Sarah allowing Hagar to have children with Abraham is a necessary means to achieve this end. He explains that

> The first lesson is in ethics and that is that it is not appropriate that man should lessen his endeavor (*hishtadlut*) towards what is necessary for him [and use] all the possible means he may need to arrive at the goal that he is aiming at. We can see that Sarai gave her maidservant [Hagar] to Abram, with the calculation that he may complete with Hagar what he intended with Sarai, which is pregnancy. The lesson that comes out of this is clear that

if man only endeavors (*mishtadel*) to the goal he is aiming at with the means that are necessary for his existence—he would miss many of the things that are necessary for him or even all of them.[112]

While Abraham's original intention was to have children with Sarah, Sarah understood that one must think creatively and proposed Hagar as a substitute, considering the possibility that she may have greater biological potency for becoming pregnant. Another example is Abraham permitting Eliezer to take a wife for Isaac from the daughters of Canaan if one from the land of Abraham would not follow Abraham back to Canaan. There he argues that

> [w]hen one cannot acquire a complete good, it is inappropriate for him to desist from the endeavor (*hishtadlut*) to obtain the next best possible good. It is appropriate for him to *yishtadel* to acquire whatever good he can. Abraham permitted Eliezer to take a wife for Isaac from the daughters of Canaan if one from the land of Abraham would not wish to follow Eliezer back to Canaan. Abraham told Eliezer that if the woman should not desire to follow him, Eliezer would be free of any guilt due to the non-fulfillment of the oath. But regardless of what would happen in this matter, Abraham did not allow Eliezer to settle Isaac outside of Canaan, for it was the will of God, may He be exalted, that Isaac stay in the Land of Canaan, due to its greater propensity for the receipt of perfection, as we have explained.[113]

Abraham's ideal wife for Isaac was one from Mesopotamia that would move to Canaan, but the second best option was accepting a wife from Canaan. Finding a wife from outside of Canaan and living outside of it was not an option for him. Similarly, Lot's daughters *hishtadlu* to perpetuate seed through their father to continue the human species[114]; and Jacob asked Laban to permit him to marry his daughter so he could have children.[115] *Hishtadlut* is also prominent in keeping babies alive when confronted by danger, such as the actions of Moses' mother Jochebed,[116] the deeds of the midwives[117] and the endeavors of the daughter of Pharaoh to find a woman to nurse the baby Moses.[118]

Ensuring the well-being of one's family is also a necessary form of *hishtadlut*. Gersonides affirms the principle that it is "appropriate for man to *yishtadel* to bequeath goods unto his children."[119] One example of this is Abraham's concern that he would have no descendants to receive his possessions after his death. Gersonides expands on the ethical utility of Abraham's concern and endeavor, stating that

It is appropriate for a man to endeavor (*yishtadel*) to bequeath what he can to his children who come after him, and should not be jealous if they exercise power over all they had worked for. Abram was worried that he would not have descendents who would acquire his possessions after his death. (This implied that he would not be jealous if his descendents themselves would take control of his possessions.) He was appeased when God informed him that his descendents would inherit him.[120]

Other examples where Gersonides attributes *hishtadlut* to working toward the well-being of one's family include Isaac's endeavor to bless Esau before death[121] and Rebecca's attempt to ensure that Jacob will be blessed.[122] This principle also works between siblings and from children to parents, as Gersonides states, "appropriate for man to help his father and relatives when has the opportunity."[123] He cites examples such as Judah's endeavor to save his brothers in Egypt,[124] Joseph's endeavor to bring his father and family to Egypt,[125] Miriam's attempt to save her brother Moses[126] and Moses' endeavor to bring Joseph's bones back to Canaan.[127]

Lastly, death and proper burial are a central part of the natural cycle of biology and its proper method is a form of *hishtadlut*. Jacob's securing a burial place is viewed by Gersonides as an appropriate preparation for death.[128] Moreover, Abraham's weeping for Sarah after her death is viewed as a suitable reflection of one's endeavor to care for relatives when sick, and his effort to bury her is an act of honor for both the living and the dead.[129] Similarly, Moses' endeavor to bring Joseph's bones back to Canaan is seen as fulfilling this natural imperative.[130]

As a result Gersonides offers different practical maxims which are contingent on the particular situation presented. This implies that there is no one correct method for all situations on how to obtain the proper end. This list of practical maxims includes

- using whatever means necessary to obtain one's goal and using the means that will make success likely,
- not settling for a less complete good,
- obtaining a next best good when one cannot obtain a perfect good,
- stopping whatever obstacles that lead one away from obtaining a right end,
- acting to obtain a good in advance before one needs it,
- initiating an action and then completing it.

One of Gersonides' lessons for action is to use whatever means are necessary to achieve the desired result. Gersonides provides the example of Sarah allowing Abraham to have a child with Hagar as an example, since if procreation is an essential form of *hishtadlut*, one must be creative in the means to achieve it.[131] He also provides the example of Abraham's minimalist negotiation tactics with Ephron for the burial plot for Sarah, asking for only what is absolutely necessary in order to make success more likely.[132] Another maxim is to not settle for less than the achievement of the complete good. For example, Miriam endeavored to find a nurse for Moses in order to save Moses in the most complete way possible.[133] Barak also ensured that no one would survive from Sisera's camp, to achieve perfect success and guarantee that the evil would not return to Israel.[134] One should also strive to obtain the next best good when one cannot obtain a perfect good. For example, Abraham permitted Eliezer to take a wife for Isaac from the daughters of Canaan if one from the land of Abraham would not follow Abraham back to Canaan.[135] Gersonides also recommends removing whatever obstacles leads one away from obtaining the right end, such as Jacob disguising himself as Esau[136] and Joseph's assuaging his father Jacob's fears about coming to Egypt, reassuring him that he possessed power in Egypt to fulfill his heart's desires.[137] Another suggestion is to obtain a good in advance before it is needed, which was Jacob's plan in securing a burial place before he became ill, when it would be more difficult.[138] Lastly, Pinchas' zealous actions represent the advice that if one begins an action, it should be completed right until the end.[139]

Another primary goal of *hishtadlut* is the endeavor of good people to successfully avoid the evils that are predetermined for them. Gersonides presents four possible options, which I argue, can be ranked from the most ideal to the least ideal method to avoid this evil. The most ideal is to actually change the action of the evil actor. The most notable example of this is that of Esther who persuaded the king that the great danger to fall upon the Jews in fact was a danger for the entire kingdom. She did so by dressing in royal clothing to win over the king, appeasing Haman by inviting him to a party, galvanizing those working for the king who harbored animosity toward Haman and then fasting at the next party so that the king would see she was in anguish and pain. In his interpretation of the story,

> [t]he thirty fifth lesson is in ethics. It is to inform that when one needs to endeavor (*hishtadel*) in a very necessary endeavorance (*hishtadlut*), to save

someone from a great evil, his endeavor (*hishtadlut*) must be in a way that when the matter continues, it will not close any doors to future endeavor (*hishtadlut*). And if [the endeavorance] can bear a useful outcome from all the opportunities for the individual [needing help], there is no reason to cut corners in the matter. Because of this, when Esther entered the inner chamber unlawfully, she wore royal clothing in a way that would find favor in the eyes of the king. Because this is one of the opportunities to her savior in coming to see him and having her words heard. And after this, she did not immediately ask the king to save her people, because Haman may have opposed her in this request. Because of this, she asked the king, before making her request, for the king and Haman to come to a party that she made for them. It was done to appease Haman, in a way which would be beneficial [to her]. And perhaps because of her appeasement of Haman, she would obtain from Haman that he endeavor (*yishtadel*) alone to save Israel from the king, after she reconciled herself [regarding Haman]. Because [Haman] was in the habit of chasing after honor and victory, and she overdid the honor in this respect. And because of this, she was given the opportunity to find many helpers against Haman as a result because the outcome would be that the rest of the king's ministers will be very jealous of him [Haman], seeing the victory that he takes for himself, such that Esther did not bring anyone with the king to the party, except for Haman. And when this matter was repeated, the king told her at the wine party [to ask her request and it will be fulfilled, even] "the kingdom."[140] But she did not yet agree to make a request, until first the king and Haman come to a party that she will make for them tomorrow. This increased the ministers' jealousy [with Haman] and also with the king. Because she showed from her words to the king that Haman has greater strength than the king....And it was due to Esther's wisdom that she knew the strength of the king's love for her, that she came to him after a lengthy fast. Accompanying her mighty fear, she appeared to the king as if she were ill and in great distress. Therefore the king was aroused to ask her "what is troubling you queen Esther?"[141] He perceived she was faint, as it is mentioned in the *Book of Jossipon*. The king's love for her awakened him to give her "even to half the kingdom"[142] to benefit her and to save her from her great distress.[143]

Only after all of this did Esther ask the king to change his decree, demonstrating to him how Haman's decree was hurting the kingdom.[144] This was also employed by Joseph who convinced the chief butler to persuade Pharaoh to release him from prison.[145] Another possible means of avoiding evil is to solidify friendships with righteous individuals. Gersonides posits that it is "appropriate for man who comes to sojourn in a place to endeavor to make friends there. These acquaintances will help him reside in the area in peace."[146] However, it is necessary that they be righteous individuals and not evil friends.[147] This is why Abraham had many friends,[148] why Jacob went to Laban, since he saw he was righteous[149] and accounts for Judah's friendship with Hirah, which helped him acclimatize in the area peacefully.[150]

According to Gersonides' ethical lessons, if one is not successful in thwarting the individual who is causing the evil or acquiring a righteous group of friends, one should strive for peace and avoid conflict (*maḥloqet*) or strife (*meriva*). This is why Abraham separated from Lot[151] and Jacob ran away from his brother Esau[152] and later attempted to make peace with him.[153] For example, in commenting on Abraham's parting of ways with Lot, Gersonides states that

> It is more appropriate for a man to choose peace and few possessions instead of many possessions and strife, as it says "burnt bread and peace is better than a house full of sacrifices and strife."[154] Abram preferred less grazing land and peace to a great deal of land and strife.[155]

Gersonides also interprets Genesis 50:16–17 as an attempt by Joseph's brothers to make peace with Joseph by fabricating a story about their father's wishes for them to achieve peaceful relations. He explains that

> [i]t is appropriate for a man to endeavor (*hishtadel*) to achieve peace as far as possible. Its benefits are wonderful for both family and society. Hence, it is inappropriate for a man to care if peace between men is achieved by a repugnant action such as lying. It is inappropriate that the desire to stay far away from lies be able to thwart the noble goal of peace. Joseph's brothers told an untrue story concerning their father's wishes in order to achieve peace between Joseph and themselves. For this reason, our Rabbis, of blessed memory, stated that it is permitted to tell an untruth for the purpose of peace.[156] In another place, they stated that it is a meritorious act (*miṣva*) to tell an untruth for the purpose of peace.[157]

Similarly, Moses ran away from Egypt when Pharaoh strove to kill him and lived outside the city as a shepherd so that no one would see him.[158] Gersonides also stresses this as a political principle in the diaspora: one should endeavor for the peace of the king that under which one lives even if one is not part of his nation, because the peace of the nation will uphold the state.[159]

However, if one cannot truly avoid the evil decree, in Gersonides' view it is preferable to choose the lesser evil and avoid the greater evil. Abraham was faced with the threat of he and his wife both starving in Canaan or the potential danger of the King of Egypt taking his wife for himself due to her beauty. Choosing the latter was the lesser of two evils since in one case they would both die, while in the other there is a chance that Sarah may be defiled, but it would be considered an unwilling sexual act (*be-'ones*). Gersonides explains that

> [w]hen it is inevitable that a person will suffer some misfortune, it is appropriate for him to discern under which circumstance he will meet with less evil and (actively) choose that course of behavior. He should not be lazy in the matter, due to the fact that in any event some misfortune will occur to him. It is preferable to choose the lesser evil and flee greater misfortune. Abram chose to travel to Egypt and flee the famine in Canaan in spite of the propensity that the (inhabitants of the) place had to defile his wife.[160]

Jacob faced a similar challenge before his confrontation with Esau, to attack with one fleet and risk all being killed or to divide his army into two and allow half to be saved if one side is attacked. According to Gersonides' interpretation of Jacob's decision, the latter is the lesser of two evils.[161] Another example is Reuben's negotiation with the other brothers over how to kill Joseph. By convincing the other brothers that it is preferable to place him in a pit and not kill him, implying that he would die through hunger and not through direct murder, Reuben guides the brothers toward the lesser of two evils.[162]

Hishtadlut, according to Gersonides, is also cultivated by the enemies of the Israelites in the Bible to obtain their desired ends. In *Wars*, Gersonides states that "there are evil men who direct all their endeavorance (*hishtadlutam*) to kill or injure others, but they succeed only rarely even though they employ skillful means in these activities."[163] For example, the Midianites endeavored to lead Israelite girls astray into idol worship[164] and Haman endeavored to destroy the Jews thinking it could be beneficial for the king.[165] But the reason Gersonides suggests that they rarely succeed is evident from his commentary on these two cases since in both examples the *hishtadlut* of the Israelites overpowered the *hishtadlut* of their enemies. For example, the Israelites responded militarily to the Midianites[166] and Esther managed to convince the king that Haman was not acting for the king's benefit, but because he hated the king and it would in fact bring great damage to the king to kill a nation that he rules over.[167]

The second virtue of self-preservation that Gersonides employs in his ethical lessons is *ḥariṣut* (diligence). In his *Supercommentary* on *De Anima*, the term *ḥariṣut* refers to the quickness of reception of the appetitive soul in receiving motion from the imaginative faculty.[168] The quickness of *ḥariṣut* to transfer the plan of the imagination into concrete desired objects within the soul may be analogous to the quickness of individuals to act based on plans in the imagination. In other words, the result of the *ḥariṣut* in their soul is the *ḥariṣut* in external actions. The term *ḥariṣut* was often quoted in a popular refrain "if the decree is true, then the diligence is absurd" (*'im ha-gezera 'emet ha-ḥariṣut sheqer*) in rabbinic and medieval sources suggesting the limitations of *ḥariṣut*.[169] Gersonides reframed this concept in an Aristotelian psychological language, while minimizing examples of worthless *ḥariṣut*. At times he uses *ḥariṣut* in the literal sense of referring to the speed of action,[170] but the most common uses of *ḥariṣut* in the biblical commentaries fall under the categories of the acquisition of specific and necessary material ends: property, wealth and food. The numerous examples that Gersonides devotes to these categories suggest that it is more than a mere coincidence.

The acquisition of property (*qinyanim*) as a form of *ḥariṣut* is presented as a necessary means toward the preservation of the body.[171] Gersonides argues that God's blessing Abraham with material success did not stop him from exercising his *ḥariṣut* in obtaining property and preserving it to the best of his ability.[172] This is why Abraham brought along all his possessions from Canaan to Egypt to ensure his maximal overseeing and maintenance of them. Gersonides expands on this, saying that

> A person must protect his possessions with as much diligence (*ḥariṣut*) as possible. Abram, in spite of his being promised success in his possessions by God, may He be exalted, endeavored (*hishtadel*) that he should bring along with him from Egypt (to Canaan) all his possessions; he did not leave behind anything. And he led his livestock patiently, in a manner that no loss should accrue to them.[173]

Similarly, the daughters of Tzelafchad exercised their *ḥariṣut* in obtaining the inheritance of their father's possessions.[174] This is also apparent in Gersonides' explanation for the commandment to cease work on the Sabbath, as it gives artisans the *ḥariṣut* to work as they know that they will have one day off at the end.[175]

This acquisitiveness also applies to food (*mezonot*) as a necessary means to preserve the body. Abraham understood that God's command to dwell in the Land of Israel implies an end goal and thus carries with it exceptions. One of those includes leaving temporarily if there is a famine to obtain more food elsewhere. The necessities of nourishing the body take temporary priority over the intellectual "divine overflow" that can most effectively take place in the Land of Israel.[176] Abraham also made food a central objective of *ḥariṣut* in providing a feast to the three guests who come to his home. Gersonides describes how

> Abraham aroused himself with great diligence (*ḥariṣut*) to bring these men into his house, spoke to them with as much honour as possible, in order that they listen to him, and provided them with a sumptuous feast.[177]

Rebecca took similar measures of *ḥariṣut* in feeding Eliezer and his camels upon greeting him.[178] Similarly, Ruth's hard work in the field exhibits her *ḥariṣut* to accumulate food.[179]

Gersonides' commentary on Proverbs demonstrates that *ḥariṣut* equally applies to wealth (*hon*). Gersonides Commentary on Proverbs 10:4, "he becometh poor that dealeth with a slack hand; but the hand of the diligent (*yad ḥaruṣim*) maketh rich" is a comment on the relationship of method and justice. Those who amass wealth with *ḥariṣut* do so justly, while those who cheat and take money from others illegally do so because of laziness.[180] Similarly, he interprets the verse "she is not afraid of the snow for her household; for all her household are clothed with scarlet"[181] as proof of the *ḥariṣut* to acquire what is needed of wealth.[182] As a result, "the hand of the diligent (*yad ḥaruṣim*) shall bear rule" (Proverbs 12:24) and "she stretcheth out her hand to the poor; yea, she reacheth forth her hands to the needy" (Proverbs 31:20) implies the necessity to acquire economic capital with *ḥariṣut* and use it to build a home, rule others and give to the poor.[183]

The third physical virtue is *hithakmut* (cunning) through which one crafts *taḥbulot* (stratagems). This is the use of slyness and ingenuity in achieving good ends by means of *'orma*, which refers to ruses, deceptions and tricks. Gersonides' usage of these terms appears to hearken back to the central application given to them by Maimonides at *Guide* III 54 and III 32.[184] In Maimonides' division of the term wisdom (*ḥokhma*) into four groupings, he defines the lowest as aptitude for stratagems (*taḥbula*) and ruses (*'orma*), providing the example of *hithakmut* of the Egyptians to enslave the Israelites so that they do not multiply and fight against them in war (Exodus 1:10). But this is only when directed to evil ends, while it can have a noble purpose when directed toward inculcating moral or intellectual virtues.[185] Nowhere is this clearer than in Maimonides' interpretation of the purpose of the sacrificial ritual, which he describes as a "gracious ruse" (*talattuf*, *'orma*) to trick the people into abandoning their pagan rituals toward a worship and greater knowledge of God, which is parallel to the Bible's leading the Israelites through the dessert for forty years to educate them in military courage.[186] Maimonides sees the construction of ruses and stratagems to lead individuals toward the cultivation of moral virtues and knowledge of God as primary, while admitting a certain necessity for ruses in physical survival. But Gersonides reverses the priorities, as he does with the other two virtues, and places greater emphasis on strategies employed for physical preservation, without rejecting ruses for intellectual purposes.[187] When *hishtadlut* cannot construct a plan to maximize our biological capacities and *harisut* cannot acquire the means to strengthen our physical defenses, deceptive means become equally important.

One fundamental reason that ingenuity in crafting stratagems is so central for good people is that those striving to do evil and hurt others have been proficient at cultivating them. Examples include Esau, Amalek, Balaam, Saul, Joab and Absalom. Gersonides interprets the description of Esau as a "cunning hunter"[188] as evidence of Esau knowing not only how to capture animals but also how to cheat people with stratagems.[189] Similarly, Amalek used craftiness to make war with Israel at a time when it thought it would win by reading stars.[190] Balaam used stratagems to convince those he blessed and cursed that he was causing it. However, in reality he was only able to predict the future and give blessings or curses depending on whatever he saw.[191] Saul also used stratagems in trying to kill David[192] and Absalom used stratagems in his attempt to kill Amnon.[193]

But as Gersonides notes, stratagems can also be used to remove or minimize evil. One of the clearest of examples is Aaron's cunning in creating stratagems when the Israelites desired to worship other gods in Exodus 32. Realizing that the Israelites would not listen and would kill him, he created stratagems to appear as if he agreed with them and thus minimize the amount of evil done. His goal was to stall until Moses returned. Aaron then suggested making a golden calf, since it is preferable to worshipping a lamb, which would return them to earlier pagan worship in Egypt. Instead, he suggested the calf since it is the closest astrological symbol and hence served as a convenient means for the Israelites to trust him. Since Moses did not return immediately, Aaron introduced other stalling tactics such as engravings, building an altar and creating a holiday to celebrate.[194]

Another crucial usage of stratagems noted in Gersonides' interpretation of the Hebrew Bible is when they are directed toward saving a life. Gersonides states this principle clearly, saying that "it is appropriate for man to use all [possible] stratagems to save a life."[195] One example that he reads in this light, is Rahab's saving the Israelite spies by hiding them in her home through a ruse to distract their pursuers.[196] Gersonides interprets Rahab's strategy as making it appear in words that you want the individual to fall into the hands of the pursuer, while at the same time allowing the individual to escape. For example, Rahab told the King of Jericho that she did not know they were Israelites and, if so, would not have helped them, but told him that they escaped at night and did not know where they went. Gersonides also deduces from Rahab's words the prudent principle that one should not completely lie in the stratagem since others will be able to see through it. For example, Rahab did not say that the Israelites did not come at all.[197] Jonathan also employs a stratagem to save David by creating a secret method of communicating with David by shooting arrows into a field.[198] Likewise, David behaved rowdily beside Achish King of Gath to trick him into thinking David was crazy and not a spy to avoid being captured.[199]

Another area for employing stratagems is in business. Efron was using a ruse in negotiating with Abraham, by first saying he would give the cave to him for free, then reversing himself by saying he was embarrassed to say how much it is worth and implying sneakily that the price is not up for negotiations.[200] Similarly Joseph employed a stratagem of cleverly gathering all the grain in the years of plenty and redistributing it later during the years of draught.[201]

Stratagems also play a necessary role in military tactics in war. Gersonides lays out this principle in expounding upon Proverbs 11:14, interpreting "where no wise direction (taḥbulot) is, a people falleth" as indicating that without stratagems in war, one will fall to one's enemies.[202] Abraham employed them in his battle with the four kings by attacking at night when they were feasting over their booty; he divided the camp into various sections, thus splitting them before they could prepare to respond.[203] Joshua also tricked the city of Ay by setting up an ambush. The people of Ay assumed they would be victorious as in the last battle and thus rushed to send all their troops out to attack the Israelites when they saw the Israelite army coming, not realizing that another group of troops was ambushing them from behind. The ambush then burned the city and attacked the forces from the other side.[204] In another example, Ehud ben Gera also used surprise ruses in killing Eglon. He approached the king by pretending to come and give him a gift and once beside the king he killed him with a short two-sided sword that he did not see.[205] Likewise, David used a stratagem of tree camouflage in attacking the Philistines so that they did not see him coming.[206]

Ultimately, Gersonides lists many cases in which one cannot respond to chance through virtue and one must simply avoid the possibility of being in a dangerous situation. Gersonides states the principle that "it is not appropriate to put oneself in danger"[207] and that it is "appropriate to run away from even the smallest possibility of life threatening danger."[208] For example, Gersonides explains Jacob's decision to stop and sleep because it is dangerous to travel at night.[209] Jacob was also angry at his sons for carrying out the murder due to the possibility that the people of the land would kill him and his family[210]; he consequently forbade his sons from being noticed by the Canaanites when attempting to buy grain fearing their retaliation.[211] Gersonides thus presents us with numerous ways to overcome or avoid the forces of chance, but ultimately admits the necessity to flee danger due to the inability to truly comprehend the possible causes and outcomes of future chance events. The prudent person keeps out of trouble.

Physical Survival in the Legal Lessons

One can also detect the influence of Gersonides' ethics of physical self-preservation on the purpose behind many of the commandments themselves. There is a rabbinic precedent for this search and Gersonides is often basing his reasoning on that of Maimonides in the *Guide of the Perplexed*, but Gersonides changes the focus to place a greater emphasis on bodily perfection. Here are five examples for the Gersonidean emphasis on physical self-preservation within his legal lessons.

The first example is the prohibition against eating milk and meat together that is derived by the rabbinic tradition from the verse "thou shalt not seethe a kid in its mother's milk."[212] Maimonides states the likely reason for this commandment is that cooking a kid in its mother's milk was part of a pagan ritual[213] and Gersonides agrees with this rationale. But he also provides an additional rationale that is related to the health of the body, that eating meat and milk together leads to indigestion, since milk digests much faster than meat. The fact this command is also mentioned in Deuteronomy 14 among the foods forbidden to eat, according to Gersonides, suggests its posing a danger for eating and is not just forbidden for theological reasons.[214]

A second example is the reason behind the commandment of male circumcision at eight days old. This commandment originates from the biblical verses "this is My covenant, which ye shall keep, between Me and you and thy seed after thee: every male among you shall be circumcised. And ye shall be circumcised in the flesh of your foreskin; and it shall be a token of a covenant betwixt Me and you."[215] While the explicit reason given is that it is a symbol of God's covenant with the Israelites, Maimonides also adds another reason: circumcision weakens the amount of sexual excitement and pleasure and therefore maintains desire within the proper amount and discourages excessive lust.[216] Thus, for Maimonides circumcision is a law that cultivates moral perfection and having one's desires at the mean amount. Gersonides agrees with Maimonides here, but slightly shifts the focus away from diminishing lust to that of channeling that desire toward reproduction and perpetuation of the species. Gersonides also defends the eighth day as the ideal day to carry out this procedure as the child is strong, but not enough to feel, the parents do not have an emotional connection to prevent it from happening and if it is done once the child gets to the age of being responsible for fulfilling commandments, the chance of the procedure being fulfilled decreases.[217] Thus, both Maimonides and Gersonides interpret circumcision medically as a technique for reducing pleasure, but Maimonides does so for the sake of moral perfection, while Gersonides does so for the sake of physical perfection.

A third example is Gersonides' scientific interpretation of the nature of the purity and impurity rituals in light of the danger of contaminating others. These impurities include leprosy (ṣar'at), abnormal seminal discharge from the male sexual organ (zav), a woman in the menstrual cycle (zava), and a woman following childbirth (yoledet). A dominant stream in rabbinic interpretation looked at leprosy as a spiritual disease which was a divine punishment for an individual who was guilty of slander or libel.[218] Contrastingly, Gersonides defines leprosy as a natural phenomenon which is a disruption in the matter of humans that causes an increase in heat and a weakening of other faculties on the human body. The banishment of the leper from society helps contaminate and prevent the spread of the illness. The three other forms of impurity listed above do not need to be sent outside the boundaries of the encampment since their forms of impurity are not contagious and dangerous to others.[219]

According to Gersonides, the method of healing a leper through slaughtering one bird is a metaphor for the destruction of the disease, and the releasing of the other live bird serves as a metaphor for the process of the leper becoming healthy.[220]

This methodology applies likewise to the fourth example of crossbreeding animals. This is derived from the command "thou shalt not let thy cattle gender with a diverse kind."[221] The Hebrew Bible does not suggest a reason for why this law is necessary. Gersonides argues (following Naḥmanides on this verse) that the Torah is against multiplying animal species since it will change the balance of different species in nature and will lead to the destruction of species since the child of a mixed-species will have difficulties reproducing.[222]

One likewise sees the same concern for human preservation in the fifth example, the scheduling of the Jewish holidays, such as Passover and the Jewish New Year. He argues that the timing of these holidays corresponds to their horoscope in one of the twelve signs of the zodiac which delineate the place of the sun, moons and planets. Passover is situated during the period of the ram, during the period known as Aries. This is a period when the sun is closest to this world and one can therefore see the influence of the sun on vegetation, which corresponds to Passover as the beginning of the barley harvest.[223] The Jewish New Year is set on the first of Tishrei to correspond to the period of the scales in the horoscope, otherwise known as Libra. This is a period when the sun is weaker, which is a symbol for the older days of man when body is weak and mind is stronger.[224] Gersonides is implying in all this that the Jewish calendar is constructed to maximize the times in nature that one can use for agricultural means for the best physical interest of humans. During the times when the stars are not aligned for the best interest of the body, this is a time that should be maximized for perfection of the mind.

CONCLUSION: THE LIMITS OF THE STRUGGLE FOR EXISTENCE

Gersonides' ethics of bodily self-preservation maximizes the arts, virtues and laws of the Torah to best obtain the physical needs of individual human beings. Is this like Spinoza's conception of nature in which the "big fish eat little ones" or like Darwin's model of nature which is a "struggle for existence?" Should one use whatever means are necessary to achieve success? Are there any limits? The ethics of self-preservation appears morally neutral in which both good and evil forces manipulate the world for their own self-interest.

Gersonides does lay out two moral limits which serve as red lines in the pursuit of material preservation that guide self-preservation toward a noble end. One such limitation is the necessity for emotional balance through the mean in moral virtue to accompany the pursuit for bodily perfection. For Gersonides, Cain's murder of Abel is a test case in what happens when scientists constructing arts for bodily perfection do not already possess a perfected character. Other than the rare exception of Noah, moral perfection was not the dominant pursuit.[225] Hence, in Gersonides' understanding of the Cain and Abel narrative,[226] both were scientists constructing different arts, Cain studying botany and Abel studying animal husbandry, but a lack of emotional discipline and control led Cain to murder Abel when he did not succeed to the level of Abel in his endeavors.[227] There is a chain reaction which began with Cain's jealousy (*qin'a*) and embarrassment (*bush*) over the failure of his experiment led to anger (*ka'as*).[228] As a result, all of Cain's research was lost and needed to be discovered from scratch by another scientist many years later.[229] Therefore a belief in technology without a perfected character is doomed to fail in its pursuit of knowledge. In this regards, Gersonides does imply a shift between the patriarchs from Genesis 12 onward and those who precede the patriarchs from Genesis 1–11.[230] The significance of this shift is not that those before the patriarchs were ignorant of scientific knowledge of the universe, but that the patriarchs discovered that ethics must be rooted in the development and perfection of character to sustain that knowledge they obtained for future generations.

A second limitation is the recognition that other individual beings are not merely competitors in a struggle to survive, but are individual beings that are in need of assistance and improvement in their lives. As important as the individual needs of the body are, there are certain collective goods that outweigh them. Imitation of God as a model of altruism provides the ideal in which the individual struggle for survival should ultimately aim. It is this theme, which we will explore further in the next chapter.

NOTES

1. *DA*, 75–77 (3.10) and *NE*, 115–116 (6.1).
2. *Comm Gen*, 85 (on Gen 2:4–3:24).

3. Gen 2:17.
4. *Comm Gen*, 85 (on Gen 2:4–3:24).
5. *Supercomm De Anima*, 28.
6. Ibid., 183.
7. *Wars*, vol. i, 166–167 (1.7) and vol. ii, 176 (4.5).
8. *Wars*, vol. ii, 176 (4.5).
9. *Wars*, vol. i, 166–167 (1.7) and vol. ii, 176 (4.5).
10. *Wars*, vol. i, 166–167 (1.7).
11. *Supercomm De Anima*, 48.
12. *Supercomm De Anima*, 18 and *Comm Song of Songs*, 69.
13. Song of Songs 5:14.
14. *Comm Song of Songs*, 69.
15. The process of the human mind coming to acquire knowledge is ambiguous at *DA* 3.5 where he posits that something passive or receptive is energized and put into action by some intellectual power which is active. Two Greek commentators, Alexander of Aphrodisias (second century AD) and Theimistius (317–390 AD), debated the nature of the passive and active element. For Alexander, the human material intellect is just a capacity that is itself empty (a "blank tablet") of which God as Agent Intellect actualizes the material intellect to think and become intellect. For Theimistius, the human material intellect is really Agent Intellect "accidentally" located in sensory collections of each human mind. Gersonides accepts Alexander's model of the human material intellect as a physiobiological capacity for knowledge, though disagrees with Alexander that the Agent Intellect is God. See Seymour Feldman, "Synopsis of the *Wars of the Lord*: Book One: Immortality of the Soul," in *Wars*, vol. I (Philadelphia, 1984), 71–84.
16. Gen 2:18.
17. *Comm Gen*, 106 (on Gen 2:4–3:24). Translation of Shlomo Pines. See Shlomo Pines, "Truth and Falsehood Versus Good and Evil. A Study in Jewish and General Philosophy in Connection with the *Guide of the Perplexed*, I, 2," in *Studies in Maimonides*, ed. Isadore Twersky (Cambridge: Cambridge University Press, 1990), 135. Gersonides' position on women is more problematic from a contemporary perspective. He is willing to accredit the snake as a metaphor, since there cannot be a speaking animal at beginning of creation and then have it placed in a lower nature. But he is not willing to read Adam and Eve as metaphors, since he is concerned

with turning the Torah into an intellectual metaphor. If it was all a parable, there would be no *to'alot* (*Comm Gen*, 114 [on Gen 2:4–3:24]). See Menachem Kellner, "Philosophical Misogyny in Medieval Jewish Thought: Gersonides vs. Maimonides," in *Y. Sermonetta Memorial Volume*, ed. Aviezer Ravitzky (Jerusalem: Magnes Press, 1998), 113–28. Also for a more positive position on women in medieval Jewish philosophy, see Abraham Melamed, "Maimonides on Women: Formless Matter or Potential Prophet?" in *Perspectives on Jewish Thought and Mysticism*, ed. Alfred Ivry, Elliot Wolfson and Allan Arkush (Amsterdam: Harwood Academic Publishers, 1998), 99–134.

18. *Comm Gen*, 106–107 (on Gen 2:4–3:24).
19. *NE*, 124 (6.7).
20. Ibid.
21. Ibid. Gersonides' presentation of the practical intellect also differs from the Thomistic ideal. Aquinas' interpretation of Aristotle highlights the more theoretical side of practical wisdom. All practical wisdom must begin in *synderesis*. *Syndresis* is a natural habit shared by all humans to know the first principle or axiom of natural law and is the end to which all our actions incline. This is the principle of "pursuing good and avoiding harm." It becomes the first principle of practical reason, which is parallel to the law of noncontradiction, the first principle of theoretical reason. See Thomas Aquinas, *Summa Theologicae*, trans. Fathers of the English Dominican Province (New York: Benziger Bros, 1947–1948), 1–2, 94, 1. Two contemporary interpreters of Aquinas, Germain Grisez and John Finnis, attempt to split Aquinas' ethics from his metaphysics and to secularize *syndresis*. See Germain Grisez, "The First Principle of Practical Reason," in *Aquinas*, ed. Anthony Kenny (New York: 1969), 340–382; John Finnis, *Natural Law and Natural Rights* (New York, 1980), 33–34; and Douglas Uyl, *The Virtue of Prudence* (New York, 1991), 99.
22. Averroes' commentary on Aristotle's *Nicomachean Ethics* sticks very closely to the text with only minor deviations. See Harvey, "The Nature and Importance," 259–260. But Christian Averroists such as Marsilius of Padua made the case for grounding of practical wisdom much more in biology. Alan Gewirth suggests that "Marsilius biologized morals and politics." See Alan Gewirth,

Marsilius of Padua and Medieval Political Philosophy (New York, 1951), 51.

23. *Comm Gen*, 85 (on Gen 2:4–3:24).

24. *Comm Gen*, 85 (on Gen 2:4–3:24). The wording of Gersonides' version is very different from Samuel ben Judah of Marseille's translation of Averroes' Commentary. The ordering of the goods in Averroes' translation is pleasure (*ta'anug*), wealth (*'osher*) and honor (*kavod*). See Averroes, *Middle Commentary on Aristotle's Nicomachean Ethics*, 63.

25. Two recent articles have investigated the question of chance in Gersonides' thought: Sara Klein-Braslavy, "Aristotle's Concept of Chance as an Investigative Tool in Gersonides' *Wars of the Lord*," *Aleph* 12.1 (2012), 65–100 and Steven Nadler, "Virtue, Reason, and Moral Luck: Maimonides, Gersonides, Spinoza" in *Spinoza and Medieval Jewish Philosophy*, ed. Steven Nadler (Cambridge: Cambridge University Press, 2014), 152–176.

26. Aristotle, *Physics* 2.5. Klein-Braslavy, "Aristotle's Concept of Chance," 67–68.

27. Maimonides predates Gersonides in identifying the biblical term *qeri* from Leviticus 26:27–28 as chance connecting *qeri* and *miqre* at *MT, Laws of Fasts Days*, 1:1–3. Though he does not identify chance with astrology like Gersonides, he does see wisdom as being able to fight against chance. Averroes' use of *tyche* was also translated as *qeri* and *miqre*. Following Averroes, Gersonides uses the expression *qeri ve-hizdamen* and *miqre ve-hizdamen* as an overarching expression for all forms of chance. See Klein-Braslavy, "Aristotle's Concept of Chance," 73n31, 75n35 and 93n79.

28. Klein-Braslavy, "Determinism, Contingency, Free Choice, and Foreknowledge in Gersonides," in *"Without Any Doubt": Gersonides on Method and Knowledge*, trans. Lenn J. Schramm (Leiden: Brill, 2011), 258.

29. *Wars*, vol. i, 146–148 (1.6) and vol. ii, 117 (3.4).

30. *Guide*, II 24 and Feldman, "Gersonides on the Possibility of Conjunction," *AJS Review* 3 (1978), 115. There is a large scholarly discussion of the "limitations of human knowledge" which begun from Shlomo Pines' article "The Limitations of Human Knowledge According to al-Farabi, ibn Bajja, and Maimonides," in *Studies in Medieval Jewish History and Literature*, ed. Isadore Twersky (Cambridge, 1979), 82–109.

31. *Wars*, vol. iii, 484 (6.2.10).
32. Gersonides writes that "God will not create a miracle, except in places that are necessary" and "nothing will be created against nature, except in times of need." See *Comm Gen*, 344 (Genesis 26:7, Ethical Lesson #3) and *Comm Early Proph I*, 231 (I Samuel 13–II Samuel 1, Lesson #15).
33. Klein-Braslavy, "Determinism, Contingency," 258.
34. *Wars* 2.2, vol. ii, 33. Please note that I reversed the order of the two clauses. Gersonides begins with a conclusion and then explains how he arrives at it, while I switched the order to make it easier to understand for the reader.
35. Ibid.
36. *Wars* 2.2, vol. ii, 31. It is this knowledge which is attained through dreams, divination, and prophecy.
37. It is important to note that even though Gersonides was slightly more idealistic than Aristotle and Maimonides about the ability to overcome luck, his model recognizes that in each of these models, there are cases that a virtue or art cannot fully prevent. For example, this would include some genetic predispositions, such as being dropped as a baby or being a Jew in Germany during the Nazi regime. Arts and virtues cannot prevent such occurrences on an individual level, but through cultivation and progress can stop their occurrence or deleterious effects for future individuals.
38. *NE*, 19–20 (1.10).
39. *Wars* 2.2, vol. ii, 33.
40. Ibid., 34.
41. Ibid., 177 (4.5).
42. Ibid., 35–36 (2.2).
43. *NE*, 119–120 (6.4).
44. Thanks to Edward Halper for helping me clarify this point. For the origin of this in Aristotle, see James G. Lennox, "Aristotle on the Biological Roots of Virtue: The Natural History of Natural Virtue," in *Biology and the Foundation of Ethics*, ed. Jane Maienschein and Michael Ruse (Cambridge: Cambridge University Press, 1999), 10–31.
45. *NE.*, 119–121 (6.4-5).
46. Ibid., 7 (1.5).
47. *Guide*, 634 (III 54).

48. Arts are mentioned briefly in Averroes' *Epitome* on the *De Anima*, trans. Deborah Black (Toronto: University of Toronto Press, 2009), Section 68, 26–27, but their significance is ambiguous:

> But since there is also some animal, namely a human being, in whose existence is not possible by these two powers alone, but by his having as well a power by which he perceives ideas abstracted from matter and composes some of them with others and discovers some of them through others, so that he constructs many arts and vocations from them which are useful in his existence, either with respect to some need he has or for the sake of excellence, therefore the need for this power, that is, the power of reason, arises in human being.

49. *Supercomm De Anima*, 46. Deborah Black in translating from the Arabic does not bring out the preservative elements that Mashbaum does in translating from the Hebrew. Mashbaum's "benefit their survival" (*mo'il bi-meṣi'uto*) and "preservation" (*haṣalat ha-ḥai*) is for Black "useful for its existence" and "healthy."
50. *Wars* 4.5, vol. ii, 177.
51. See Chap. 5.
52. *Comm Gen*, 117 (on Gen 4:1–26).
53. Gen 3:18.
54. *Comm Gen*, 110 (on Gen 2:4–3:24).
55. Ibid., 104–105.
56. *Comm Song of Songs*, 86.
57. *Wars*, vol. iii, 313–316 (6.1.15).
58. *Comm Gen*, 69 (on Gen 1:20–23).
59. *Wars*, vol. i, 94 (Intro).
60. *Wars*, vol. iii, 313–316 (6.1.15). Leo Strauss shrewdly notices the tension of Gersonides' approach between the "belief in the possibility of the progress of science," but "not a belief in infinite progress." See Leo Strauss, *Philosophy and Law: Contributions to the Understanding of Maimonides and His Predecessors* (Albany: State University of New York Press, 1995), 94 and n30.
61. Gen 3:21.
62. *Comm Gen*, 102 (on Gen 3:21).
63. Onkelos on Genesis 3:21 refers to the garments as "vestments of honor" (*livushin diqar*).

64. Ibid.
65. *Wars*, vol. iii, 495 (6.2.12) and Eisen, *Gersonides on Providence*, 22–28.
66. *Comm Gen*, 110–111 (on Gen 2:4–3:24).
67. Shame has a very tentative status in *NE*, 38 (2.7). It has a temporary role in an early stage in development of character, like in early stage in a child's development.
68. *Comm Gen*, 123 (on Gen 4:1–26).
69. Ibid., 125.
70. Ibid., 125.
71. Ibid., 123–124.
72. Ibid., 125. Gersonides actually uses the logical principle of *min temurat ha-kolel*, where one infers a general principle from a specific case. Gersonides already warns in the Introduction (Ibid., 6 [Intro]) that he will use this principle as the first of his *meqomot* (*topoi*).
73. Ibid., 123.
74. Ibid., 124.
75. Ibid., 125.
76. Ibid., 126.
77. Maimonides model of the "divine will" can be understood as a metaphor for nature, where the "divine" acts are the "natural" acts (*Guide*, III 32). See Avraham Nuriel, "The Divine Will in More Nevukhim," *Tarbiz* 39, no. 1 (1969), 39–61 and Roslyn Weiss, "Natural Order or Divine Will: Maimonides on Cosmogony and Prophecy," *Journal of Jewish Thought and Philosophy* 15, no. 1 (2007), 1–26.
78. *Comm Gen*, 126–127 (on Gen 4:1–26).
79. Gen 3:20.
80. *Comm Gen*, 129 (on Gen 4:1–26).
81. Gen 3:17 and Ibid.
82. Gen 3:21 and *Comm Gen*, 129 (on Gen 4:1–26).
83. Gen 3:22 and *Comm Gen*, 129 (on Gen 4:1–26).
84. *Comm Gen*, 162 (on Gen 6:9–7:17).
85. Ibid., 183–184 (on Gen 11:1–9).
86. Ibid., 184 (on Gen 11:1–9).
87. Ibid., 117 (on Gen 4:1–26).
88. *Wars*, vol. iii, 314 (6.2.15) and Menachem Kellner, "Maimonides and Gersonides on Astronomy and Metaphysics," in *Torah in the*

Observatory: Gersonides, Maimonides and Song of Songs (Atlanta: Academic Studies Press, 2009), 149–151.

89. *NE*, 33–36 (2.6) and 120–121 (6.5).
90. Ibid., 19–20 (1.10).
91. *Supercomm De Anima*, 59–60.
92. Gersonides understood Maimonides' moral virtues in Ibn Tibbon's Hebrew translation. It is unclear if or to what extent he would have had access to the Judaeo-Arabic original.
93. *Comm Gen*, 212–213 (Gen 14:14–15, Ethical Lesson #3–4).
94. Ibid., 293 (Gen 21:25, Ethical Lesson #10).
95. Ibid., 213 (Gen 14:22–23, Ethical Lesson #7) and 204 (Gen 13:14–18, Ethical Lesson #12).
96. Charles Manekin is one of the first to notice this array of virtues. See Charles Manekin, "Freedom Within Reason?: Gersonides on Human Choice," in *Freedom and Moral Responsibility: General and Jewish Perspectives* (College Park: University Press of Maryland, 1997), 185. David Horwitz argues that these three are in fact identical and synonyms. My reading shows the difficulties in this and differences between them. See David Horwitz, "*Ha-Haritzut Emet*: Ralbag's View of a Central Pragmatic/ Ethical Characteristic of Abraham," in *Hazon Nahum: Studies in Jewish Law, Thought, and History Presented to Dr. Norman Lamm*, eds. Yaakov Elman and Jeffrey S. Gurock (New York: Yeshiva University Press, 1997), 268n13. He is basing this on Jacob Klatzkin's medieval Hebrew philosophic dictionary. Klatzkin may have been correct about general medieval philosophical usage, but Gersonides was too scientific and nuanced to make this assumption. See Jacob Klatzkin, *Oṣar ha-Munaḥim ha-Filosofi- yyim* (repr. New York, 1968), vol. i, 330. As you can see from Klatzkin, Gersonides does not invent these Hebrew terms and their usages, but takes them and makes them into a central part of an ethics centered on physical self-preservation.
97. One notable exception: Horwitz, *Gersonides' Ethics*, 228.
98. Mishnah Avot 2:5, 4:20.
99. *BT* Pesaḥim 113a.
100. *Guide*, III 51, 618.
101. Ibid. 621.
102. Ibid. *Hishtadlut* also plays a role in both Judah Halevi's *Kuzari* 3.8 and 5.10 and Bahya Ibn Pakuda's *Duties of the Heart* 4.3. The

reason I focus on the *Guide* is that Gersonides views his work as a response to Maimonides, while Halevi and Bahya are not mentioned. Even if Warren Zev Harvey is correct that Halevi model of the *hishtadlut* of nature played a role influencing the translator of Averroes, it is less clear if this part of Halevi's work was a direct influence on Gersonides. See Warren Zev Harvey, "Gersonides and Spinoza on Conatus," *Aleph* 12, no. 2 (2012), 283.

103. The centrality of Maimonides as Gersonides' philosophic predecessor and opponent can be seen in his Introduction to *Wars*, where he states "the glorious jewel of the sages of our Torah, Moses ben Maimon have not investigated this question in the way [that we propose]" (*Wars*, vol. i, 94 [Intro]).

104. This has been developed in two recent studies on Gersonides' *Supercommentary* on Averroes' *Commentary* on the *Book of Animals*. See Harvey, "Gersonides and Spinoza on Conatus" and Ahuva Gaziel, "Gersonides' Naturalistic Account of Providence in Light of the *Book of Animals*," *Aleph* 12, no. 2 (2012), 243–271.

105. Aristotle, *Generation of Animals* 3.2, 760a–b and *Supercomm De Animalibus*, Ch 17, MS. Vatican, 127a. Referenced by Harvey, Ibid., 278.

106. Aristotle, *Parts of Animals* 1.1, 642a and *Supercomm De Animalibus*, Ch 11, 99. Referenced by Harvey, Ibid., 279. Editing of Gersonides' *Supercommentary* on *Book of Animals* thanks to Ahuva Gaziel's edition and translation into English thanks to Warren Zev Harvey's article.

107. Harvey, Ibid., 276.

108. *Comm Song of Songs*, 48 (3:3).

109. *Supercomm De Anima*, 19 and 21.

110. One study to begin to analyze *hishtadlut* in the biblical commentaries is Carmiel Cohen, "Human Endeavor and Trust of God in Gersonides' Biblical Commentaries," *Megadim* 45 (2007), 109–123.

111. *Comm Gen*, 227 (Gen 15:2–3, Ethical Lesson #2) and *DH*, 417.

112. *Comm Gen*, 233 (Gen 16:2, Ethical Lesson #1).

113. Ibid., 325 (Gen 24:8, Ethical Lesson #5) and *DH*, 429.

114. *Comm Gen*, 267 (on Gen 19:31–32).

115. Ibid., 395 (Gen 29:21, Ethical Lesson #13).

116. *Comm Exod*, vol. i, 13 (on Exod 2:2).

117. Ibid., 7 (on Exod 1:17).

118. Ibid., 15 (on Exod 2:9).
119. *Comm Gen*, 356 (Gen 27:1–4, Ethical Lesson #1).
120. Ibid., 227 (Gen 15:2–6, Ethical Lesson #3) and *DH*, 417.
121. *Comm Gen*, 356 (Gen 27:1–4, Ethical Lesson #1).
122. Ibid., 356 (Gen 25:28, 27:1–10, Ethical Lesson #2).
123. Ibid., 520 (Gen 45:9–13, 23, Ethical Lesson #5) and *DH*, 452.
124. *Comm Gen*, 501 (on Gen 44:14).
125. Gen 45:9–13, 23.
126. *Comm Exod*, vol. i, 19 (Exod 2:7, Ethical Lesson #3).
127. Ibid., 235–236 (Exod 13:19, Ethical Lesson #2).
128. *Comm Gen*, 538 (Gen 47:29–31, Ethical Lesson #1).
129. Ibid., 308 (Gen 23:2, Ethical Lesson #1 and Genesis 23:3–20, Ethical Lesson #2).
130. *Comm Exod*, vol. i, 235–236 (Exod 13:19, Ethical Lesson #2).
131. *Comm Gen*, 233 (Gen 16:2, Ethical Lesson #1).
132. Ibid., 309 (Gen 23:8–18, Ethical Lesson #5).
133. *Comm Exod*, vol. i, 19 (Exod 2:7, Ethical Lesson #3).
134. *Comm Early Proph I*, 88 (Judg 4:16, Lesson #5).
135. *Comm Gen*, 325 (Gen 24:8, Ethical Lesson #5).
136. Ibid., 357 (Gen 27:11–12, 15–16, Ethical Lesson #3).
137. Ibid., 520 (Gen 45:9–13, 23, Ethical Lesson #5).
138. Ibid., 538 (Gen 47:29–31, Ethical Lesson #1).
139. *Comm Numbers*, 454 (Numb 34:1–15, Lesson #6).
140. Esther 5:3.
141. Ibid.
142. Ibid.
143. *Comm Megillot*, 160 (Esther, Lesson #35).
144. Ibid., 157 (Esther, Lesson #25).
145. *Comm Gen*, 472 (Gen 40:14, Ethical Lesson #7).
146. Ibid., 460 (Gen 38:1, Ethical Lesson #1).
147. Ibid., 398 (Gen 30:27, Ethical Lesson #27).
148. Ibid., 194 (Gen 12:3, Lesson #2).
149. Ibid., 398 (Gen 30:27, Ethical Lesson #27).
150. Ibid., 460 (Gen 38:1, Ethical Lesson #1).
151. Ibid., 204 (Gen 13:8–9, Ethical Lesson #8).
152. Ibid., 357 (Gen 27:42–45, Ethical Lesson #6).
153. Ibid., 409 (on Gen 32:4).
154. Prov 17:1.
155. *Comm Gen*, 204 (Gen 13:8–9, Ethical Lesson #8) and *DH*, 413.

156. *BT* Yevamot 65b.
157. *Comm Gen*, 564 (Gen 50:16–17, Ethical Lesson #12) and *DH*, 463.
158. *Comm Exod*, vol. i, 45 (Exod 2:14–15, 3:1, Ethical Lesson #3).
159. *Comm Megillot*, 155–156 (Esther, Lesson #18).
160. *Comm Gen*, 203 (Gen 12:10–13, Ethical Lesson #3) and *DH*, 410.
161. *Comm Gen*, 411 (on Gen 32:8–9) and 417 (Gen 32:8–9, 33:1–2, Ethical Lesson #3).
162. Ibid., 453 (on Gen 37:21–24).
163. *Wars*, vol. ii, 36 (2.2).
164. *Comm Numbers*, 336 (on Numb 25:17–18).
165. *Comm Megillot*, 140–141 (on Esther 3:8–11).
166. Numb 25:17–18.
167. *Comm Megillot*, 146 and 157 (on Esther 7:5–6 and Esther, Lesson #25).
168. *Supercomm De Anima*, 183. Thanks to David Horwitz for making this connection. See Horwitz, *Gersonides' Ethics*, 226–236. The context of Averroes' discussion: "The failure of the appetitive soul to receive movement from the imaginative form is called 'paralysis' and slow reception is called 'laziness' while quickness of reception is called 'agility' " (from Mashbaum's translation).
169. Horwitz, "*Ha-Haritzut Emet*," 267.
170. Examples of Gersonides' usage of *ḥarisut* as referring to speed of desire for the object includes Lot's advice at Sodom (*Comm Gen*, 274 [Gen 19:17, Ethical Lesson #22]), Lot's daughter's getting up after sleeping with father (*Comm Gen*, 267 [on Gen 19:33–35]), Abraham's following God's command to sacrifice Isaac (*Comm Gen*, 298 [on Genesis 22:3]), and Abraham's endeavor to bury Sarah (*Comm Gen*, 308 [Gen 23:3–20, Ethical Lesson #2]).
171. *Comm Gen*, 195 (Gen 12:5, Ethical Lesson #3).
172. Ibid.
173. Ibid., 203 (Gen 13:1–3, Ethical Lesson #6) and *DH*, 411.
174. *Comm Numbers*, 360 (Numb 27:1–7, Lesson #6).
175. *Comm Exod*, 375 (Exod 20:8–10, Legal Lesson #10).
176. *Comm Gen*, 202 (Gen 12:10, Ethical Lesson #1).
177. Ibid. (Gen 18:2–8, Ethical Lesson #2) and *DH*, 419.
178. *Comm Gen*, 326 (Gen 24:12–25, Ethical Lesson #7).
179. *Comm Megillot*, 5 (on Ruth 2:7).

180. *Comm Proverbs*, 44 (on Prov 10:4).
181. Prov 31:21.
182. *Comm Proverbs*, 150 (on Prov 31:21).
183. Ibid., 57 and 150 (on Prov 12:24 and 31:20).
184. Eisenmann, "Social and Political Principles," 242.
185. *Guide*, III 54, 632–633.
186. Ibid., III 32, 526–531. Shlomo Pines points out that the Arabic term *talattuf* is used six times in different contexts in *Guide* III 32. Pines translates as "gracious ruse" and "wily graciousness." Ibn Tibbon translates as both *'orma* and *taḥbula*. See Shlomo Pines, "The Philosophic Sources of *The Guide of the Perplexed*," in *Guide*, lxxii–lxxiii.
187. To counter Maimonides and highlight the non-esoteric character of *Wars of the Lord*, Gersonides stresses how *Wars of the Lord* was not written with intellectual stratagems, concealing from masses so that only few will understand (*Wars*, vol. i, 101 [Intro]). Though in his *Commentary on Proverbs* he praises intellectual stratagems. See *Comm Proverbs*, 94–95 (on Proverbs 20:18–19).
188. Gen 25:27.
189. *Comm Gen*, 335 (on Gen 25:27).
190. *Comm Exod*, 287–289 (on Exod 17:16).
191. *Comm Numbers*, 287 (on Numb 22:6).
192. *Comm Early Proph I*, 202 (on I Sam 18:9–13).
193. Ibid., 256–257 (on II Sam 13:24–27).
194. Exdous 33:4–5; *Comm Exod*, 393–394 (on Exod 31:18–32:12); and 440 (Exod 32:1–6, Ethical Lesson #11).
195. *Comm Early Proph I*, 236 (on I Sam 13–II Sam 1, Lesson #34).
196. Josh 2:1–9.
197. *Comm Early Proph I*, 20–21 (Josh 1–5, Lesson #7–8).
198. Ibid., 234–235 (I Sam 13–II Sam 1, Lesson #32).
199. Ibid., 236 (I Sam 13–II Sam 1, Lesson #34).
200. *Comm Gen*, 307–308 (on Gen 23:14–15).
201. Ibid., 502 (Gen 41:48, Ethical Lesson #1).
202. *Comm Proverbs*, 51 (on Prov 11:14).
203. *Comm Gen*, 212–213 (Gen 14:15, Ethical Lesson #4).
204. *Comm Early Proph I*, 33 (on Josh 8:1, 8:14).
205. Ibid., 76 (Judg 1–3, Lesson #6).
206. Ibid., 246 and 248 (on II Sam 5:7–8, 22–25).
207. *Comm Gen*, 440 (Gen 34:30, Ethical Lesson #8).

208. Ibid., 503 (Gen 42:1, Ethical Lesson #4).
209. Ibid., 364 (Gen 28:11, Ethical Lesson #3).
210. Ibid., 440 (Gen 34:30, Ethical Lesson #8).
211. Ibid., 503 (Gen 42:1, Ethical Lesson #4).
212. Exod 23:19.
213. *Guide*, III 48, 599.
214. *Comm Exod*, vol. ii, 123–125 (on Exod 23:19). Gersonides very cleverly uses the fact that this command is stated three times in the Hebrew Bible, at Exod 23:19, 24:26 and Deut 14:21 as a hint that there are three different reasons for the commandment.
215. Gen 17:10–13.
216. *Guide*, III 49, 609–610.
217. *Comm Leviticus*, vol. ii, 123–124 (Lev 12, Legal Lesson #3).
218. BT Shabbat 97a and James Diamond, "Maimonides on Leprosy: Illness as Contemplative Metaphor," *Jewish Quarterly Review* 96, no. 1 (2006), 95–122.
219. *Comm Leviticus*, vol. i, 307–308 (on Lev 11).
220. Ibid., 314–315.
221. Lev 19:19.
222. *Comm Leviticus*, vol. ii, 253–254 (on Lev 19:19).
223. Ibid., 385 (on Lev 22–23).
224. Ibid., 390.
225. *Comm Gen*, 146 (on Gen 6:9).
226. Ibid., 129 (on Gen 4:1–26).
227. Ibid., 123, 124, and 126.
228. Ibid., 126–127 (on Gen 4:1–26).
229. Ibid., 129.
230. Robert Eisen argues that Gersonides' understanding of Abraham's being the first to receive God's special covenant, the Covenant of the Pieces, is a form of inherited providence which continues throughout Jewish history. See Eisen, *Gersonides on Providence*, 43–52. This shift form of providence appears to contain an ethical teaching.

CHAPTER 3

Altruism and the Beneficent Virtues

Another key difference between the ethics of Maimonides and Gersonides is on the nature of altruism and beneficence. Both accept the Aristotelian description of God as intellect but reject the implications that God is simply self-contemplating. In synthesizing Aristotle and the Bible, Maimonides and Gersonides both describe the universe as originating from God for no self-interested benefit, but derive different human lessons from God's altruism. For Maimonides, the overflow to others is merely an outcome of one's own perfection and thus humans feel the same impulse to imitate God's loving kindness and spread the "overflow" of their private contemplation to forms of political leadership. Contrastingly, for Gersonides, altruism is not merely a passive outcome, but an active duty. Furthermore, it takes the form of a nonpolitical universal and altruistic ethics whereby humans are obliged to cultivate the virtues of loving kindness (*ḥesed*), grace (*ḥanina*) and beneficence (*haṭava*) in knowledge and action.

ARISTOTLE ON THE INSEPARABILITY OF EGOISM AND ALTRUISM

Aristotle describes God in the *Metaphysics* as an unmoved mover who causes the motion of the rest of the cosmos without himself moving. God causes the motion of the cosmos by being the object of love of all other beings, but has no need to love others: "The final cause, then, produces motion as being loved, but all other things move by being moved."[1] In Aristotle's model, God's love and benefit for others is an unintended consequence of

© The Author(s) 2016   63
A. Green, *The Virtue Ethics of Levi Gersonides,*
DOI 10.1007/978-3-319-40820-0_3

God's own self-love and self-contemplation and by the love and contemplation of others of God. Though among humans, according to Aristotle, personal self-interest is always tied to the concern for a greater collective, and the greater collective always works toward the interests of individuals. For example, in the *Nicomachean Ethics*, laws must cultivate the moral virtue of individuals and the individual moral virtues are perfected by exercising them in relation to another person.[2]

However, the relationship between the individual and the collective in Aristotle's ethical thought has been challenged by one of the major criticisms launched against Aristotelian virtue ethics over the last century—its supposed egoism.[3] This critique centers on the ability of an agent to be motivated by purely self-interested or egoistic reasons, in contrast to the view that an agent can be motivated by altruistic reasons that are not in any way in the agent's interest. Scholars who make the case against Aristotle's egoism argue that, for him, ethics is "ultimately selfish" in contrast to morality, which is "essentially unselfish"[4] and that "self-interest, more or less enlightened, is assumed to be the motive of all conduct and choice."[5] The case for defending Aristotle as an egoist can be based on ideas spread throughout the *Nicomachean Ethics*. He begins the work by presenting the goal of politics (*politike*) as that which guides people to individual happiness and then goes into detail about what happiness consists of.[6] The development of moral virtue is focused on the development of emotions in the soul of an agent such as ensuring good habits, and achieving the mean in relation to pleasure and pain.[7] In his discussion of friendship, Aristotle notably argues that the root of the love of others is actually the love of one's self.[8] The example he gives is of a mother who loves her child, seemingly for the sake of the child, but actually because the child is her own creation and is a piece of herself.[9] The book ends with the most egoistic conception of the ideal form of happiness which is the individual's pure contemplation leading to autonomy and self-sufficiency.[10]

Many recent scholars of Aristotelian ethics have responded to this portrait by arguing that it is a selective caricature, and in fact a careful reading of Aristotle reveals that he is actually an altruist.[11] Julia Annas asserts that "Aristotle's discussion in the *Nicomachean Ethics* is often abused as reducing friendship and all apparent altruism to egoism" and Richard Kraut states that "pure egoism is incompatible with the ideal of human relationships that Aristotle puts forward in his discussion of friendship."[12] This would be consistent with a reading of ethics as part of the political art, where the cultivation of individual happiness is merely one part of the larger collective. In rejection of the egoist reading in which the goal of politics (*politike*) guides people to individual happiness,[13] the altruist would claim that Aristotle introduces that discussion with one which defends the good of the city as greater and more complete than the individual good, referring to it as more noble and more divine.[14] Aristotle also presents justice as an inseparable part of moral virtue[15] and offers models of political justice, such as distributive and corrective justice, which transcend selfish human interest.[16] Moreover, in Aristotle's discussion of friendship, the defenders of the "altruistic" Aristotle would respond to the egoists by separating the reduction of the love of others to the love of self in Book 9 from the possibility of an altruistic friendship in Book 8.[17] There Aristotle discusses friendship where one acts for the good of the other person for their sake and not as a means to some personal goal for oneself.[18] Kraut interprets the phrases "for the sake of another" as leaving open a possibility of a complex motivation and a purely altruistic reason being one possibility.[19] Kraut even minimizes Aristotle's self-interested ideal of pure contemplation not as the best life for all, but as one possible way of life.[20]

The inherent difficulty of this discussion is that the categories of egoism and altruism are modern ones that contemporary interpreters of Aristotle are imposing onto the text. They cannot help but twist Aristotle's statements in order to fit them into these modern classifications. The modern approach stems from its focus on the primacy of the individual who predates the agreement of the social contract and the creation of the state. All individuals are equal in this state of nature, but the framework of the social contract depends on the nature of the pre-political individual. Two major answers dominated modern thinking on the nature of the individual in the state of nature. This individual may be inherently egoistic concerned with his own physical self-preservation and signs a contract with others to preserve this purpose, as Hobbes suggested, or the individual is intrinsically concerned with the pity (and thus well-being) of others and agrees to the contract to legislate compassion, as Rousseau argued.

Aristotle, though, did not present the ethics of the individual as limited to either of these categories. For Aristotle, personal self-interest is always tied to concern for the greater collective and the greater collective always works toward the interests of individuals.[21] Or as Hardie articulates it, "when every move has been made to reconcile egoism and altruism, there remains a conflict between the extreme demands of political morality, including readiness to be killed, and the attainment of happiness in a 'complete life'. Aristotle can abandon neither."[22] The reason this choice is problematic is that Aristotle argues that our true self is the intellect, and wisdom is a property that is universal to everyone. Thus by creating a friendship of the good (as opposed to friendship of utility or pleasure), one is helping both oneself and the other, hence making the divide between egoism and altruism collapse, which is the sign of the highest form of friendship.[23] This is represented through the image of maternal love for a child (as discussed earlier), which he presents as both egoist and altruistic. This tension is also exemplified in the last five chapters of Book 10 of the *Nicomachean Ethics*. Aristotle begins by presenting the secluded contemplative life as ideal and the moral-political life as only secondary.[24] But right after highlighting this model, he then presents a critique of it, shows how unrealistic it is, and suggests the necessity to return to the city to legislate good laws. Read in this light, the tension between the good of the individual and the good of the collective is not one with an easy solution in Aristotle's thought.

Divine Altruism in Saadya and Maimonides

The model of God as self-less and altruistic in creating the world for no self-interested purpose finds expression in the thought of Saadya Gaon and Moses Maimonides. In constructing a Jewish natural theology, Saadya Gaon presented the first systematic description of God as an altruistic creator of the universe. According to Saadya, creation was God's first act of loving kindness (*fadl, ḥesed*) which was executed through bringing beings into existence from nonbeing.[25] As he states in his Introduction to his *Commentary on Job*,

> [p]lainly, his bringing creation into being from nothing is the ultimate act of grace. For he created the entire world and settled it with human beings for their benefit....Likewise, his giving us life, and the other acts of providence by which he governs us and order the passage of our lives are all expressions of grace and bounty.[26]

God's revelation of a divine law is His natural and loving response to lovingly creating the universe. Although Saadya contends that the truths of revelation are not suprarational and can in theory be attained by humans through their own effort, he suggests that such a situation is difficult and rare for both reasons of nature, in that not everyone has the capabilities, and nurture, in that not everyone will want to take the time and exert the effort. This is why God needs to give humanity a divine law as it is a kind of instruction manual and shortcut to reaching natural truths.[27] Thus God's generosity in creating humanity necessitates the same generosity as expressing itself in revealing a law.

Maimonides presents a similar presentation of God as a loving and altruistic creator, but understands the implications of creation differently: God's actions serve as a model for virtue ethics within a state. In doing so, he quotes Jeremiah 9:23, "for I the Lord act with loving-kindness (*ḥesed*), justice (*mishpaṭ*) and righteousness (*ṣedaqa*) in the world."[28] Maimonides interprets this verse as suggesting that once one has completed the four perfections of possessions, body, moral traits and intellect, one can imitate God's divine actions in the world. Maimonides is obscure about the meaning of these divine actions, and divergent interpretations have been proposed by interpreters. Are they practiced in the form of moral virtues that are cultivated by a law within a state, or are they a form of morality that arises from a metaphysical study of God and are thus trans-political?

Interpreters of Maimonides who have been influenced by the thought of Immanuel Kant have read Kant's critique of metaphysics and the primacy of a universal ethics into these chapters in Maimonides' *Guide*. This was first developed by Hermann Cohen who read Maimonides' usage of Jeremiah 9:23 as evidence that God is primarily moral and hence imitating God's moral actions is the greatest form of divine worship.[29] This point is repeated later by Steven Schwartzchild who states that according to Maimonides, "man's purpose is to 'know God', but the God who is to be known is knowable only insofar as He practices grace, justice and righteousness in the world."[30] Shlomo Pines makes a similar point in his much debated article "The Limitations of Human Knowledge According to al-Farabi, ibn Bajja, and Maimonides." He interprets Maimonides' thought as an early version of what Kant would develop in more complexity much later, suggesting that there are some limitations to the ability of the mind to conceptualize objects of traditional metaphysics, thus leading to the primacy of the life of action.[31] Even Alexander Altmann, who criticizes Pines on restricting the amount of metaphysical knowledge possible according to Maimonides, proposes a trans-political morality in imitating divine actions that differs from the moral virtues. He states that "Maimonides obviously distinguishes between the moral virtues...on the one hand and the imitation of the Divine attributes, which, unlike the moral virtues, is not the result of practical reasoning, but follows from theoretical, metaphysical considerations."[32]

All these interpretations assume that Maimonides believed in a universal moral law revealed by God that transcended the political. However, a careful reading of these chapters reveals that Maimonides held that God desires an imitation of his loving kindness (*ḥesed*) in creating the world through the establishing of political structures where the moral virtues are cultivated. Part of the problem in *Guide* III 53–54 is that Maimonides does not state a political definition of loving kindness explicitly and is quite ambiguous over who should imitate God's loving kindness and in what form. But if one extracts Maimonides' hermeneutic strategy from his ideas that are spread throughout the work then one finds that it is the job of the reader to connect the dots, and one must read III 53–54 in light of I 53–54.[33] (The numbering parallel of the chapters is also not coincidental).[34] There he states that one imitates divine actions for the sake of "governance of cities" something which was exercised by Moses in obtaining the knowledge of God's actions for the sake of "governing them."[35] Furthermore, this is consistent with Maimonides' understanding of the prophet as combining the roles of the philosopher and the politician.[36] If the absolute loving kindness of God is in creation of the universe and bringing everything into existence, then the loving kindness of the prophet is in the creation of a political society where humanity can fulfill its social and political nature through cultivating moral virtues. For as Maimonides argues in II 40, in following Aristotle, "man is political by nature and that it is his nature to live in society."[37]

Moreover, Maimonides suggests that the purpose of loving kindness in the realm of politics results from the limitations of human knowledge of the supralunar world. In other words, the inability to obtain certain knowledge beyond this world leads to a prioritization of ethics and politics. This position lends Maimonides a strong position on negative theology, where terms referring to both God and human beings are "equivocal," having a different meaning when referring to different objects. It allows one to perceive God's ethical and political actions, while recognizing God as distant and "wholly other."[38] Thus Maimonides is not aiming to prove creation with epistemological certainty, but argues that creation needs to be the foundation for the divine law revealed by a prophet, which is a political law.[39] In doing so, one imitates God's loving creation of the world through order and justice, by creating a political society through revealing a law based on God's attributes.

ASTRONOMY AND ACTIVE BENEFICENCE OF KNOWLEDGE

In contrast to Maimonides' model, Gersonides rejects the political form of divine altruism. Instead, he presents a universal ethics of enlightenment aimed at imitating God's altruistic attributes through increasing wisdom for others in a way that is not restricted by political boundaries.[40] The Provençal Maimonideans already began the interpretation of (and divergence from) Maimonides that ascetic contemplation takes priority over political rule and cultivation of the ethical virtues. One dominant feature of their interpretation of Maimonides was the superiority of intellectual study over political rule and the critique of political *imitatio dei* for intellectual *imitatio dei*.[41] As Aviezer Ravitzky sums it up,

> [w]e are dealing here with a purposeful effort to marginalize (or overcome entirely) the social aspect of the *Guide*'s teachings and focus attention on the individual aspect, on the elevation of the individual person. According to this critical view, there is no escaping the harmful effects of political involvement on the perfection of the personality. Such involvement distracts and dispirits anyone who becomes a communal official.[42]

We see this in the works and commentaries of Samuel Ibn Tibbon who idealized the ascetic contemplation of Enoch, Noah and Adam, before his sin.[43] Similarly, he interprets loving kindness, justice and righteousness in Jeremiah 9:23 as part of God's knowledge and not as attributes of action.[44] The exact motivation for this shift is not certain, but Ravitzky surmises that Ibn Tibbon witnessed the controversy and excommunication associated with Maimonides' philosophic writings and was discouraged by the communities' lack of understanding and general disinterest in the project.[45]

For Gersonides, intellectual altruism is an imitation of God's anthropocentric construction of cosmology. One witnesses this through astronomy that demonstrates the operations of the supralunar world that are constructed to benefit humanity.[46] By studying the stars, one comes to know the laws of the physical universe and can determine how the stars are constructed to affect beings in the physical world, especially humans. In doing so, one increasingly obtains the different parts of the plan of the universe, the Agent Intellect. Specifically, from studying the stars one recognizes God's beneficence and how it is evident in the structure of the heavens. Through studying the structure and movements of the stars one can understand God and the laws of the universe—the Agent Intellect. He says that

> [i]t is evident in a general way that the determinate order obtaining amongst generated things in the sub-lunar world derives from the heavenly bodies. Since this order is constant and regular, and from it different things follow others at different times..., it follows that the cause of this order must be continuous and that it is operative in different things at different times.[47]

In this regard, Gersonides rejects a key component of the Maimonidean pursuit of divine wisdom, that the knowledge of metaphysics, or ultimate principles of being as exemplified in the Account of the Chariot (*ma'ase merkava*), can be acquired through conceptual reasoning alone.[48] Maimonides is very skeptical about the ability to obtain knowledge of God through astronomy, stating that "regarding all that is in the heavens, man grasps nothing but a small measure of what is mathematical....I mean thereby that the deity alone fully knows the true reality, the nature, the substance, the form, the motions, and the causes of the heavens."[49] Contrastingly, Gersonides argues throughout his writings that all knowledge should be acquired empirically by means of the senses through the method of experience, trial and error.[50] This is consistent with Gersonides' own experience, having himself invented an instrument he named "Jacob's Staff" to measure distance between celestial objects. The pursuit of metaphysics though is not recommended by Gersonides because of both the difficulty of the process and the uncertainty of the result, describing the premises as remote commonly accepted premises.[51] This is also consonant with the shift in epistemology at the end of the thirteenth century and beginning of the fourteenth century away from metaphysics toward a stronger empiricism.[52]

Gersonides sees this anthropocentric altruism of the cosmos exhibited in the beginning part of the creation narrative of Genesis 1. Throughout Gersonides' reading of the Hebrew Bible he interprets narratives as empirical scientific case studies.[53] In doing so, days one, two and four of creation are all metaphors for three different descending levels in the hierarchy of the supralunar world. Day one represents the separate intellects (*sekhalim nifradim*) as the light in Gen 1:3.[54] Gersonides explains that light is an appropriate metaphor since light is also used in the context of intellect and understanding. He is also following Maimonides in attributing angels to the separate intellect or the light described here.[55] The separate intellects are free of matter and serve the purpose of both contemplating the divine and causing the motion of the celestial spheres. Day two symbolizes the celestial spheres (*galgalim*), which are the multiplicity of rotating spheres that cause the motion of the planets. He describes the division of the firmament (*raqi'a*) as a metaphor for a sphere, of which there is a multiplicity, and observes that the "matter that does not preserve its shape" ensures these spheres do not interfere with one another.[56] Lastly, day four embodies the heavenly bodies (*geramim shamaymiyyim*) or what today is referred to as the planets. Day four is a return to discussing the supra-lunar world, after a brief discussion of the sublunar world in day three. These stars serve the function of perfecting the sublunar world. As an overflow of their own perfection, they influence the sublunar realm. As a result, the details of the heavenly bodies, such as the motions, size, location, are constructed to influence what is lower.[57] Gersonides interprets the examples of Genesis 1:14–18 as evidence of this beneficent construction. The first example is signs (*'otot*).[58] The stars influence the sublunar world in many ways and reveal themselves to humans through certain signs in dream, divination and prophecy. It is, however, up to humans to interpret those signs and use the knowledge acquired.[59] The second example is that of seasons (*mo'adim*).[60] Here he is referring to the fact that every star presents different influences at different times, according to its location with respect to the earth and time of day, which all are dependent on the cycle of time.[61] Lastly, he presents the sun (*ha-ma'or ha-gadol*) and moon (*ha-ma'or ha-qatan*) as having the strongest influence.[62] This is because Gersonides rejects Averroes' argument that the efficient cause of motion in the terrestrial world is the motion of the stars and instead argues that it is light or radiation, which emanates from the stars, the most powerful being the sun and moon.[63]

Gersonides also makes a case for the necessity of obtaining this knowledge through empirical study through his reading of the punishment after the Garden of Eden in Genesis 3. The objective of the theoretical intellect is to acquire knowledge of the natural world, but that man after being rejected from Eden had to "till the ground"[64] is a metaphor for the need to obtain intelligible knowledge through empirical study of matter.[65] Unlike Maimonides who reads "the fall" in the Garden of Eden as a metaphor for the influence of the imagination on the intellect,[66] Gersonides interprets the story as the necessity to use the material intellect to comprehend the Agent Intellect. Thus Gersonides describes how the pursuit of theoretical knowledge begins with the material intellect which is a physiobiological capacity for knowledge inherent in human body acquiring pieces of knowledge over time. The material intellect abstracts "material forms" embedded in physical substances.[67] Through piecing together these different fragmented parts, we put together the larger structure of the Agent Intellect.[68] The ethics derived from this form of knowledge is based on the fact that one must pass on what one has obtained in order to help others obtain it since it is inherently incomplete and fragmented.[69] In this way, one can come closer to a complete picture of the Agent Intellect which one needs to build on from one's predecessors and colleagues.[70]

God in the Hebrew Bible thus becomes a model for altruistic imitation through his critique of Maimonides' negative theology and usage of equivocal terms to describe the relationship of God and the world, where the same term would have completely unrelated meanings with respect to God and the world.[71] Gersonides rejects this model and replaces it with "figurative" or "metaphorical" terms that begin with a primary meaning and derive a secondary meaning from the primary meaning, so that an attribute is ascribed to God primarily and to other creatures secondarily.[72] Gersonides suggests that Maimonides' negative theology does not work, since when one is presenting a negative description of an attribute of God one is in fact reliant on a continuity of the meaning of the attribute between God and humanity *even* in the process of negating.[73] He thus states that

> [i]f the terms used in affirming predicates of Him were absolutely equivocal, there would be no term applicable to things in our world that would be more appropriate to deny than to affirm of God or [more appropriate] to affirm that to deny of Him.[74]

Thus, if one wanted to completely negate a term with respect to God, one could not use it all, even in a negative sense and one would have to be completely silent with respect to discussing God! As a result, as David Horwitz phrases it, "one can find language in his biblical commentaries, language concerning God that Rambam would not find philosophically acceptable. Robert Eisen points out that from a philosophical point of view, Ralbag can legitimately accept biblical descriptions of God that Rambam would maintain are anthropomorphic."[75] Hence, Gersonides makes the God of the Hebrew Bible a *direct* model for imitation, where God's different character traits and positive actions represent his various intellectual virtues that human beings must imitate. As a form of *imitatio dei*, God's attributes and actions are outcomes of His essence and His relationship to the world.

Through his astronomical model, Gersonides takes the contemplative focused project of his Provençal Maimonidean predecessors further than they did by making educational altruism an active and necessary duty. Gersonides argues that this enlightenment ethics is carried out by individuals who in every generation imitate God in rationally desiring to direct others to perfection. This, according to Gersonides, explains the prominence of the role of the shepherd and the prophet described in every generation in the Bible.[76] These unique individuals understand their place in the cosmos to be fulfilling the same role as that of the stars relative to God, as imitating God's beneficence in disseminating wisdom to those lacking it. They do so through teaching and writing books and through these exercises; they present the best means to guide other individuals toward achieving knowledge of God, nature and also their eternality.[77]

THE BENEFICENT VIRTUES

Gersonides describes the prophet and shepherd as imitating God in spreading knowledge generously to others, but is God's altruism a model for imitation in actions in interpersonal relations that are not purely focused on spreading knowledge? This can be argued by looking at how God's three altruistic attributes of loving kindness (*ḥesed*), grace (*ḥanina*) and beneficence (*haṭava*) represent not merely the structure and form of the universe in the Agent Intellect, but also God's action in bringing it into being and maintaining its being.

The first divine attribute worthy of imitation according to Gersonides is loving kindness (*ḥesed*). There is already a rabbinic precedent of imitating God's attribute of loving kindness through the obligation to clothe the naked, visit the sick, and comfort the mourner.[78] But Jewish philosophers have been debating the nature of how one can derive this attribute from God's essence or actions. Saadya and Maimonides derive God's loving kindness from the fact that he created the world for no personal interest, claim of justice or necessity. However, Gersonides builds on this to add an additional element. For Gersonides, God's loving kindness is expressed in his construction of the heavenly bodies, which are designed to benefit the sublunar world in the best possible way. Gersonides presents this teaching in his combining the following biblical verses in his Invocation to *Wars*:

> All the bright lights of the heavens (Ezekiel 32:8) He brings forth for loving-kindness (*ḥesed*) to do whatever He commands them (Job 37:12–13). He establishes them as his government upon the earth (Job 38:33).[79]

This loving kindness is a form of divine providence for humanity, as exemplified in one of God's 13 attributes,[80] by the giving of goods and protecting from evils through the order (*ma'arekhet*) of the stars.[81] The celestial bodies are constructed anthropocentrically through their perfect structure, motion and rays.[82]

Humans can imitate God's loving kindness by teaching those who know less to help increase the intellectual perfection of those beings, a form of imitation of the loving altruism of the celestial bodies which emanate knowledge to lower levels of reality. He begins to explain in the Introduction to *Wars* that

> [i]t is not proper for someone to withhold what he has learned in philosophy from someone else. This would be utterly disgraceful. Indeed, just as this entire universe emanated from God for no particular advantage to Him, so too is it proper for someone who has achieved some perfection to try to impart it to someone else. In this way he is imitating God as best he can.[83]

He expands upon the parallel between human and divine altruism in *Wars* Book 2 stating that

> [i]t is the nature of perfection, which is possessed by such a man, that when he has reached the point where he can disseminate his knowledge to others, he has a desire to transmit it....In this way reality is perfected, i.e., out of love (*ḥesed*) and grace (*ḥanina*) superior beings desire to give for their perfection as much as possible to those inferior to it. For example, were it not for the loving and gracious will of God (may He be blessed) to bestow as much as possible some perfection upon beings inferior to Him, were it not for the loving and gracious wills of the separate intelligences to mutually influence each other, and were it not for the loving and gracious will of the heavenly bodies and the Agent Intellect to influence the sublunar world—there would be no such world, all the more so would it not be perfect.[84]

God's loving kindness also takes place in the form of structuring perfectly the order of the celestial bodies. For humans to imitate this action of God's loving kindness may be by imitating the balancing effects of the celestial bodies in the practical realm. The celestial bodies are ordered by

God's loving kindness with the goal of preserving a balanced equilibrium (*shivvui*) between the different elements, though sometimes there is an accidental imbalance of one element that forms.[85] So humans can strive to imitate God's use of the heavenly bodies by carrying out actions of loving kindness that imitate this original equilibrium that God intended and emulate the correction of imbalances by creating peace between individuals. Acts of *ḥesed* therefore strive to equalize an imbalance in power that unjustly occurred. If God's *ḥesed* lays out the ideal form of distributive justice, humans imitate God's *ḥesed* in their own acts of *ḥesed* through corrective justice in working toward repairing the unjust imbalances of this world.

Gersonides presents sporadic interpretations of this model of loving kindness throughout his biblical commentaries through examples of Moses, Saul, Mordechai, David and Boaz. The first example is that of Jethro giving his daughter to Moses as a form of repayment for Moses' kindness in saving his daughters and flock from the nearby shepherds. There he states that

> [t]he tenth lesson is in ethics and that it is appropriate for man to endeavor (*hishtadel*) to repay good to one who delivered good to you because from this complete justice arises, until this characteristic is recompensed in people, in other words that you will pay back the loving-kindness (*ḥesed*) bit by bit, which according to their opinion they were already repaid. Because of this we find that Reuel [Jethro] criticized his granddaughters when they abandoned the man [Moses] without bringing him home to reward him for his action. And he commanded them to call him to come eat bread.[86]

Gersonides stresses that the principle behind Moses' act of kindness is that it is appropriate for man to help the weak because they have no strength. In the previous lesson he expands on the nature of this *ḥesed*:

> The ninth lesson is in ethics and that it is appropriate for a man to arouse himself to help the weak and to save them from their oppressors because they lack their own strength for this. In this matter, justice and the good of the political association are perfected and the necessary help arrives bit by bit. This is the reason that Moses, peace be upon him, aroused to save the Jethro's daughters from the shepherds and to water their flock. Moses was aroused to save the Israelite from the one who was beating him for the same reason.[87]

The implication of this judgment is that Moses is correcting a natural imbalance in power relations in which ideally the good should prosper and work for the sake of peace and the just should not suffer at the hands of their oppressors. A second example of loving kindness is Saul's sparing of the Kenites right after God commanded him to destroy all of Amalek.[88] While God commanded Saul to wipe out Amalek, Saul took one exception, showing kindness to the Kenites due to the fact that they were the tribe of Jethro, Moses' father-in-law, who helped Moses and the Israelites on their departure from Egypt. Gersonides explains:

> "For you showed kindness to all the Israelites, when they came up out of Egypt." This is the loving-kindness (*ḥesed*) when Jethro came to Moses in the desert and was happy with Israel's success and advised Moses to create officers to judge the people [as opposed to doing it all himself], as was discussed in Parshat Jethro.[89]

Thus, according to Gersonides, Saul endeavored to remove the relatives of Moses (in-laws) from Amalek, imitating the kindness they showed to the Israelites, so that during the war with Amalek, they would not be harmed.[90] Gersonides' reading implies that Saul had to correct God's blanket decree and adjust it to fit the nuances of the situation. A third example of biblical loving kindness is Ahasuerus' rewarding Mordechai for saving him from the nefarious assassination plot of Bigthana and Teresh. The lesson we learn from this, according to Gersonides, is that

> [i]t is appropriate to constantly remember the kind acts done to him (*ḥasidim ha-na'asim lo*) so that one can justly repay them.[91]

This act of kindness was a just response to Mordechai's original justification, which, according to Gersonides, is that one should endeavor for the peace of the king, even if the king is not part of his nation.[92] Mordechai's act of *hishtadlut* led to the king's act of kindness to him, which was crucial for the Jews in a time of need. A fourth example of kindness is David's compassion toward his friend Jonathan after his death which he expressed through rewarding his son Mephibosheth.[93] This corrects the imbalance of David's unfulfilled covenant to Jonathan.[94] The fifth and last example is that of Boaz toward Ruth. Boaz saw his taking Ruth in marriage as an act of kindness that resulted from Ruth's kindness to Naomi, a wife of his deceased relative.[95] This also fits well with Gersonides' interpretation of Boaz as one whose priority was to establish peaceful relations with all, including slaves and workers.[96] However, Gersonides is also very critical of forms of false kindness that are not directed toward peace and the success of the good. For example, Absalom's kindness was deceptive as it was contrived in order to kill David and become the king himself.[97] Gersonides also laments the difficulty of truly cultivating loving kindness. One act is certainly not sufficient, since one must behave with loving kindness consistently throughout one's life. In commenting on "Most men will proclaim to everyone his own kindness (*ḥasdo*),"[98] he states that

> [y]ou will find many people who will proclaim their own loving-kindness (*ḥasdo*) when they say, "I did this act of kindness (*ḥesed*) to so-and-so" and they think because of this that they are truly kind people....Accordingly, it is not possible to call this person a kind person based on one act of kindness he has done, unless they act this way in all matters.[99]

In this way, the human imitation of divine loving kindness helps to correct the accidental imbalance in the natural order and restores the natural order to its original just state. If it is left uncorrected, it allows evil to prosper thwarting the natural goal of peace between men.

The second and third divine attributes worthy of imitation by Gersonides are grace (*ḥanina*) and beneficence (*ḥaṭava*). These two operate together, as God's grace is imitated in humans through beneficence. If loving kindness is creating an ordered system and maintaining its well-ordered nature, grace and beneficence are the acts of providing an object to another that is not necessary to live, but improves one within that system. Therefore Gersonides expounds how God's "activity that derives from him—beneficence (*ḥaṭava*) and grace (*ḥanina*)—is i.e. giving form to existent things in [a] most perfect way."[100] Thus humans cannot just imitate God's ordering of nature in loving kindness (*ḥesed*), but must also emulate his desire to perfect creatures through imitating his grace (*ḥanina*) in acts of beneficence (*ḥaṭava*).

The nature of God's grace and beneficence is evident to Gersonides in his creation of animal biology. God does so in such a way that adds to animals many parts that are not necessary for their existence, but yet improves them. Consequently, in describing God's thirteen attributes, he defines gracious (*ḥanun*) as "[h]e gives to some of the beings certain things by way of graciousness, that is, things that are not necessary for their existence but are present in them by way of betterment, as demonstrated in the *Book of Animals* [*Generation of Animals*, II, 1, 731b]."[101] He likewise begins his *Commentary on the Torah* by praising God who through his wisdom and graciousness (*ḥanina*) created existence and desired to give benefit (*le-heṭiv*) to man by perfecting him through "the structure of his limbs, his faculties, and his organs, which He gave him to preserve his existence."[102] This is evident in Gersonides' commentary on Aristotle's examples in his *Supercommentary on Averroes' Commentary on De Animalibus* where he adds the quality of beneficence in the purpose of eyelids, spleen and heat. In discussing eyelids, he stresses that they are not necessary for sight, but if they are missing, nature endeavors to benefit (*le-heṭiv*) sight by increasing the speed of fluttering.[103] Similarly, with regard to the spleen, the utility of black bile going from the liver to the stomach is to benefit (*le-heṭiv*) digestion and to awaken the desire to eat; and the purpose of natural heat is to benefit (*le-heṭiv*) sensation.[104]

Moreover, Gersonides concludes that God's grace and beneficence to humanity is apparent in his imbuing humans with a procreative power that is superior to that of other natural creatures. In this regard, he interprets the fact that Genesis only reports the story of human birth and does not do so for other creatures as hinting to the distinctiveness of human reproduction, following Aristotle's discussion in *De Generatione Animalium* 2.1.[105] He points out that sea creatures reproduce themselves by fertilizing an incomplete egg, flying creatures fertilize a complete egg and walking creatures develop their kin outside the body. He adds that God gave humans one additional advantage, which is the ability to choose (*beḥira*) whether one will actualize reproduction or not.[106] At the same time, Gersonides shows that despite the fact that God created nature in order to give humans and other creatures these tools, it results in no personal benefit to God himself. In fact, this perfect ability to procreate by humans is understood by biblical characters to be the result of God's grace and beneficence. Thus when they attribute their progeny to the grace or beneficence of God, they imply that God generously gave them the tools to perfect this ability. For example, Gersonides interprets Abraham's initiative in complaining to God about his lack of progeny as reflecting God's beneficence.[107] Similarly, Gersonides interprets God's giving Abraham a son, Isaac, at such an old age as an act of God's grace.[108] Similar accreditation is given by Rachel and Leah to their success at having children[109] and by Jacob in identifying his children to Esau.[110] God's grace and beneficence though cannot be controlled to serve a particular human interest. He advises that it is not appropriate to ask for grace and beneficence because God may withhold the beneficence completely. For example, this is why Rachel, in asking for another son, did not ask for multiple children, since one should not ask from God more than what is appropriate.[111]

Gersonides also deduces from the biblical stories that man imitates God's graceful actions through acts of beneficence to others. In interpreting Proverbs 20:23, he explains how God dislikes using different character traits in relation to different people and recommends instead imitating the acts of God. This is done by acting in such a way as to better others (*le-heṭiv*).[112] It should be noted, however, that for Gersonides this imitation is an outcome of intellectual contemplation. As proof, he cites the verse "let thy springs be dispersed abroad"[113] to show that contemplation of the nature of God leads one to desire one to benefit (*le-heṭiv*) others which means encouraging others to learn sciences and be guided to perfection.[114] But the most common examples of *haṭava* are in daily life. Gersonides mentions several biblical examples of human imitation of divine beneficence. Abraham's bestowing goods on the three visitors who come to visit him is described as follows:

> The third lesson is in ethics and it is appropriate for one who *yaṭiv* (bestows good) upon other men to demonstrate to them that he is actually receiving a good from him. One should not boast about the fact that he *yaṭiv* (has bestowed goods); it is evident that such behavior is a vice. Abraham showed the men that they were giving him a present by coming into his house to receive *haṭavato* (his beneficence).[115]

Thus, Abraham is not helping these three men because of a sense of obligation, but is doing so in order to benefit them and thus makes an effort to demonstrate that it is his pleasure to do so. Similarly, Mordechai's giving knowledge of the plot of Bigthana and Teresh to the king is another example of *haṭava*. Gersonides describes how

> [t]he nineteenth lesson is to inform us that it is appropriate that the one who does good (*meṭiv*) through love and honor should endeavor (*hishtadel*) that the receiver should know the good that [the giver] *heṭiv* (bestowed) on him. This will clarify to him that he *heṭiv* (bestowed good) to him through love and not by chance and without intention. And this will strengthen the love between them. And this will also direct the receiver of good to reward the bestower of good for this [benefit]. Therefore we find that Mordechai informed Esther that Bigthana and Teresh sought to harm King Ahasuerus,

in order that she will pass on this information in his name. And this reward will be kept for him until the right time.[116]

Mordechai's work to benefit the king by saving his life was not intended for a direct self-interested benefit, but it is an outcome of it. Other examples include Jacob's working for Laban when not financially necessary[117] and Joseph's helping out his relatives.[118]

The first quality of beneficence is that giving should be universal and one should give to everyone. In reading Proverbs 20:23, Gersonides interprets the proper way to benefit others as imitating God's universal giving.[119] His exegesis on "bountiful eye shall be blessed, because he giveth bread to the poor"[120] suggests that the bountiful eye is he who rules people with the intent to benefit them and is blessed because he gives food to those in need.[121] Similarly, the verse "if thine enemy be hungry, give him bread to eat, and if he be thirsty, give him water to drink"[122] is taken by Gersonides to mean that it is a praiseworthy trait to benefit all people, whether they be friend or enemy.[123] While Gersonides does not expound on the universal qualities of Abraham, Jacob, Joseph and Mordechai, one can easily extrapolate it from their deeds. Abraham generously welcomes the three guests into his tent without any knowledge of who they are or why they have come; Joseph assists his brothers after selling him into slavery; and Mordechai helps save the life of a foreign king.

The second feature of beneficence is that it must work to improve the receiver of the gift. The message of "the tongue of the wise useth knowledge aright,"[124] is taken by Gersonides to imply that the knowledge of the wise improves (*teṭiv*) the hearers of the words and makes them wiser.[125] However, he does present the warning that it is inappropriate to bestow good upon bad people and instead one must stay far away from them.[126] The necessity of avoiding bestowing good upon bad people at Genesis 15:1 may appear to contradict Gersonides' interpretation of Proverbs 25:21 as the necessity to benefit one's enemies. The difference between the two is that one should aim to benefit those enemies whom one thinks have the potential to be improved, while those who are hopelessly wicked should be avoided. This is expanded upon in his commentary on the phrase, "blessings are upon the head of the righteous, but the mouth of the wicked conceals violence"[127] where he notes that the righteous mind is always on the good and the wicked always on the bad.[128]

A third element of beneficence is the methodological qualification that the gift should not serve as a burden on the receiver. One example of this is Abraham's method of preparing the food for his three guests. Gersonides interprets Abraham's hurrying in order to beneficently prepare the food in as little time as possible as resulting from the observation that they were in a hurry to leave.[129] Abraham also inquired if the guests were lacking anything or need anything when eating with him, since the guests, due to their modesty, may not ask for what they need and thus the goods Abraham bestowed could become a burden.[130] Gersonides provides another example of the drinking party given by Ahasuerus in the Book of Esther. He suggests that it is not appropriate that those enjoying the party should have to ask for what they need, since they may be embarrassed to ask. Instead the host should honor them with his beneficence. This explains why the party was designed: "[S]o the king had appointed to all the officers of his house, that they should do according to every man's pleasure."[131]

The fourth characteristic of beneficence is that self-interest for the giver should not serve as the primary motive of the gift. Aristotle, as was discussed above, argues though that all love of others stems from self-love and thus altruism is connected with egoism in some form.[132] Gersonides, like Aristotle, recognizes a self-interested motive in many cases, but strives to not make it the primary impetus. In commenting on verses in Proverbs, he argues that human acts of grace lead to this-worldly rewards. He concurs with Solomon that grace leads to personal happiness as derived from his maxim: "[H]e that is gracious unto the humble, happy is he."[133] As Gersonides infers, God rewards with happiness those who imitate his grace by giving to the poor, seeing this exemplified in the adage "[h]e that is gracious unto the poor lendeth unto the LORD; and his good deed will He repay unto him."[134] This also extends into the realm of punishment, since, as Gersonides points out, whoever does not practice grace toward the poor, God will act toward him in the same way that he acted toward the poor. Gersonides derives this from the phrase "whoso stoppeth his ears at the cry of the poor, he also shall cry himself, but shall not be answered."[135]

Although Gersonides admits to the fact that there is some personal reward for beneficent action, he comments on the actions of biblical characters to show that it is not the primary motive. In Abraham's act of beneficence to the three guests, Gersonides interprets Abraham's technique as constructed to avoid the reward of honor that those who bequeath goods to others enjoy. Thus Gersonides suggests that in bestowing good upon these three men, it is appropriate for Abraham to demonstrate that *he* is the one who is actually receiving a good from them, rather than the other way around. This allows him to avoid boasting about the fact he has bestowed goods, which is a vice. Abraham suggests to the men that they were giving him a "gift" by coming into his house to receive his beneficence.[136] This is why Abraham beseeches them with the following words: "If I have found favor in thy sight,"[137] stressing the *apparent* personal benefit he receives by serving them, according to Gersonides' reading. This is also revealed in Abraham's technique of carrying out a great number of actions with little speech, since talking a great deal about the benefits he wishes to bestow upon others implies that the donor is more interested in helping himself rather than others.[138] This explains Abraham's paucity of words when the guests arrive; instead, he runs to the tent to prepare bread and to fetch a calf so as to provide meat and milk.[139] This is also exemplified in the actions of Jacob, who runs away from Esau to his Uncle Laban, and proceeds to work to raise cattle for him, even though he could live in his home for free without shame as a relative. Gersonides interprets Jacob's actions as a form of beneficence on the part of Laban, who goes on to reward him with his daughters, even though the reward was not Jacob's primary motive.[140] One also finds an example of this in David's action toward an Egyptian man he found on his path who was hungry and thirsty and he gave him water and food. While Gersonides points out that he demonstrated the good trait of mercy (*ḥemla*) and received a reward for it, David's primary motivation was to benefit the Egyptian man he found.[141] This is also true in Mordechai's beneficence in passing on his knowledge of Bigthana and Teresh's plot to kill Ahasuerus. His primary motive in this case was ensuring the peace of the kingdom, but recognized that there may be benefits and reward for himself and the Jewish people as a result of his action.[142] Hence, he made sure to deliver the information along with his name, so that he could reap the reward at the appropriate time.[143] Lastly, Gersonides points out that Nehemiah acted beneficently toward the Jews and the deputies by inviting them to his table to eat; he prepared some of the highest quality animals for the meal, without asking the people to pay, since he argued that they were already paying too much tax.[144] His motive was to teach them about the good of God's providence and did so by imitating this providence for their benefit.

CONCLUSION

Pure altruism is ultimately an ideal that God exemplifies, but which no human can ever completely fulfill as a physical creature. Humans are limited by their bodily nature and can never justify selflessness that ignores the bodily demands that require preserving itself. One example of this is Gersonides' commentary on the command to love thy neighbor as thyself,[145] in which he suggests that one loves another person like one loves one's own body. One should choose what is best for the other and guide him away from what is deleterious for him to the extent one can. This does not mean, he continues, that one should give up one's own work for the sake of the work of the other since the love of oneself precedes the love of the other.[146] But how does one know when to choose one or the other? By what standard does one judge the different merits of competing goods? This theme will be expanded upon in the next chapter.

NOTES

1. *Metaphysics*, 1072a27 (12.7).
2. *NE*, 229–235 (10.9) and 92 (5.1).
3. Egoist interpretations of Aristotle include that by Guy Cromwell Field, *Moral Theory* (London: Methuen & Company, 1921), 109, 111; David Ross, *Aristotle* (London: Methuen & Company, 1923), 231; Donald James Allan, *The Philosophy of Aristotle* (Oxford: Oxford University Press, 1970), 189. We find this critique also in the thought of the Jewish thinker Samuel David Luzzato (1800–1865) who, according to Dov Nelkin, "rejected what we might term 'Aristotelian virtue ethics' for its focus on an ideal life *for the individual* instead of on other-directed virtues, he understood other-directed virtues as being necessary for one's own happiness" (Dov Nelkin, "Virtue," in *The Cambridge History of Jewish Philosophy*, eds. Martin Kavka, Zachary Braiterman and David Novak [Cambridge: Cambridge University Press, 2012], 748).
4. Field, *Moral Theory*, 109, 111.
5. Allan, *The Philosophy of Aristotle*, 189.
6. *NE*, 2–6 (1.2-4).

7. Ibid., 26–36 (2.1-6).
8. Ibid., 200–202 (9.8).
9. Ibid., 175–176 (8.8) and 199–200 (9.7).
10. Ibid., 223–226 (10.7).
11. Altruist interpretations of Aristotle include that by Julia Annas, "Plato and Aristotle on Friendship and Altruism," in *Mind* 86, no. 344 (1977), 532–544 and Richard Kraut, *Aristotle on the Human Good* (Princeton: Princeton University Press, 1989), 78–154.
12. Annas, "Plato and Aristotle," 539 and Kraut, *Aristotle on the Human Good*, 78.
13. *NE*, 4–6 (1.4).
14. Ibid., 3 (1.2).
15. Ibid., 90–95 (5.1-2).
16. Ibid., 95–99 (5.3-4). Ernest Weinrib interprets Aristotle's use of mathematics in describing corrective and distributive justice very literally, seeing arithmetic and geometric proportion as objective ideals based on the intelligibility of mathematics. See Ernest Weinrib, "Aristotle's Forms of Justice," *Ratio Juris* 2, no. 3 (1989), 220.
17. Ibid., 193–196 (9.4) and 202–205 (9.9).
18. Ibid., 169–170 (8.4).
19. Kraut, *Aristotle on the Human Good*, 79.
20. Ibid., 103–104.
21. These two readings challenge the boxing of Aristotle into egoism or altruism and strive to show how the two are in tension. W. F. R. Hardie, *Aristotle's Ethical Theory* (Oxford: Clarendon Press, 1980), 325–335 and Charles Kahn, "Aristotle and Altruism," *Mind* 90, no. 357 (1981), 20–40.
22. Hardie, *Aristotle's Ethical Theory*, 333.
23. Kahn, "Aristotle and Altruism," 34, 39.
24. *NE*, 223–229 (10.7-8).
25. Saadya Gaon, *Book of Beliefs and Opinions*, trans. Samuel Rosenblatt (New Haven: Yale University Press, 1989), 137–138 (III Exordium).
26. Saadya, *The Book of Theodicy: Translation and Commentary on the Book of Job*, trans. Lenn E. Goodman (New Haven: Yale University Press, 1988), 124.
27. Saadya, *Beliefs and Opinions*, 31–33 (Intro VI).

28. Jeremiah 9:23, cited by *Guide*, III 53–54.
29. Hermann Cohen, "Charakteristik der Ethik Maimunis," in *Jüdische Schriften*, vol. 3, ed. Bruno Strauss (Berlin: Ayer Co, 1924), 246.
30. Steven Schwarzschild, "Moral Radicalism and 'Middlingness' in the Ethics of Maimonides," in *The Pursuit of the Ideal: Jewish Writings of Steven Schwarzschild*, ed. Menachem Kellner (Albany: State University of New York Press, 2009), 144.
31. Pines, "The Limitations of Human Knowledge," 110–111.
32. Alexander Altmann, "Maimonides' 'Four Perfections'," in *Essays in Jewish Intellectual History* (Hanover: Brandeis University Press, 1981), 73.
33. *Guide*, 15 (Intro).
34. This method is employed by Daniel Frank in his exegesis. See Daniel Frank, "The End of the *Guide*: Maimonides on the Best Life for Man," *Judaism* 34 (1985), 495. Cf. Altmann, "Maimonides' 'Four Perfections'," 73.
35. *Guide*, 125 and 128 (I 54). See also Lawrence V. Berman, "The Political Interpretation of the Maxim: The Purpose of Philosophy is the Imitation of God," *Studia Islamica* 15 (1961), 60.
36. *Guide*, 234 (II 37).
37. *Guide*, 381 (II 40). This is very similar to Aristotle, *Politics* 1.2, where he states that "it is evident that the state is a creation of nature, and that man is by nature a political animal. And he who by nature and not by mere accident is without a state, is either a bad man or above humanity." While Maimonides does not source Aristotle, his first line of *Guide* II 40 is almost an exact quotation from the beginning of Aristotle's *Politics*.
38. Ehud Benor, "Meaning and Reference in Maimonides' Negative Theology," *Harvard Theological Review* 88, no. 3 (1995), 339 and 341n8.
39. *Guide*, 329 (II 25).
40. *Wars*, vol. ii, 55 (2.6). Menachem Kellner develops the contrast between Maimonides and Gersonides well here. See Kellner, "Politics and Perfection" and "Maimonides and Gersonides on Mosaic Prophecy," *Speculum* 52, no. 1 (1977), 62–79.
41. Thank you to Haim Kreisel for reminding me of this important link.

42. Aviezer Ravitzky, "The Political Role of the Philosopher: Samuel Ibn Tibbon versus Maimonides," in *Maimonidean Studies*, vol. 5, eds. Arthur Hyman and Alfred Ivry (New York: Yeshiva University Press, 2008), 347.

43. Ibid., 354.

44. Samuel Ibn Tibbon, "Preface to translation of Maimonides, Commentary on *Avot*," trans. Menachem Kellner in Menachem Kellner, "Maimonides and Samuel Ibn Tibbon on Jeremiah 9:22–23 and Human Perfection," in *Studies in Halakhah and Jewish Thought Presented to Rabbi Professor Menahem Emanuel Rackman on His Eightieth Birthday*, ed. Moshe Beer (Ramat-Gan: Bar-Ilan University Press, 1994), 54 and Ravitzky, "The Political Role," 361.

45. Ravitzky, "The Political Role," 370–371.

46. Gad Freudenthal argues that Gersonides' concept of astronomy is closer to astrophysics than astrology. See Gad Freudenthal, "Human Felicity and Astronomy: Gersonides' War against Ptolemy," *Da'at* 22 (1989), 59.

47. *Wars*, vol. iii, 29 (5.1.1).

48. For Maimonides' discussion of the Account of the Chariot see *Guide* III 1–7. Ruth Glasner surmises that the absence of any manuscripts on Gersonides' Supercommentary on the *Metaphysics* is due to his never completing it as a result of a growing sense of empiricism and metaphysical skepticism. See Ruth Glasner, "Gersonides' Lost Commentary on the Metaphysics," *Medieval Encounters* 4 (1988), 130–157.

49. *Guide*, 326–327 (II 25).

50. *Supercomm De Animalibus*, 106 and *Comm Song of Songs*, 21 and 89. See also Gaziel, *The Biology of Levi Ben Gershom*, 54–70 and Freudenthal, "Human Felicity and Astronomy."

51. *Comm Song of Songs*, 10 and 90. Cf. Menachem Kellner, "Translator's Introduction," in *Comm Song of Songs*, xxx. Kellner argues that Gersonides' criticism of metaphysics is polemical with the intent of scaring away would-be-philosophers. The difficulty with this conclusion with regard to this point is that Gersonides stresses the importance of empiricism and shies away from direct metaphysical speculation in his other writings as well.

52. Ernest Moody, "Empiricism and Metaphysics in Medieval Philosophy," *Philosophical Review* 67 (1958), 145–163.

53. Manekin, "Conservative Tendencies," 316: "Gersonides is content to appeal to the biblical narrative as testimony for the truth of certain doctrines....Since the miracle-reports contained in Scripture are confirmed by the authority of the prophets and the men of their day, the acceptance of these reports is no less founded than Aristotle's and Ptolemy's acceptance of the observations of their predecessors."
54. *Comm Gen*, 41 (on Gen 1:3) and *Wars*, vol. iii, 435–438 (6.2.5).
55. *MT, Book of Knowledge, Laws of the Foundations of the Torah*, 9–10 (2.3-4).
56. *Comm Gen*, 50 (on Gen 1:6) and *Wars*, vol. iii, 34–37 (5.2.2).
57. *Comm Gen*, 63 (on Gen 1:19) and *Wars*, vol. iii, 34–41 (5.2.2-3).
58. Gen 1:14.
59. *Comm Gen*, 56 (on Gen 1:14).
60. Genesis 1:14.
61. *Comm Gen*, 57–58 (on Gen 1:14) and *Wars*, vol. iii, 455–459 (6.2.8).
62. *Comm Gen*, 58 (on Gen 1:15).
63. *Wars*, vol. iii, 38–41 (5.2.3). See also Tzvi Langermann, "Gersonides on the Magnet and the Heat of the Sun," in *Studies on Gersonides*, ed. Gad Freudenthal (Leiden, 1992), 280 and 282.
64. Gen 3:23.
65. *Comm Gen*, 111 (on Gen 2:4–3:24).
66. *Guide*, 23–26 (I 2).
67. *Wars*, vol. i, 144–145 (1.5).
68. Ibid., 146–164 (1.6).
69. Ibid., 218–222 (1.12).
70. *Comm Song of Songs*, 23 and Seymour Feldman, "Gersonides on the Possibility of Conjunction with the Agent Intellect," *AJS Review* 3 (1978), 99–120.
71. The equivocal terms are *mushtaraka* in Arabic and *meshutafim* in Hebrew.
72. The derivative terms are *musta'ara* in Arabic and *mush'alim* in Hebrew.
73. *Wars*, vol. ii, 107–115 (3.3). See also Harry Wolfson, "Maimonides and Gersonides on Divine Attributes as Ambiguous Terms," in *Mordecai M. Kaplan Jubilee Volume, on the Occasion of His*

Seventieth Birthday, English Section (New York: Jewish Theological Seminary of America, 1953).

74. *Wars*, vol. ii, 110 (3.3).
75. Horwitz, *Gersonides' Ethics*, 339. The reference to Eisen is from Eisen, *Gersonides on Providence*, 157–167.
76. *Wars*, vol. ii, 55 (2.6) and *Comm Song of Songs*, 22, 30, 52 and 63.
77. Robert Eisen makes a similar point in his chapter on esotericism in Eisen, *Gersonides on Providence*, 104: "There are strong indications that Gersonides has confidence that the gap separating the elite from the masses is one that can be overcome. Gersonides seems to feel that the masses can be brought to a level of philosophical sophistication, provided that there is proper and skillful guidance. His fear that harm might come about by revealing philosophical truths to the masses appears to be limited to those cases in which philosophical truth is revealed indiscriminately and without proper instruction. It is only in these instances that the imparting of philosophical truth can be detrimental to the uneducated masses."
78. BT Sotah 14a and Warren Zev Harvey, "Grace or Loving-Kindness," in *Contemporary Jewish Religious Thought: Original Essays on Critical Concepts, and Beliefs*, eds. Arthur Cohen and Paul Mendes-Flohr (New York: Charles Scribner's Sons, 1987), 300–302 and "Love: The Beginning and the End of the Torah," *Tradition* 15, no. 4 (1976), 5–22.
79. *Wars*, vol. i, 88 (invocation).
80. Exod 34:6.
81. *Comm Exod*, 424–425 (on Exod 34:6–7) and *Comm Numbers*, 134 (on Numb 14:18–19).
82. *Wars*, vol. iii, 38–41 (5.2.3).
83. Ibid., vol. i, 97.
84. Ibid., vol. ii, 55 (2.6).
85. Ibid., 168–169 (4.3).
86. *Comm Exod*, vol. i, 21 (Exod 2:20, Ethical Lesson #10).
87. Ibid. (Exod 2:11–13, 17, Ethical Lesson #9).
88. I Sam 15:3, 6.
89. *Comm Early Proph I*, 192–193 (on I Samuel 15:6).
90. Ibid., 130 (I Sam 15:6, Lesson #9).
91. *Comm Megillot*, 136 (Esth 2:21, 6:3, Lesson #21).
92. Ibid., 135–136 (Esth Lesson #18).

93. *Comm Early Proph I*, 288 (II Sam 9, Lesson #39).
94. I Sam 20:14–15.
95. *Comm Megillot*, 10 (Ruth, Lesson #9–10).
96. Ibid., 9 (Ruth, Lesson #6).
97. *Comm Early Proph I*, 292 (II Samuel 2–21, Lesson #56).
98. Prov 20:6.
99. *Comm Proverbs*, 92 (on Proverbs 20:6).
100. *Wars*, vol. iii, 232 (6.1.4).
101. *Comm Exod*, 424 (on Exodus 34:6). Thanks to Warren Zev Harvey for this translation. See Harvey, "Gersonides and Spinoza on Conatus," 286.
102. *Comm Gen*, 1 and Harvey, "Gersonides and Spinoza on Conatus," 283.
103. *Supercomm De Animalibus*, 138.
104. Ibid., 166, 182.
105. *Comm Gen*, 65 (on Gen 1:20–23).
106. Ibid., 66.
107. Gen 15:2–3 and *Comm Gen*, 222 (on Gen 15:2–3).
108. *Comm Gen*, 289 (on Gen 21:8).
109. Ibid., 385 (on Gen 30:5–8).
110. Ibid., 416 (on Gen 33:6–7).
111. Ibid., 398 (Gen 30:24, Ethical Lesson #25).
112. *Comm Proverbs*, 95 (on Prov 20:23).
113. Prov 5:16.
114. *Comm Proverbs*, 27 (on Prov 5:16).
115. *Comm Gen*, 269 (Gen 18:3, Ethical Lesson #3) and *DH*, 419.
116. *Comm Megillot*, 156 (Esth, Lesson #19).
117. *Comm Gen*, 394 (Gen 29:14, Ethical Lesson #7).
118. Ibid., 508 (on Gen 44:21).
119. *Comm Proverbs*, 95 (on Prov 20:23).
120. Prov 22:9.
121. *Comm Proverbs*, 104 (on Prov 22:9).
122. Prov 25:21.
123. *Comm Proverbs*, 118 (on Prov 25:21).
124. Prov 15:2.
125. *Comm Proverbs*, 66 (on Prov 15:2).
126. *Comm Gen*, 227 (on Gen 15:1).
127. Prov 10:6.
128. *Comm Proverbs*, 45 (on Prov 10:6).

129. *Comm Gen*, 269 (Gen 18:6–8, Ethical Lesson #4).
130. Ibid., 270 (Gen 18:8, Ethical Lesson #6).
131. *Comm Megillot*, 152 (Esth 1:8, Esther Lesson #3).
132. By contrast, Kant proposed that the categorical imperative should ideally be carried out for its own sake and not for any other personal motive. Kant, *Groundwork of the Metaphysics of Morals*, trans. Herbert James Paton (New York: Harper and Row, 1964), 60 [1.3] and "On a Supposed Right to Tell Lies from Benevolent Motives," in *Kant's Critique of Practical Reason and Other Works on the Theory of Ethics*, trans. Thomas Kingsmill Abbott (London: Longmans, Green and Co., 1889).
133. *Comm Proverbs*, 64 (Proverbs 14:21).
134. Ibid., 88 (Proverbs 19:17).
135. Ibid., 100 (Proverbs 21:13).
136. *Comm Gen*, 269 (Gen 18:3, Ethical Lesson #3).
137. Gen 18:3.
138. *Comm Gen*, 269 (Gen 18:3, Ethical Lesson #3).
139. Gen 18:5–8.
140. *Comm Gen*, 394 (Gen 29:14, Ethical Lesson #7).
141. *Comm Early Proph I*, 240 (I Sam 30:11–12, Lesson #48).
142. *Comm Megillot*, 135–136 (Esth, Lesson #18).
143. Ibid., 156 and 161 (Esth Lesson #19, 36).
144. *Comm Early Proph II*, 40 (Neh 5:17–19, Lesson #11).
145. Lev 19:18.
146. *Comm Leviticus*, 252–253 (on Lev 19:18).

CHAPTER 4

Justice and the Practical Wisdom of the Individual

An outcome of the difference between Maimonides and Gersonides on self-preservation and altruism is the authority of justice as ordering the value of competing goods and the role of the individual to independently deliberate. Maimonides defines the Torah as imposing a standard of political justice and leaves less space for individuals to make their own moral calculation. Only those jurists who are trained in the science of the religious law have the freedom to deliberate. As a result, one absence in the writings of Maimonides is an explicit discussion of practical wisdom as a virtue and the necessity for practical deliberation over different competing goods and interests in an individual's decision-making process. In contrast, for Gersonides, he does not give the Torah complete authority to mete out justice as part of its mandate. Gersonides' ethics can be distinguished here from Maimonides' through the former's greater focus on competing practical goods with a method for how to decide between them. He interprets the narrative of the Hebrew Bible as a chronicle of cases where three different goods conflict: human physical needs such as family and property; peace and the cessation of conflict; and obeying God's commands. He thus views the ethical stance of the Bible as seeking not to avoid conflict but rather endeavoring to create a tradition of demonstrating how to deal with serious practical conflicts.

In untangling the relationship of conflicting goods in Gersonides' ethics, we need to begin by analyzing the association of justice and practical wisdom as the principles underlying the resolution of conflicts. We must then seek to determine why these specific goods are constantly clashing

© The Author(s) 2016
A. Green, *The Virtue Ethics of Levi Gersonides*,
DOI 10.1007/978-3-319-40820-0_4

and how one prioritizes different ones at different times. This will be achieved by examining specific examples in Gersonides' interpretation of biblical texts.

THE STANDARD OF JUSTICE

Gersonides' definition of justice requires situating its unique place in the history of ancient and medieval understandings. How one defines justice is also relevant for how one proposes a solution to moral conflicts, since the mitigation of moral conflict depends on weighing the relative importance of different goods through a unified standard of justice.[1]

Plato and Aristotle debate to what extent there is a unified definition of justice and how much it is guided by a wise ruler or lawgiver. Plato describes the meaning of justice by constructing the ideal city in speech, as a form of giving everyone what they deserve through the wisdom of the philosopher who orders society according to its best perfection.[2] Plato subsumes justice and practical wisdom under the all-encompassing wisdom of the philosopher.[3] The overarching wisdom of the philosopher endows him with the unique ability to balance the conflicting demands and goods within a state. In opposition to Plato, Aristotle strives to present a more practical and generic definition of justice that can apply to multiple nonphilosophically guided regimes. The structure of Aristotle's argument in *Nicomachean Ethics* Book 5 reflects the presupposition that justice operates separately as an individual moral virtue and as a political law governing the arrangement of the regime.[4] As a law, justice is both distributive and corrective, in which every regime distributes external goods according to the standard of fairness of the specific regime. For example, conflicts would be differently reconciled in a democracy than in an oligarchy, as they have highly different models of fairness.[5]

Medieval Jewish, Christian and Islamic philosophers adapted this model of justice to that of their scriptural traditions, which present a God who claims to be perfectly just. Indeed, justice is assumed to be an essential attribute of God, grounded in such proclamations as "shall not the Judge of all the earth do justly?"[6] and "the Lord is a God of justice."[7] In attempting to reconcile divine and human justice, divine law, according to medieval philosophers, represents a type of philosophic regime, following Plato's model in the *Laws*. At the same time, medieval Jewish, Christian and Islamic philosophers each strove in different ways to delineate the relationship between divine and human justice.

For Aquinas, humans imitate divine justice by following a natural human instinct. He argues that justice cannot be taught simply as a moral virtue by the political regime, but is a habit or *synderesis*, which is shared by all individuals. It allows them to know the first principle of practical reason or axiom of natural law and is the end to which all their actions incline. This is the principle of "pursuing good and avoiding harm."[8] From this first principle, one deduces universal conclusions or secondary principles. These precepts, such as not to kill or steal are derived from the first principle not to harm but, unlike the first principle, are not grasped by everyone.[9] Yet it is from these primary and secondary principles that a system of "natural law" is derived, guiding specific political regimes to act in accordance with its precepts.

Contrastingly, human justice for Al-Farabi and Maimonides is a political imitation of divine justice. Both argue that the prophet as both a philosopher and a lawgiver has to first study God's principles of Being, the natural world that emanates from Him; following that, he will be able to construct the principles of human justice in imitation of these principles and thus create a political society. Al-Farabi utilizes both *The Perfect State (al-Madina al-Fadila)* and *The Attainment of Happiness (Tahsil al-Saadah)* to demonstrate how political science and ethics are the imitation of divine science and metaphysics, in which the prophet emulates the divine in formulating the rules of the state.[10] Similarly, Maimonides ends the *Guide* with a description of how *ṣedeq* and *ṣedaqa* in the Bible refer to both justice as fairness, in the sense of equitably giving everyone what they deserve. He points out that God exercises this virtue through his creation of the forces of nature.[11] In a similar fashion, the prophet imitates this divine action in constructing a political law that strives to ensure that everyone receives their due.

Gersonides distinguishes his conception of justice from his predecessors by construing divine justice as an ideal that cannot be fully imitated by the prophet within a unified human political or legal framework. Divine justice is simply equivalent with the order and laws of the natural world, of which God's rational justice is referred to as *yosher*. Various scholars have proposed translating Gersonides' usage of *yosher* as organization, arrangement, regularity, rightness or equilibrium.[12] This signifies that the laws of the perfect plan of the universe are fashioned through the perfect equilibrium of the Agent Intellect and the divine mind. In fact, Gersonides frequently refers to God's relationship to the world by using the expression "law, order and equilibrium" (*nimus ve-ha-seder ve-ha-yosher*). He states that

[s]ince it has been demonstrated that there is a separate existent that is the agent of sub-lunar generation and that in addition it is the law (*nimus*), order (*sidram*), and rightness (*yoshram*) of these phenomena, it is evident that the First Intellect is the law, order, and rightness of existent things in the absolute sense. We have indicated that this is the view of Aristotle, as expressed in Book XII of the *Metaphysics*: for all of reality constitutes a unitary system. Accordingly, you see that the domain of the spheres provides, in the best way possible, for the sub-lunar world, and by means of this domain this separate agent performs its activities. This indicates that this [whole process] is ordered by something that has a total comprehension of this order.[13]

God's conception of justice in the moral sense is tied in with his ordering of the universe in the scientific sense. This reading challenges that of Menachem Kellner who argues that Gersonides saw no form of divine justice in this world. Kellner states that

[i]n denying that all matters of this world are governed in accord with justice, Levi is clearly flying in the face of the near-absolute rabbinic unity behind the claim that God orders everything justly....There can be no doubt that in denying the principle of measure for measure in rewards and punishments in this world, Gersonides is stepping out of the mainstream of normative rabbinic Judaism.[14]

The universe is fair in the order of God's construction of it. Hence, for Gersonides, moral justice is a natural phenomenon, making divine justice something which operates through the just construction of nature and does not require human law to impose it. The implication is that there is an enduring standard of divine justice at work in the universe.[15] This divine justice operates through the construction of nature since it was through it that God created the world beneficently for humanity.

Like those who follow the Rabbinic tradition, Gersonides describes divine justice as a form of "measure for measure" (*midda ke-neged midda*), but does so in a way that views punishment as built into nature itself.[16] One of the examples he uses to illustrate this point is Cain's punishment for killing Abel. Since Cain was a tiller of the earth, Gersonides describes the punishment he receives as "measure for measure," in that the land would no longer yield produce for him. This compelled Cain to wander to far-off places in order to find a fertile place to grow his plants.[17] While at first it may sound as if the punishment is supernatural in nature, Gersonides' understanding of "measure for measure" is that it is purely natural: God chose Abel's art since animal husbandry is more effective at producing food for humans than agriculture. In Cain's murder of Abel, God's lesson to him is that he also destroyed the most effective source of producing food and is thus forced to rely on agriculture alone. Indeed, this is a less stable form of sustenance, and this explains why his punishment compels him to wander to search for fertile soil. Another example given by Gersonides centers on the complaints of the Israelites regarding the lack of bread and water.[18] Gersonides points out that this complaint was senseless, since they already had both. In fact, he discerns that they were not complaining about their lack at that moment, but about the general nature of the desert. Gersonides thus interprets the punishment of fiery serpents sent to bite the people as a fitting punishment, since unlike carnivorous animals, snakes do not bite others for the sake of obtaining their prey, but purely for the sake of hurting others.[19] The nature of the snake imitates that of the complaint in that both have no goal other than to hurt others. Since Gersonides defines providence naturalistically in *Wars* Book 4, the implication is that Moses understood the natural biology of the various creatures inhabiting God's world and made use of this knowledge, as evidenced by his method of punishment.[20]

In denying the centrality of a political role for the prophet in imposing a just order on society, Gersonides gives a greater place to the individual in imitating God's just ordering of nature. This can be seen in the specific choice of term that Gersonides chooses to attribute to individuals acting justly. Unlike Samuel ben Judah of Marseilles in his translation of Averroes' *Commentary on the Nicomachean Ethics* and *the Republic*, Gersonides does not use *ha-shivvui* (for "just," *dikaiosune*) and *lo shivvui* (for "unjust," *adikias*) to refer to the political principle of justice. Instead, in Gersonides' model, only individuals can imitate God's justice through individual acts of justice.[21] For example, Gersonides attributes the quality of *yosher* to Joseph, citing that when he was in charge of distributing Egypt's food during the famine, he returned the money his father paid for it and gave his father lots of grain.[22] He explains that

> [t]he twelfth lesson is in ethics and it is what we learned from the attribute of justice (*yosher*) of what is told about Joseph. And that is that Joseph refused to take the money that had been sent to him and sent it back to his father, for Pharaoh had already obtained possession of it, even though Joseph was the cause of all the good that came to Pharaoh. Indeed, he returned the money that his father had sent him personally, and sent his father utensils full

of grain, for Pharaoh had already given Joseph full reign over the distribution over the grain, to give or to sell to whomever he pleased. The Egyptian
(king) had said, "Go to Joseph: you shall do what he tells you."[23]

Was it fair to everyone else that Joseph gave his father free grain? And why
is Gersonides suggesting that it was more just for Joseph to give his father
free grain? While Gersonides does not say this explicitly, it may be that
Gersonides is suggesting that since one owes a debt to their parents for
bringing them into being and raising them, in this instance Joseph is simply repaying that debt. Aristotle raises this point in the *Nicomachean Ethics*
about the imbalanced nature of friendship between parent and child and
the inability of a child to truly repay the parent for what he has given him.
He says that "it would seem well that one ought to provide sustenance
especially to parents, on the grounds that we are in their debt and that it
is nobler thus to provide for those who are the causes of our being than
to provide for ourselves."[24] The implication is that according to natural
justice, the debt that a son owes to his father outweighs what he owes to
the people he is ruling. But Joseph's *yosher* does not mean that he unca-
priciously gave his father and brothers whatever they desired without concern for the desires and needs of Pharaoh or others in Egypt. Gersonides
expands upon Joseph's sense of justice in his actions:

> The sixth lesson is in ethics that it is inappropriate for someone who exer-
> cises control over another's possessions to simply do with them as he pleases,
> for example, by giving his friends some of these possessions. One should
> only give the amount that the owner of the possessions wants. This should
> be so even though the owner of the possessions achieved them due to the
> efforts of the one who has control over them. In spite of the fact that Joseph
> was the ruler over Egypt, he did not give his family a stake in the choice land
> of Egypt without the command of Pharaoh. This is why Scripture states: "So
> Joseph settled his father and his brothers, giving them holdings in the choic-
> est part of the land of Egypt...as Pharaoh had commanded."[25] Moreover,
> the grain was under the authority of Joseph to give to whomever he desired.
> Yet, he did not want to give the members of his father's household any
> more grain than they needed; this is the point of the verse "Joseph sus-
> tained his father, and his brothers, and father's entire household with food,
> down to the little ones."[26] Pharaoh obtained the grain because of Joseph.
> Nonetheless, Joseph did not want to give his loved ones any more than they
> needed. For this was the will of Pharaoh when he said: "And you shall eat
> from the fat of the land,"[27] that is to say, that he permitted them to eat the

choice food that was in Joseph's hand. All of this teaches the attribute of justice (*yosher*) of Joseph and his refusal to take an excess. This is why he did not ask Pharaoh to give to his father any more food than the amount that Pharaoh himself had authorized."[28]

The justice that is praised is that of Joseph's balancing a wise and equal distribution to Egyptian society with the distribution to his own family which is based on a standard that is not rooted in any specific written law. Similarly, Gersonides regards Moses as possessing the quality of *yosher* for defending an Israelite who was being unjustly beaten by an Egyptian task-master and saving the daughters of Jethro, in both cases using his strength to defend the weaker party.[29] Likewise, Gersonides ascribes this quality to David which he sees in his gracious actions to Jonathan and Hanun ben Nahash[30] and which he also sees evident in David's limiting his numbers of wives.[31] While these individuals are leaders of political communities, their *yosher* arises from their own character and not that of the regime.

This marginalization of justice as a goal for the political community and the abandonment of it solely to individuals in Gersonides' thought are parallel to a common critique employed by the nominalist (and Franciscan) thinkers aimed at scholastic (and thus papal) ethics and political theory in the fourteenth century.[32] Placing Gersonides within his Christian historical context may help explain his critique of earlier models of medieval Jewish thought. For example, William of Ockham (1288–1348) argues against the existence of a rational and teleological system of universal principles, replacing it instead with an ontological individualism where every existing being is a radically unique creation of God himself.[33] Similarly, Marsilius of Padua (1275–1342) designates peace or tranquility as the goal of the state as opposed to justice or education, making a biological analogy between the operational harmony of different parts of animal biology and the various facets of the state.[34] Political justice is only derived from nature very minimally, in interpreting *Nicomachean Ethics* 5.6, as natural principles such as respecting parents are rules that are only metaphorically referred to as "natural," but are conventionally imposed for the sake of political stability.[35] Furthermore, Marsilius interprets Aristotle's interpretation of justice as an individual moral virtue for the ruler, but leaves out the political side of justice that is concerned with fairness and distribution.[36]

The limitations of political justice also appear in the fourteenth century Franciscan commentaries on the *Nicomachean Ethics* by Gerald Odonis (1285–1348), who was known as the *doctor moralis* and by John Buridan

(1300–1358), who built upon and popularized many of Odonis' ideas in his own commentary.[37] In his *Commentary on Book V of the Nicomachean Ethics* Odonis made the observation that free agreement between exchanging parties was a greater path toward equality than the decision of a judge. In this way, he lessened the necessity for a judge to intervene in order to achieve corrective justice in cases of economic exchange, thus returning to the fair distribution Aristotle presented as distributive justice. This seems to demonstrate that Odonis had greater faith in the actions of good men in economic transactions than in the construction of good laws.[38] Buridan followed Odonis on this point in limiting the judge's role in establishing equality. Buridan takes Odonis' argument a step further by contending that an exchange should be considered just even in economic exchanges in which one party has obtained an unequal advantage. He argues that it is a natural part of the financial world, where one side will always have an advantage, and should not be considered unjust. Odonis and Buridan both reject the notion of justice as an overarching principle that aims for equality and is moderated by a political law. Instead, they support the concept of allowing a free market of individuals to exercise their own self-interest.[39]

PRACTICAL WISDOM: DELIBERATION AND CHOICE

Aristotle argues that every political community distributes goods according to the standard of fairness determined by nature of the regime. He says that

> [f]or all agree that what is just in distributions ought to accord with a certain merit. Nevertheless, all do not mean the same thing by *merit*; rather, democrats say it is freedom, oligarchs, wealth; others, good birth; aristocrats, virtue.[40]

But a religious law whose authority derives from God and imposes a standard of political justice leaves less space for individuals to make their own moral calculation. Only those jurists who are trained in the science of the religious law have the freedom to deliberate. Gersonides' model radically differs in that the law does not impose a complete standard of political justice on all realms of life, instead leaving space for individuals to pursue their own self-preservation and intellectual education independent of the law, and as a result leaves practical deliberation to the individual to weigh and decide upon the value of competing goods.

Gersonides' return of practical wisdom to ethics may be a response to its apparent absence in the writings of Maimonides. Scholars have examined Maimonides' entire corpus and have not found a segment of the soul called "practical reason," or the virtue of "practical wisdom" known as *phronesis (ta'aqul)*.[41] In neglecting to discuss practical wisdom in the *Guide of the Perplexed*, Maimonides draws a clear distinction between reason, which is concerned with theoretical issues, and the imagination, which deals with all practical concerns. Through a careful reading of Maimonides' discussion of the Garden of Eden narrative, one can see that this absolute distinction between theoretical reason and the imagination is more superficial than meets the eye, and that there appears to be a hidden doctrine of practical wisdom contained within it. In addition, a careful look at his use of some quotations in *Guide* I 2 reveals that he may be subtly hinting at a form of practical wisdom at work. The first of his three quotations from Genesis 3 is "the tree was good for food and it was a delight to the eyes."[42] He uses this as an example in order to show Adam's choice of the desires and corporeal pleasures of the imagination over intellectual apprehension. But he neglects to quote the rest of the verse, which is crucial: "and that the tree was to be desired to make one wise," which would be a hint at a form of practical wisdom.[43] He also alludes to the role played by practical wisdom in ethics by proposing that the middle way is the way of the wise men, *derekh ḥakhamim* and that people with a sick soul are healed by wise men, who are physicians of the soul.[44] However, the question is: Why would Maimonides have downplayed the importance of practical wisdom to the point of virtual concealment? As Howard Kreisel puts it, Maimonides may have concealed his doctrine for "pedagogic reasons."[45] Indeed, scholars have surmised two reasons for why Maimonides may have hidden his discussion of practical wisdom. One is to highlight the centrality of the divine law (argued by Raymond Weiss and Jonathan Jacobs) and the other is to stress the theoretical nature and ends of the intellect (presented by Howard Kreisel).[46]

Gersonides' approach is to make practical wisdom a separate virtue from both theoretical wisdom and the divine law. He adapts the term *kisharon ha-ma'ase* (excelling in action) from Ecclesiastes 4:4 ("I considered all labour and all excelling in action") as the biblical equivalent of practical wisdom.[47] The association of *kisharon ha-ma'ase* with practical wisdom is also evident from his definition of the term at Ecclesiastes 7:19–20, as to "take the appropriate [action] in *kisharon ha-ma'asim*, according to the [appropriate] time, place, matter, receiver and actor."[48] This definition of *kisharon ha-ma'ase* is very similar to Aristotle's criteria of practical wisdom in the *Nicomachean Ethics* as "to feel them when one ought and at the things one ought, in relation to those people whom one ought, for the sake of what and as one ought."[49] In Gersonides' *Commentary on Esther*, his discussion of the "wisdom" (*ḥokhma*) of Mordechai and Esther in practical success indicates that he refers to "practical wisdom" simply as "wisdom" in that context.[50] Later, in his commentaries on the Pentateuch, he moves toward discussing the specific steps of practical wisdom such as consideration (*hityashvut*), deliberation (*histaklut*) and choice (*beḥira*).

Gersonides' conception of practical wisdom is not subservient to the legal parts of the Torah, but part of an independent narrative stream of the Bible, from which independent ethical lessons can be derived and imitated in the practical wisdom of others.[51] This model of practical wisdom is also clearly separate from theoretical wisdom and not in any way subservient to it. In commenting on "and a man of wicked devices is hated,"[52] Gersonides interprets the wicked individual as one who spends too much time thinking about whether a course of action is worth pursuing or not. Because of this long consideration, he will not achieve a conclusion and in doing so, will confuse matters even more. Thus, Gersonides argues that someone who thinks through every matter, whether worth doing or not, will not carry out what is necessary.[53]

Gersonides follows Aristotle in defining the first stage of practical decision making as that of deliberation (*bouleusis*).[54] In Aristotle's model, deliberation is a step-by-step inquiry about the means to achieve an end. One does not deliberate about the ends themselves, but instead they are rationally known or educated through habit. For example, Aristotle provides the case of a doctor who does not deliberate whether he will cure someone, but instead finds the means to do so. If there is more than one means to a given end, then one deliberates which means will allow it to come about most easily and beautifully.[55] Gersonides similarly refers to deliberation (*histaklut*), as the activity of consultation (*'eṣa*) about the best possible means to achieve the correct end.[56]

The first element of deliberation, according to Gersonides' interpretation, is the ability to learn from others through consulting with individuals of expertise in a specific practical area. For example, he interprets the verse, "hear counsel (*'eṣa*), and receive instruction (*musar*), that thou mayest be wise in thy latter end,"[57] as recommending the receiving of instruction from individuals of stature (*gedolim*).[58] He also differentiates between the method of the fool and the wise man in that "the way of a fool is straight in his own eyes; but he that is wise hearkeneth unto counsel (*'eṣa*)"[59] proposing that the wise man is open to hearing the *'eṣa* of others, while the fool is confident in his own beliefs.[60] Furthermore, in his interpretation of the passage, "with the well-advised (*no'aṣim*) is wisdom,"[61] he suggests that someone who is wise will find those are well-advised because it is the path of wisdom to get advice.[62] It is noteworthy that these principles are evident in Gersonides' *Commentary on Esther* in both the actions of King Ahasuerus and Haman. He observes that not only does Ahasuerus not act without the consultation (*'eṣa*) of proper advisors,[63] but also the treacherous Haman employs a similar strategy by consulting many individuals and not ceasing to look for advice from friends and wise individuals.[64] We also learn from this that even evil men strategically consult those with practical experience in a similar way to those who strive to do so for good ends.

A second part of the process of deliberation is to do so in a manner that is not rushed and to exert the effort to investigate all matters carefully. In other words, one should look for the best means to achieve an end through careful research. In order to describe the process of deliberation, Gersonides uses the metaphor of swimming in deep water. He derives this metaphor from the verse "counsel in the heart of man is like deep water; but a man of understanding will draw it out"[65] to indicate that it is not easy to perceive the proper courses of action. Like a swimmer in deep water, it is hard to reach the bottom, but it is attainable after much effort.[66] Once again, Gersonides makes a distinction between a wise man and a fool, this time in regard to the speed and exactness of deliberation. He derives this from the verse: "he that trusteth in his own heart is a fool; but whoso walketh wisely, he shall escape,"[67] explaining that a fool does not sit and think over matters before acting. In fact, he is so confident in his heart that he needs no consultation (*'eṣa*) that it leads to evil action. This is unlike one who follows wise advice and thus avoids all evil.[68] Gersonides also points out that the impatient individual lacks the patience to deliberate before acting, which he draws from the statement, "seest thou a man that is hasty in his words? there is more hope for a fool than for him."[69] The ethical principles that Gersonides derives from his exegesis of assorted verses of Proverbs are applied to specific examples in Genesis. Jacob, on hearing how Hamor had defiled Dinah, did not rush to show anger, but waited until the right time to respond; indeed, Jacob was silent until his sons came to consult him and discuss the best course of action with him.[70] Jacob furthermore criticized Reuben for acting hastily without deliberation in sleeping with Bilah, Rachel's maid (as reported at Genesis 35:22).[71] What Gersonides may be suggesting in attributing Jacob's criticism of Reuben's sin to a lack of deliberation is that he thought only about his immediate pleasure and did not consider possible negative outcomes (based on Chronicles 5:1 and Lesson #13), thus causing him to lose his birthright. Gersonides also shows how Jacob refused to depart from Canaan to Egypt on Joseph's request until he received the best possible advice. He argues that

> [t]he sixth lesson is in ethics and that is that it is inappropriate for a man to perform important acts hastily, but should first deliberate (*yityashev bahem*) until the most perfect plan of action is arrived at. Jacob refused to leave the land and agree to the request of Joseph until he had received the best possible advice concerning this. Therefore, he performed activities designed to obtain prophecy, in order that through prophecy he could discover if it was appropriate for him to travel to Egypt, as (the Torah) had previously mentioned.[72]

Even the injudicious King Ahasuerus paused to deliberate in his moment of anger, a detail noted by Gersonides.[73]

The goal of deliberation is to determine the means that will meet the least evil and avoid the greatest amount of misfortune. The principle of determining the lesser evil among a multiplicity of evils is a common trope in medieval Christian ethics and is employed by Gersonides in his description of the biblical characters and how they practice deliberation.[74] Hence, Abraham faces a famine in Canaan and must deliberate between two alternatives: staying in Canaan and starving with no risk to his wife, but risking starvation for everyone versus risking his wife's abduction, but having food for everyone and the greater potential to stay alive. Abraham chose the second possibility since it is in that situation he could pretend his wife is his sister and even if she was defiled, it would be an unwilling sexual act.[75] Jacob also had to weigh two possible evils while seeing Esau approaching with 400 men, fearing that Esau was coming to kill him. In choosing between being all killed and only a portion being killed, Jacob divided the camp into two so that only half will be killed, which would be the lesser of two evils.[76] Joseph's brother Reuben made a similar calculation in endeavoring to minimize Joseph's fate in his brothers' plot to kill him. By suggesting to put him in a hole rather than kill him (so that he would die of hunger rather than being murdered directly), he tried to convince the brothers to select the lesser form of murder.[77] In another example, Gersonides describes Joseph as having practiced *'eṣa* in ensuring there was an ample supply of bread in Egypt. He does not describe what the calculation is exactly, but it seems to be a decision made between the lesser evil of having a smaller amount of food during the years of plenty to ensure a balanced supply in the years of famine versus the worse evil of having no food at all during the drought years.[78] Gersonides also interprets the destruction of the First Temple as a result of a miscalculation in the weighing of evils. King Zedekiah was faced with the terrible circumstance of being ruled by the Babylonians and the greater evil of being exiled by them. Yet Zedekiah did not listen to Jeremiah's warning that the latter catastrophe would fatefully occur (which was a much worse fate), and thus Zedekiah made a gross error in judgment which led to the destruction of the First Temple and the subsequent exile of the Jews. He interprets "Happy is the man that feareth always; but he that hardens his heart shall fall to evil"[79]:

> "Happy is the man that feareth always" refers to one for whom it is appropriate to fear because this is a reason to become cunning in taking fitting advice to avoid evil from which you fear. However, one who hardens his heart and attributes to God the matters that are appropriate to fear, he will fall to evil. Do you not see that hardening of the heart destroyed the First and Second Temples? That is if Zedekiah would not have hardened his heart and would have bent his neck underneath the yoke of the King of Babylonia, [the Israelites] would not have been exiled from their land then. Similarly with the Second Temple, [if they did not harden their hearts, the Israelites] would not have had to submit to another kingdom and [had to bend their necks] underneath their burden.[80]

Gersonides attributes this to the fact that "he that hardens his heart shall fall to evil," for in stubbornly refusing to listen to the advice of Jeremiah who was wiser than he, Zedekiah and his kingdom suffered the disastrous consequences.[81]

However, according to Gersonides, one can also use deliberation toward a positive goal of acquiring the best possible good. Even if one cannot acquire the ultimate best good, Gersonides insists that one should not be discouraged. In fact, one should not desist from effort but instead strive to acquire whatever positive good one can. Gersonides derives this lesson from the example of Abraham who listened to Sarah's advice (*'eṣa*) that he should take Hagar and impregnate her since Sarah was facing difficulties conceiving. This shows that when faced with the conflict between not having children with one's spouse and having children with another woman, it was better for Abraham to have children even if it was not with his beloved wife. Even Sarah thought this may have been the only way of fulfilling God's promise and as a result she recommended the best means to do so.[82] In fact, later in the biblical narrative, Rachel made the same deliberation, following Sarah's model.[83]

The second step in the process of practical decision making is that of choice (*prohairesis*), which is the desire and hence decision to act upon the means deliberated upon.[84] For the action to take place, one cannot simply want to complete an action and find the means to do so, but must also have the physical desire that arises from the appetitive faculty. This is why Aristotle says that choice is "either intellect fused with desire or desire fused with thinking."[85] Gersonides follows Aristotle in describing choice (*beḥira*) as a synthesis of deliberation (*histaklut*) and desire (*hit'orerut*),[86] but brings out the element of conflict and the different goods that are in conflict more strongly than Aristotle does. The language of choice, *bahar* and *beḥira*, plays a role as well in Gersonides' ethical lessons in Genesis where Abraham chooses to go down to Egypt to avoid the famine over staying in Israel to obey God's command[87] and also chooses fewer possessions for the sake of peace with Lot.[88]

CASES OF CONFLICT: PROPERTY, PEACE
AND THE DIVINE LAW

In Gersonides' model of deliberation and choice, there are three conflicting goods: human physical needs such as family and property; peace and the cessation of conflict; and obeying God's commands. However, as Gersonides argues, choosing between these three alternatives is not a tragic dilemma with no rational method of deciding. Gersonides does not envision choice in moral conflicts in this light, but suggests that one can resolve such moral conflicts based on a hierarchy of goods. All three goals are important, but when in conflict, certain goods take priority over others depending on which two are in conflict. Human physical needs such as family and property take priority over God's commands, since the need for physical preservation is a prerequisite for fulfilling those commands. Peace takes priority over the physical desire for property, since although property is a necessary basis for physical preservation, it is not the ultimate end; in fact, peace allows for contemplation more effectively if one has the opportunity for it. Yet, when God's commandments and the pursuit of peace come into conflict, there are times when one must follow God's ordinances and other times when one must pursue peace. One must note that these are not strict rules, but are a set of guidelines and recommendations for how to deliberate and choose between competing goods in the majority of cases.

The following diagram illustrates the relationship between the three conflicting goods and shows how each of these three conflicts can be reconciled (Fig. 4.1).

From a historical perspective, Gersonides may have been influenced by ethical discussions of his Christian contemporaries with regards to moral deliberation. Christian thinkers were not beholden to an all-encompassing divinely revealed law, and thus understand ethics as part of a natural law. Moral conflicts are a result of an ethical reasoning that is independent of

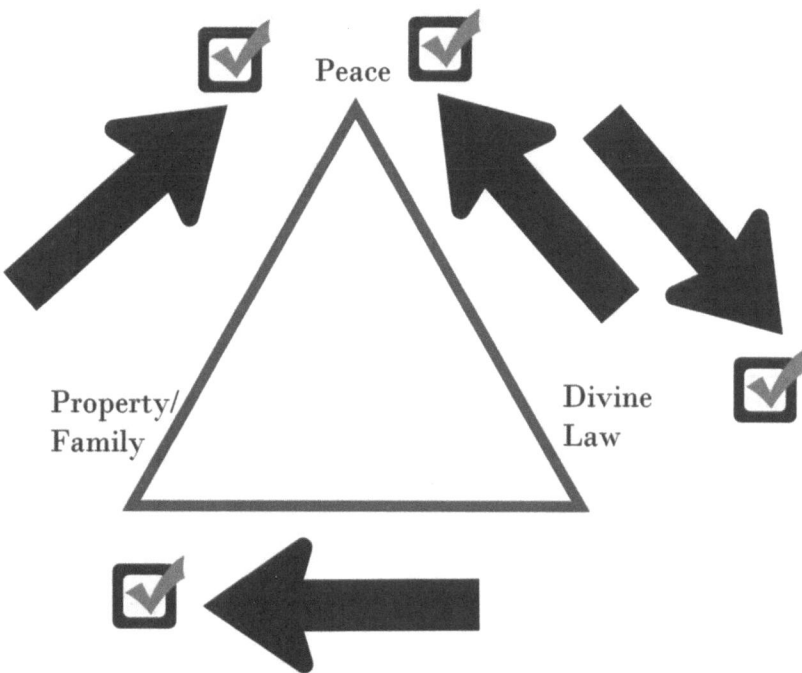

Fig. 4.1 The deliberation between conflicting goods

legal reasoning. However, whether Gersonides was directly influenced by Christian thinkers who dealt with similar conflicts is difficult to discern.

One significant moral dilemma that Gersonides addresses is the conflict between materialistic and bodily necessities—such as maintaining property, ensuring the proper amount of food and expanding the number of progeny—versus the divine commands. In the following cases of conflict, Gersonides recommends prioritizing physical needs, since it is impossible to follow God's command if one's bodily requirements are not taken care of. The first example of this, as shown through Gersonides' ethical lessons, is the famine in Canaan right after Abraham arrived there, after following God's command to leave Mesopotamia.[89] Medieval commentators ask in hindsight whether Abraham should have remained in Canaan and trust that God will provide food *or* whether he was right to depart for Egypt and ignore the divine command? Gersonides praises Abraham's choice of the latter, proposing that it is not, in fact, a complete rejection of God's command, since he knew that God speaks in generalities and that the command to dwell in Canaan does not apply to every circumstance. He presents the dilemma as follows:

> The first lesson is also in ethics and that is that a man should obtain food and similar necessities needed for bodily preservation with diligence (*ḥariṣut*). God had already promised Abram success with respect to the acquisition of possessions. Nonetheless, Abram roused himself because of the famine that existed in the land of Canaan to go to the land of Egypt, and did not desist going there because God, may He be exalted, had [previously] commanded him to dwell in the land of Canaan. For the commandments of God, may He be exalted, are to bestow good upon man, not that he would die because of them. And because of this Abram knew that the will of God, may He be exalted, was that he should turn away from there [Canaan] for the pursuit of food. Moreover, the intention of Abram's journey to the land of Canaan was in order that he should be more prepared to receive the Divine overflow that would cling to him, and this would not be conceivable in a state of famine and lack of food. And for this reason it was the greater good that (Abram) should leave that place [Canaan] to the place where food would be found until the famine should cease.[90]

Remaining in Canaan was especially not wise in his present circumstances, since due to what Gersonides interprets as the current celestial conditions, a temporary move to Egypt was required for the sake of physical self-preservation.

In a second example of conflict, continuing in Genesis 12, Abraham must deliberate between staying in Canaan and risking starvation for everyone, against going to Egypt to obtain food for the people, but risking his wife's abduction by the Egyptian Pharaoh and his being killed by him to obtain his wife. He expands the point as follows:

> The third lesson is also in ethics and that is when it is inevitable that a person will suffer some misfortune, it is appropriate for him to discern under which circumstances he will meet with less evil, and [actively] choose that course of behavior. He should not be lazy in the matter, due to the fact that in any event some misfortune will occur to him. It is preferable to choose the lesser evil and flee greater misfortune. Abram chose to travel to Egypt and flee the famine in Canaan in spite of the propensity that the [inhabitants of the] place had to defile his wife. It is appropriate to know that Abram did not sin in this matter. [Had the Egyptians forced Sarai to commit a sexual act] Sarai would have committed the act of [sexual] defilement unwittingly, and as a result would not have been consequently prohibited to her husband even after the subsequent giving of the Torah, as the Rabbis, of blessed memory said concerning Esther: "Esther was considered as earth."[91] If Abram would have chosen to (stay in the land of Canaan and) suffer under the famine, he might have died. Choosing this course of action, as opposed to entering Egypt and risking the unseemly happening that might have occurred to Sarai, would have been classified as foolish piety, as they [the Rabbis] say in the third [chapter] of [tractate] *Sotah* (21b), "What is an example of a foolish pietist (*ḥasid shote*)? When he sees a woman drowning in the river, he says, 'It is inappropriate to save and [thereby] look at a woman'."[92]

Abraham chose the second possibility since it provided the greater potential for staying alive. Moreover, he did so in a way that allowed him to pretend his wife is his sister so that even if she was defiled, it would be an unwilling sexual act. Gersonides defends this decision by quoting the talmudic criticism of the "foolish pietist" (*ḥasid shote*) who is pious in meticulously following ritual laws, while ignoring basic human necessities. The talmudic example is of a man who witnesses a woman drowning in the river, but will not rescue her since he would have to immodestly look at her body (BT Sotah 21b).[93] This story implies that the laws of modesty are overruled by the necessity to preserve a human life. Abraham's choice, in Gersonides' eyes, is one which values survival over piety, since Abraham would not be able follow God's commands if he did not first ensure that his physical needs were taken care of.

Gersonides also quotes the case of the foolish pietist in the dilemma Jacob faces over whether he should challenge his Uncle Laban to give Rachel to him for a wife. Gersonides sees that on the one hand, Jacob fulfilled his part of the commitment with Laban and desires to produce progeny; on the other hand, perhaps he is embarrassed and thinks he should withhold himself from endeavoring in such matters, respecting the wishes of his future father-in-law. In the end, Gersonides praises Jacob for following the former course of action and attributes any embarrassment he might feel to a form of foolish piety.[94] In another example cited by Gersonides, the two and a half tribes of Ruben, Gad and half of Menashe were also conflicted about choosing between the material benefit of the fertile pasture on the opposite side of the Jordan, and the intellectual and spiritual benefits of living in Canaan. Gersonides suggests that their actions were justified as they gave priority to their material needs in setting up their pasture on the opposite side of the Jordan.[95]

In a similar fashion, Gersonides illustrates the conflict between material needs and the pursuit of peace, where if one has the opportunity for peace, one should choose it over increasing the amount of property or food. By peace, Gersonides here is referring to the cessation of hostilities, a temporary truce, and not necessarily a lasting and ideal peace.[96] Maimonides describes how lasting peace is an intellectual ideal, which results from contemplative understanding as opposed to the less controllable power of the passions. In fact, Maimonides ends with a much larger conclusion: that in fact the entire purpose of the Torah is for the sake of peace! In the last paragraph of the *Mishneh Torah* itself Maimonides connects peace and knowledge positing that "there will be neither famine nor war, neither jealousy nor strife…the one preoccupation of the whole world will be to know the Lord."[97] Gersonides agrees with Maimonides about the intellectual basis of the ideal, stating that at the time of the Messiah, there will be peace since there will not be conflicting beliefs (*'emunot miteḥalefot*), implying that the truth will be known and clear,[98] but in his ethical lessons, he proposes an important method for a nonintellectual cessation of hostilities.[99]

Gersonides gives a few examples in his ethical lessons to defend such a prioritizing of a cessation of conflict over the pursuit of material goods. The Bible describes how Abraham endeavored to acquire possessions, but when faced with a conflict with Lot, his decision to part ways with him indicates, according to Gersonides, that it is better to choose peace with few possessions than many possessions with strife. Abraham preferred less grazing land and greater peace over an abundance of land and strife.[100] He argues that

> [i]t is more appropriate for a man to choose peace and few possessions instead of many possessions and strife, as it says "burnt bread and peace is better than a house full of sacrifices and strife."[101] Abram preferred less grazing land and peace to a great deal of land and strife.[102]

Similarly, when Abraham had a child with his maidservant Hagar and at that time had no children with Sarah, he agreed to exile Hagar to heed his wife's request for the sake of peace in the home (*shalom bayit*). Gersonides elucidates how

> [t]he fourth lesson is in ethics and that it is appropriate for a man to allow room for others (to do as they see fit) in the interests of family peace (*shalom bayit*). Abram allowed Sarai with her maidservant, in spite of the fact she was pregnant from Abram and he had no other seed. He did this, however, to appease Sarai his wife.[103]

Maintaining Hagar and Ishmael within his family was Abraham's original intention in having a child with her, since he desired to perpetuate his family through children and ensure that he could pass on his possessions to his descendents. He explains his reasoning in an earlier lesson:

> The third ethical lesson is that it is appropriate for man to *hishtadel* to bequeath what he can to his children who come after him, and should not be jealous if they exercise power over all that he had worked for. Abram was worried that he would not have descendents who would acquire his possessions after death.[104]

But, in the end, he was willing to give up this opportunity for *hishtadlut* for children and *ḥariṣut* to maximize the transference of his possessions in order to have peaceful relations with his wife.[105]

Gersonides likewise applies this ethical principle to war, viewing it as advisable for man to pursue peace and avoid conflict and war, even if one believes that one will win with God's help. For example, the Israelites made an offer of peace to Sihon before killing in war and likewise with all nations Joshua conquered.[106] This may appear to be merely an obvious implication of the biblical verses,[107] but Gersonides develops and strengthens this into a principle which is consistent with his larger emphasis on peace. He states that

> [t]he fifteenth lesson is to inform us that it is appropriate for man to pursue peace and to distance himself from conflict and war, even if it becomes clear to him that he will win. We see that God, may He be exalted, desired that they send a peace offering to Sihon before they whet their appetite for war and even though he hardened his spirit and strengthened his heart. This was done to all the nations that Joshua conquered because God, may He be exalted, hardened their spirits and strengthened their hearts in order that Israel destroy them, as was explained there [in the Book of Joshua]. [This was done] in order to realize in our hearts that it is appropriate in all places to pursue peace, to whatever extent possible, because God, may He be exalted, does not desire the death of the wicked.[108]

The priority of peace over conquest is also apparent in his exegesis on "remove not the ancient landmark, which thy fathers have set."[109] In his understanding, the meaning of this verse is

> [d]o not change the boundaries that the founders set with regard to land so that you can exploit one's neighbor's pastures and increase one's land. This is also a warning not to change early borders that the founders set because they all have a utility.[110]

Here, Gersonides discerns that early borders and fences have a purpose for their existence and one should not try to break them down for the sake of conquest and self-interest. He is implying that it is better to leave things according to the status-quo if there is no serious reason for a change.

Another interesting case is the example of Abraham's challenge to King Abimelech over the act of theft committed by his servants (Genesis 21:25) where he only chastised Abimelech over his loss of property once he was certain he was not hostile to him and his life was not in danger. This example reconciles peace and self-interest, but still prioritizes the ensuring of avoiding conflict before receiving the material benefit. He explains that

> [t]he ninth lesson is in ethics that it is appropriate to stay as far as possible away from acts of theft and harm. Abraham chastised Abimelech, in spite of the fact that the latter was a king, on account of the theft that his servants had committed; for Abraham surmised that they had committed the deed according to his instructions.[111]

Abraham could have ignored the matter and not mentioned it to the king, but instead decided it was worthy of mention in order to chastise Abimelech because of the necessity of preserving his possessions.[112] The fact that Gersonides makes the statement "in spite of the fact that the latter was a king" suggests that there are reasons to consider not criticizing a king, such as the threat of him killing you for challenging his authority. In such cases, avoiding conflict would have been a better option. Gersonides only challenged Abimelech once he was certain that it would not be a threat to his life. He expands upon this in the next lesson:

> The tenth lesson is in ethics that it is appropriate to be courageous at the appropriate time and fearful at the appropriate time. At first, Abraham our patriarch was fearful of Abimelech, and because of this told him that Sarah was his sister, out of fear lest Abimelech kill him. Subsequently, he strengthened himself to chastise him concerning the theft of his servants, once it became clear to him [Abraham] that he would not receive harm from speaking in this manner, as Abimelech was seeking peace with him.[113]

Abraham correctly calculated that this is the right time to courageously critique the king for the sake of obtaining his goal because Abimelech would not hurt him and thus he could emerge unscathed.

Here we have an interesting parallel to Averroes's Commentaries on both the *Ethics* and the *Republic*, where he adds similar comments to the discussion about striving for peace, not as a result of common intellectual perfection, but as the cessation of hostility. In Averroes' legal code, *Bidayat al-Mujtahid*, "Book of Jihad" Chapter 10.1.6 (which Gersonides would not have read), Averroes brings out the tension between commands for war and peace in the Quran. He shows that Quran 9:5 and 9:29, which argues for a constant war to slay polytheists, contradicts Quran 8:61, which advocates for peace if the enemy agrees to it.[114] Averroes implicitly proposes a solution to this difficulty in his *Commentary on Aristotle's Nicomachean Ethics* where, using Aristotle's theory of equity in 5.10 (1137b24), he brings this example in as a case study for his discussion.[115] There Aristotle demonstrates that law is universal in its application, and cannot be fitted to all particular cases, but he maintains that there are certain cases which the lawgiver would have inserted into the law if he were there. Averroes adds the following comment:

> And you can add this with respect to the laws laid down with respect to war in the law of the Muslims because the command pertaining to war in it is

very general to such a point that they destroy root and branch whoever differs with them. Now there are times in which peace is to be more preferred than war. However, since the Muslim masses make this edict of war generally valid despite the impossibility of destroying their enemies completely great damage has attained them on account of their ignorance of the intention of the Lawgiver, the blessings of God be upon Him. It is therefore proper to say that peace is preferable at times to war.[116]

For Averroes, the contradiction between the Quranic verses is such a case, where war is a general principle in Islam, but the intention of God and the lawgiver was not to suggest that war is always preferable, since many times peace is preferable. Furthermore, another limitation on war hinted at by Averroes in his *Commentary on Plato's Republic* is the possibility of virtue existing in non-Greek nations. If the purpose of war is to spread virtue to other nations and if these nations already contain it, then war may not always be necessary.[117]

The tension between the requirements of following divine commands and the necessity of peace is more complicated.[118] There are times when divine commands must overrule any initiative to end conflict and push for a peaceful resolution. In other situations, finding a method for a peaceful negotiation is more important than the divine law. One case of a biblical character standing up for God's law in the public sphere against leaving the issue alone for the sake of a peaceful resolution is Mordechai's unwillingness to bow down to Haman. Mordechai could have simply avoided creating needless strife with Haman by bowing down to him for the sake of peace. Mordechai knew the danger associated with not bowing down to him yet he did not seek a peaceful compromise. Why did he not do so? The biblical text is ambiguous and does not explicitly suggest a reason for Mordechai's refusal to bow down to Haman. It simply states that "for he had told them that he was a Jew."[119] Commentators have been perplexed by why being a Jew forbid Mordechai from bowing down to Haman, since there is no Jewish law forbidding one from bowing down to a king. Prominent rabbinic interpretations are that he wove an image of an idol on his clothes, making bowing down to him idolatry,[120] or that Haman considered himself a god.[121] Gersonides appears to be building on this and develops it into a calculation that weighs two goods:

> The twenty-third lesson is to inform us that it is inappropriate for anyone under any circumstance to bow down to and prostate oneself before a god

other than the one God, may He be exalted, even if it leads him to fear royal authority. Even if Mordechai could predict what danger would [arise] as a result of not bowing down to and prostrating himself before Haman, he would still not have agreed to do it.[122]

Mordechai recognized that bowing down to Haman was a form of idolatry and it is one of the three commandments for which one should die rather than transgress ("be killed but do not transgress") and thus refused to peacefully submit to Haman's request. Gersonides argues further that the reason Mordechai did not explain his reasoning for not bowing down is that he would have to explain to the king's servants that the king's law is trumped by God's law during certain occasions and they would not have accepted this limitation on the king's authority.[123]

Gersonides also recognizes cases where the necessities of peace trump divine commands. One such case is Joseph's brothers' willingness to break the prohibition on lying for the sake of peace and reconciliation with their brother.[124] Joseph's brothers fabricated a story about how their father commanded them to report to Joseph after his death, in order to forgive them for their sins. Gersonides states that in this case it is "appropriate for man to endeavor to achieve peace as far as possible" and that it is "inappropriate that the desire to stay far away from lies be able to thwart the noble goal of peace."[125] In fact, Gersonides cites the talmudic principle that one is permitted to tell a lie for the sake of peace as justification for their behavior, which cited this example.[126]

Another case used by Gersonides in which this principle is employed is when Jacob chastises the vengeful actions by his sons Simeon and Levi against Shechem for the rape of their sister Dinah. He states that

> [t]he eighth lesson is in ethics and that it is not appropriate for anyone to put himself in danger. Even though God promised to constantly protect him,[127] he feared greatly [for his life] when his children committed that foreign act, and he feared that the people of the land will wipe him out along with his house.[128]

Jacob reprimands them for not prioritizing peace over revenge; even though Hamor strongly violated the divine command against rape, Jacob characterizes his sons' act of revenge as breaking a basic principle of the Torah. He argued that the Canaanites and Prizites are large nations and we are merely a small nation. Thus they will wipe us out if we do not attempt to have peaceful relations with them.[129]

The deliberation and choice of peace against following the divine law is situated in the calculations of the individual with practical reason, who must weigh the ability to put God's law into practice in the world without sacrificing peace and the weight of the specific command that he would consider violating. Gersonides shows that Mordechai calculated successfully that they could stand up for God's commands without creating a war, while Joseph and Jacob acted on the conviction that avoiding conflict was a priority in their specific situations.

Conclusion

Gersonides' ethics represents a shift from understanding justice as a political virtue to that of purely an individual virtue. Weighing the importance of competing goods and demands takes on a greater significance in the hands of individuals. God does not involve Himself in the actions of individuals who are in competition and cooperation for the necessary goods. This greater individualism requires an even stronger emphasis on the cultivation of practical wisdom since it is up to individuals to reconcile conflicting demands for competing goods in the world. Gersonides presents a unique set of guidelines in deliberation for balancing these competing demands such as physical needs, peace and the divine law.

The individualism of Gersonides' ethics at first glance appears to reject any conception of how the state should be ordered. But as we will see in the next chapter, Gersonides redefines the political through a new beginning point of the individual. Idit Dobbs-Weinstein is thus correct to state that "Gersonides is a (if not the) decisive link between another Aristotelian tradition, the Arabic and Judaeo-Arabic one and Modernity as well as its first and last Jewish voice" in that like early modern thinkers, it is not the state that shapes individuals, but individuals that form the state.[130]

Notes

1. This is exemplified in the image of the ancient Greek god of justice who is represented with scales.
2. *Republic*, 113 (434c), 123 (443b), and 153 (473d).
3. However, there are three opinions on the definition of justice in Book 1 of the *Republic*: Cephalus avers that justice represents one's ancestral traditions; Polemarchus states that justice is defined as helping friends and hurting enemies; and Thrasymacus suggests

that justice is the advantage of the stronger. Yet, although these undoubtedly signify important features of justice, they are nonetheless transcended by the justice of the philosopher.

4. *NE*, 90–93 (5.1). One is a disposition or active condition (*hexis*) of character that does not include the opposite condition within it, while the other is the action that can be discerned in contrast to its opposite result. David O'Connor clarifies this distinction through a medical analogy. The disposition is a form of etiology in which the doctor looks at the patient's psychic state and focuses on the underlying causes of a disease, such as a viral or a bacterial infection. The action is symptomological whereby the concentration is on the symptoms of a disease, such as a sore throat or aching joints. See David K. O'Connor, "The Aetiology of Justice," in *Essays on the Foundations of Aristotelian Political Science*, eds. Carnes Lord and David O'Connor (Berkley: University of California Press 1991), 137.

5. Both Plato and Aristotle overemphasize the unification or separation of justice, practical wisdom, and theoretical wisdom. Plato attempts to artificially unify these under one concept of wisdom, while Aristotle attempts to artificially separate these. I argue that these concepts can neither be fully separated or unified, but are in constant tension.

6. Gen 18:30.

7. Isa 30:18.

8. Aquinas, *Summa Theologiae*, 1–2, 94, 1.

9. Ibid., *Summa*, 1–2, 94, 4 and 95, 2.

10. Majid Khadduri, *The Islamic Conception of Justice* (Baltimore: John Hopkins University Press, 2001), 83–88.

11. *Guide*, 631 (III 53).

12. Harry Wolfson, *Crescas' Critique of Aristotle: Problems of Aristotle's Physics in Jewish and Arabic Philosophy* (Cambridge: Cambridge University Press, 1971), 349; Norbert Samuelson, *The Wars of the Lord. Treatise Three: On God's Knowledge*, trans. Norbert Samuelson (Toronto: Pontifical Institute of Mediaeval Studies, 1977), 100; Touati, *La pensée*, 105; Staub, *The Creation of the World*, 335n390; Gad Freudenthal, "Cosmogonie et physique chez Gersonide," *Revue des études juives* 145 (1986), 305n26; *Comm Song of Songs*, 103n15, 131n29.

13. *Wars*, vol. iii, 136 (5.3.5).

14. Gersonides, "Providence and the Rabbinic Tradition," 681–682.
15. *Comm Leviticus*, 233 (Lev 18:24–30, Intellectual Lesson #9).
16. BT Sanhedrin 90a and Nedarim 32a.
17. *Comm Gen*, 127 (on Gen 4:1–26).
18. Num 21:5.
19. *Comm Numbers*, 269–270 (on Num 21:5).
20. Though in this case, Gersonides does not use the term "measure for measure," though it is implied through the example.
21. *Wars*, vol. iii, 182 (5.3.12) and *Comm Proverbs*, 11–12 (on Prov 2:9).
22. *Comm Gen*, 504–505 (Gen 42:25, Ethical Lesson #12).
23. Gen 41:55, *Comm Gen*, 504–505 (Gen 42:25, Ethical Lesson #12) and *DH*, 448.
24. *NE*, 191 (9.2).
25. Gen 47:11.
26. Gen 47:12.
27. Gen 45:18.
28. *Comm Gen*, 528 (Gen 47:11–12, Ethical Lesson #6) and *DH*, 455–456.
29. *Comm Exod*, 21 (Exod 2:11–13, 17, Ethical Lesson #9).
30. *Comm Early Proph I*, 288 (II Sam 8:15, Lesson #39).
31. *Comm Early Proph II*, 13 (I Kgs 1:4, Lesson #2).
32. The creation of modernity as arising from an internal Christian theological debate, nominalism versus scholasticism, has been very nicely argued by both Michael Gillespie and Louis Dupre. See Gillespie, *Theological Origins of Modernity*, 19–43 and Louis Dupre, *Passage to Modernity: An Essay on the Hermeneutics of Nature and Culture* (New Haven: Yale University Press, 1995).
33. Gillespie, *Theological Origins of Modernity*, 22–23.
34. Marsilius of Padua, *Defender of the Peace*, trans. Alan Gewirth (New York: Columbia University Press, 1956), 8–9 (1.2) and 89–97 (1.19).
35. Ibid., 190 (2.12).
36. Ibid., 56 and 58 (1.14).
37. James J. Walsh, "Some Relationships between Gerald Odo's and John Buridan's Commentaries on Aristotle's Ethics," *Franciscan Studies* 35, 237–275. A critical edition and English translation do not exist for either commentary. Buridan's Commentary on Book 10 of the *Nicomachean Ethics* has been translated into English.

See Jean Buridan, "Jean Buridan, Questions on Book X of the *Ethics*," ed. and trans. John Kilcullen, in *The Cambridge Translations of Medieval Philosophical Texts. Volume II: Ethics and Political Philosophy*, ed. Arthur Stephen McGrade, John Kilcullen and Matthew Kempshall (Cambridge: Cambridge University Press, 2001), 498–586.

38. Joel Kaye, *Economy and Nature in the Fourteenth Century: Money, Market Exchange and the Emergence of Scientific Thought* (Cambridge: Cambridge University Press, 1998), 129–130.

39. Ibid., 132.

40. *NE*, 95 (5.3).

41. Pines, "Truth and Falsehood Versus Good and Evil," 127 and Kreisel, *Maimonides' Political Thought: Studies in Ethics, Law, and the Human Ideal* [Albany: State University of New York Press, 1999], 63 (from his chapter on "Practical Reason").

42. Gen 3:6.

43. Marvin Fox, *Interpreting Maimonides: Studies in Methodology, Metaphysics, and Moral Philosophy* (Chicago: University of Chicago Press, 1995), 186.

44. *LC*, 30–31 (2.1).

45. Kreisel, *Maimonides' Political Thought*, 64.

46. Ibid.; Weiss, *Maimonides' Ethics*, 30, Jonathan Jacobs, "Aristotle and Maimonides: The Ethics of Perfection and the Perfection of Ethics," in *American Catholic Philosophical Quarterly* 76, no. 1 (2002), 151 and Parens, "Prudence, Imagination," 35n26.

47. *Kisharon ha-ma'ase* is only used in the context of Ecclesiastes in Gersonides' writings, likely because of its existence in Ecclesiastes in 4:4.

48. *Comm Megillot*, 46 (on Eccles 7:19–20: "take the appropriate [action] in practical wisdom (*kisharon ha-ma'asim*), according to the time, place, matter, receiver and right actor."

49. *NE*, 34 (2.6).

50. Ibid., 155 and 161 (Esther Lesson #17, 36).

51. *Comm Gen*, 2.

52. Prov 14:17.

53. *Comm Megillot*, 164 (on Prov 14:17). Touati, *La Pensée*, 514. This argument is reminiscent of John Buridan's plan for a non-theoretical ethics. In his Introduction to *Question on the Ethics*, Buridan separates the ethics of the *Nicomachean Ethics* and the

Politics which teach the meaning of a good life, from the ethics of the *Rhetoric* and the *Poetics* which teach the necessary means toward achieving the goals of human passions through a special "moral logic" (*Logica moralis*), which is distinguished from "moral philosophy" (*moralis Philosphia*). See John Buridan, *Quaestiones super decem libros Ethicorum Aristotelis ad Nicomachum* (Paris, 1513), Prooemium, 2 and James J. Walsh, "Nominalism and the Ethics: Some Remarks about Buridan's Commentary," *Journal of the History of Philosophy* 4, no. 1 (1966), 9.

54. *NE*, 48–50 (3.3).
55. Ibid.
56. Gersonides states that they are intertwined at his Ethical Lesson #2 on Genesis 12:11–13 (*Comm Gen*, 202–203). This term *histaklut* is spelled both with a *sin* and *with a sameh*, but it is translated as deliberation in the context of both usages. See *histaklut* with a *sin* appears in Gersonides' *Supercomm De Anima*, 172 and *histaklut* with a *sameh* in Ethical Lesson #1–3 on Genesis 12:10–13 (*Comm Gen*, 202–203). His usage of *'eṣa* as consultation is based on many verses in Proverbs and used by Samuel ben Judah to translate the Arabic equivalent of *bouleusis* in his Hebrew translation of Averroes' *Commentary on Aristotle's Nicomachean Ethics*.
57. Prov 19:20.
58. *Comm Proverbs*, 88 (on Prov 19:20).
59. Prov 12:15.
60. *Comm Proverbs*, 56 (on Prov 12:15).
61. Prov 13:10.
62. *Comm Proverbs*, 59 (on Prov 13:10).
63. *Comm Megillot*, (Esther lesson #7).
64. Ibid., (Esther lesson #39).
65. Prov 20:5.
66. *Comm Proverbs*, 92 (on Prov 20:5).
67. Prov 28:26.
68. *Comm Proverbs*, 132 (on Prov 28:26).
69. Prov 29:20.
70. *Comm Gen*, 439 (Gen 34:5, Ethical Lesson #5).
71. Ibid., 562 (Gen 49:4, Ethical Lesson #2–3).
72. Ibid., 518–519 (Gen 46:1–3, Ethical Lesson #6) and *DH*, 453.
73. *Comm Megillot*, 153 (Esther Lesson #7).

74. M.V. Dougherty, *Moral Dilemmas in Medieval Thought: From Gratian to Aquinas* (Cambridge: Cambridge University Press, 2011), 2.
75. *Comm Gen*, 202 (Gen 12:11–13, Ethical Lesson #2–3).
76. Ibid., 417 (Gen 32:7–9, Ethical Lesson #2–3).
77. Ibid., 453 (on Gen 33:21–24).
78. Ibid., 480 (on Gen 41:54).
79. Prov 28:14.
80. *Comm Proverbs*, 129 (on Prov 28:14).
81. Ibid.
82. *Comm Gen*, 232 (on Gen 16:3) and 234 (Intellectual Lesson #2).
83. Ibid., 384–385 (on Gen 30:1–4).
84. *NE*, 46–47 (3.2) and 116 (6.2): "choice is longing marked by deliberation." Richard Sorabji argues that choice is of ends everywhere except 3.2–3.3, where it is of means. I do not see that at 6.2 where he is discussing means, even though desire aims at an end. See Richard Sorabji, "The Role of Intellect in Virtue," in *Essays on Aristotle's Ethics*, ed. Amélie Rorty (California: University of California Press, 1980), 202.
85. *NE*, 116–117 (6.2).
86. *Supercomm De Anima*, 172.
87. *Comm Gen*, 203 (Gen 12:10–13, Ethical Lesson #3).
88. Ibid., 204 (Gen 13:8–9, Ethical Lesson #11). For a discussion of Gersonides on choice, see Manekin, "Freedom within Reason?"
89. Gen 12:10–11.
90. *Comm Gen*, 202 (Gen 12:10, Lesson #1) and *DH*, 409.
91. BT *Sanhedrin* 74b.
92. *Comm Gen*, 202 (Gen 12:11–13, Ethical Lesson #2–3) and *DH*, 410–411.
93. "What is a foolish pietist like?—E.g., a woman is drowning in the river, and he says: 'It is improper for me to look upon her and rescue her'" (BT Sotah 21b).
94. *Comm Gen*, 395 (Gen 29:21, Ethical Lesson #13).
95. *Comm Numbers*, 415 (on Numb 32:1–5). Gersonides though also admits the limitations of this move, in this case, where they experienced regret years later after conquering the land, which removed them from God. As a way of returning to God, they had to build an alter that described in Joshua 22.

96. See Immanuel Kant, "Toward Lasting Peace: A Philosophical Sketch," in *Kant's Political Writings*, ed. Hans Reiss (Cambridge: University of Cambridge Press, 1991), 93.

97. *MT, Laws of Kings and their Wars*, 420 (12.5).

98. *Comm Deut*, 352 (Deut 33:10, Lesson #19).

99. This discussion contributes to Robert Eisen's study *The Peace and Violence of Judaism: From the Bible to Modern Zionism* where he examines the idea of peace in medieval Jewish philosophy (Eisen, *The Peace*, 111–128) and concludes that "medieval Jewish philosophy implicitly develops the peaceful emphasis even further by accentuating a universalism predicated on the notion that intellectual perfection is the ultimate goal for all human beings" (Ibid., 206). Gersonides model provides an alternative philosophic model to that of Maimonides that focuses on the cessation of hostilities and not just the ideal of intellectual perfection as a means to peace.

100. *Comm Gen*, 204 (Gen 13:8–9, Lesson # 8).

101. Prov 17:1.

102. *Comm Gen*, 204 (Gen 13:8–9, Ethical Lesson #8) and *DH*, 413.

103. Ibid., 234 (Gen 16:6, Lesson #4) and *DH*, 417.

104. Ibid., 227 (Gen 15:2–6, Lesson #3) and *DH*, 417.

105. The following questions could be asked: Why is peace with Sarah more important than peace with Hagar and Ishmael? What claim does she have that they do not have? Gersonides expands on another facet of his reasoning in *bi'ur diverei ha-parasha* on Chapter 16. There he explains that Hagar's belittling of Sarah beyond tolerance was a negative trait and the decision to banish her was a result of Sarah's rebuke and education of Hagar. This indicates that if one is going to sacrifice their material self-interest for the sake of peace, it is preferable to combine peace with perfection of character.

106. *Comm Deut*, 30 (Deut 1–2, Lesson #15).

107. Deut 20:10–12.

108. *Comm Deut*, 30 (Deut 1–2, Lesson #15).

109. Prov 22:28.

110. *Comm Proverbs*, 106 (on Prov 22:28).

111. *Comm Gen*, 293 (Gen 21:25, Ethical Lesson #9) and *DH*, 423.

112. Ibid. (Ethical Lesson #9, 11).

113. Ibid. (Ethical Lesson #10) and *DH*, 423.

114. Compare Quran 9:5: "Slay the idolaters wherever you find them, and take them, and confine them, and lie in wait for them at every place of ambush" to Quran 9:29: "And if they incline to peace, do

thou incline to it; and put thy trust in God; He is the All-Hearing, the All-knowing." See Noah Feldman, "War and Reason in Maimonides and Averroes," in *The Ethics of War: Shared Problems in Different Traditions*, eds. Richard Sorabji and David Rodin (United Kingdom: Routledge, 2006), 102–104.

115. Averroes, *Middle Commentary on Aristotle's Nicomachean Ethics*, 199–200.
116. Quoted and translated to English in Lawrence V. Berman, "Review of Averroes Commentary on Plato's *Republic* by E.I.J. Rosenthal," *Oriens* 21 (1968–1969), 439.
117. Averroes, *Commentary on Plato's Republic*, trans. Ralph Lerner (Ithaca: Cornell University Press, 1974), 13–14 (27:1–14). Or as Ralph Lerner puts it (Ibid., xviii), "if Plato is correct about the potentiality for virtue among non-Greek nations, then there is no call for waging a war to bring civilization to them."
118. By "divine commands" I do not mean, part of Jewish law, but God's directly commanding something. This conflict that I am laying out may appear fallacious if one were to respond that one can find parts of Jewish law that command one to make a living, provide food for yourselves and to make peace with others. For Gersonides, these ethical virtues are first and foremost imitations of the natural order set up by God, while Jewish law is merely is a way of cultivating and enforcing these natural virtues. In spite of this, the Bible describes commands which are not directly connected to the natural order, and it is herein where the conflict lies.
119. Esther 3:4.
120. *Esther Rabbah* 7:6.
121. Rashi on Esther 3:2.
122. *Comm Megillot*, 156 (Esther Lesson #23).
123. Ibid., 156–157 (Esther Lesson #24).
124. Lev 19:11.
125. *Comm Gen*, 564 (Gen 50:16–17 Lesson #12).
126. BT Yevamot 65b.
127. Gen 28:15.
128. *Comm Gen*, 440 (Gen 34:30, Ethical Lesson #8).
129. Deut 22:25.
130. Idit Dobbs-Weinstein, "Gersonides' Radically Modern Understanding of the Agent Intellect," in *Meeting of the Minds: The Relations Between Medieval and Classical Modern European Philosophy*, ed. Stephen F. Brown (Belgium: Brepols, 1998), 192.

CHAPTER 5

The Ethics of Divided Political Institutions: King, Priest and Prophet

The relationship of the ethical and the political is another issue that unites and divides Maimonides and Gersonides. Both understand ethics and politics as inherently linked and in that regard follow Aristotle in describing the *Ethics* and the *Politics* as two parts of the same project. But Maimonides and Gersonides differ on the priority of the two. For Maimonides, the prophet is a philosophic-legislator that legislates a divine (political) law that cultivates different moral and intellectual virtues. Different divine laws advocate different virtues. For Gersonides, the virtues of physical preservation and of beneficence are central and are an individual responsibility in imitation of nature. But they are amplified toward the collective through institutions, which serve to actualize physical preservation and of beneficence on a larger scale. Therefore, in Gersonides' scheme, there is an institutional separation between the "secular" political body of the kingship and the "religious" (or intellectual) political body of the priesthood, while giving the prophet the means to criticize and challenge both.[1]

DEFENDING GERSONIDES AS A POLITICAL THINKER: A RESPONSE TO HIS CRITICS

Interpreters of Gersonides' political thought have had trouble placing him on the philosophical map and have consequently missed the significance of his political model and how it relates to his ethical thought. I will begin elucidating my reading by placing it in opposition to the four existing scholarly interpretations. First, the interpretation of Charles

© The Author(s) 2016
A. Green, *The Virtue Ethics of Levi Gersonides*,
DOI 10.1007/978-3-319-40820-0_5

123

Touati is a historicist reading of Gersonides' political thought. He argues that Gersonides' political philosophy applies only to biblical and messianic times, but not to the current state of the Jews in exile. He argues as follows:

> Mais il faut dès l'abord faire observer que cette politique tirée des Ecritures ne vaut que pour les temps bibliques. Gersonide, non plus que les autres théologiens juifs, n'a édicté ou tiré des textes sacrés du judaïsme une politique pour les temps de la dispersion, dont on ne trouve pratiquement les linéaments que chez les *halakhistes*. Autrement dit, les vues de Gersonide ne sont valables que pour le passé ou pour le futur eschatologique, mais non pour l'entredeux.[2]

The problem with this analysis is that it posits that Gersonides' description of political ideas in the Hebrew Bible is purely historical, while at the same time, it sees the ethical and scientific lessons from scripture as rooted in nature and thus constantly relevant. It is unclear why a different hermeneutic would apply to these two realms. True, Gersonides may be describing the political framework in relation to a kingship that no longer exists. However, if Gersonides is also interpreting the Bible with Platonic and Aristotelian political philosophy in mind, based on the assumption that philosophic ideas transcend historical time periods, it is unclear why some of those lessons would not be universally true.

A second interpretation of Gersonides' political thought is the idealist reading, as presented by Menachem Kellner.[3] Kellner argues that unlike Plato, Aristotle and Maimonides who argue that philosophic contemplation must lead to some form of political activity in the state, Gersonides conceives of the end of perfection as the imitation of God through teaching and spreading wisdom to others.[4] He is thus seen to be disinterested in politics and his lessons that fall under political philosophy are in fact mostly with respect to ethics.[5] Kellner's reading is limited by the fact that he restricts his conception of politics to the Maimonidean model, from which Gersonides diverges. But, as will be shown below, Gersonides follows a different political model focused on the separation of institutions; indeed, the idealistic ethics to which Kellner subscribes is part of the institution of the priesthood, as outlined in Gersonides' formulation.

A third interpretation of Gersonides' political thought is the intellectualist reading, as presented by Warren Zev Harvey.[6] Harvey argues that Gersonides considered the scientific study of the cosmos to be his primary object of study and that political involvement was merely a distraction, though sometimes a necessary one. He makes this case based on three arguments. First, in terms of his biography, Gersonides lived a scientifically focused life and did not get involved in political leadership, or at least we have no knowledge of him taking on a public position.[7] Second, he did not write a *Supercommentary* on *Averroes' Commentary on Plato's Republic*, likely indicating that he was not interested in the subject. Third, Gersonides makes many comments in his biblical exegesis that are critical of political power, such as his remarks on Deuteronomy 17:14–15.[8] Each of these points is partially correct, but more complicated than meets the eye. Gersonides did not take a position in public office, but this does not indicate that he was not concerned with the public sphere. In fact, his writing offers a model of political structure which, if properly instituted, is designed to ensure peace and stability through the creation of political institutions. It is also true that Gersonides did not write supercommentaries on Averroes' commentaries on Aristotle's practical works. However, it is my contention that Gersonides used the narrative framework of the biblical text as a replacement for the commentary form to teach about practical issues, since examples and cases may be a more effective way to teach ethics and politics than a commentary or a treatise. Thus, he similarly did not write a commentary on Aristotle's *Nicomachean Ethics*. Lastly, it is true that Gersonides makes disparaging comments about political power, but each of these points must be looked at in context, as he is often critical of one political model, while advocating another in its place.

The last interpretation of Gersonides' political thought is the analysis by Esti Eisenmann.[9] Her work in fact is the first to characterize Gersonides as an independent thinker who formulated his own political philosophy. For Eisenmann, Gersonides is primarily a critic of the model of ideal political leadership represented by the prophet as philosopher-king as advocated by Al-Farabi and Maimonides.[10] Political leadership is thus restricted to the secular leadership of the king who has limited power,[11] resulting from a complete separation of practical philosophy from the theoretical sciences.[12] This interpretation, however, does not adequately look at the origin and purpose of the two political institutions in the two different models of ethics, physical preservation and altruism. Indeed, it is my view that the prophets fit into this paradigm not as part of the religious institution (which is the role of the priesthood), but serve as a vital check on the power of both institutions.

CRITIQUE OF THE PROPHET AS PHILOSOPHER-KING

Gersonides' political philosophy must be read first as a critique of the Maimonidean concept of prophecy in which the ideal leader is a philosopher-king. This prophet contemplates the nature of existence and transforms that knowledge into parables and laws to guide individuals in the city.[13] Indeed, Maimonides interprets the biblical story of Jacob's ladder[14] as a parable for the relationship of the philosopher to society in Plato's analogy of the cave.[15] Gersonides appraises Maimonides' prophet as being an unrealistic prototype for imitation and proposes a different model upon which to base the relationship of the prophet to the political leader. Gersonides' critique takes two methods: one method, in *Wars of the Lord*, makes use of subtle references and comments about Plato's *Republic* (*Medina ha-Hashuva*) and to political philosophy (*filosofiya medinit*); and the other method, in his biblical commentaries, is done indirectly by describing the challenges Moses faced in combining the intellectual and the political. In both cases, Gersonides does not mention Maimonides by name, but allows his comments to allude to his ideas through redefining the meaning of prophecy and politics.

It may in fact be argued that Gersonides' *Wars of the Lord* is focused primarily on responding to theological questions that he believed Maimonides did not adequately answer in the *Guide* with little role for political philosophy in the structure of *Wars of the Lord*. But within Gersonides' theological analysis one can put together a critique of the Maimonidean political ideal through piecing together these sparse comments. During Gersonides' writing of *Wars of the Lord*, a Hebrew translation of Averroes' *Commentary on Plato's Republic* was published by Samuel ben Judah of Marseille and this is most likely what Gersonides is referring to when he mentions the *Republic* and political philosophy.[16] One example arises in Gersonides' comparison of the difference between the Agent Intellect and the material intellect. He notes that distinct from the object of study of the Agent Intellect, the subject matter of the material intellect is defective and imperfect, of which political philosophy is an example.[17] Another example occurs in his discussion of the role that the heavenly bodies play in human affairs. According to Plato, every individual's job or "craft" in society, such as being a farmer, a builder, or a weaver, is dependent on the constitution of one's soul and it is the role of the philosophic ruler to construct society in such a way as to assign everyone their most appropriate task.[18] Gersonides takes the role of the philosophic ruler and assigns it to the direct emanation of the heavenly bodies, which more effectively perform the task of optimizing the division of labor in society. He argues that "all the crafts are perfected in a more superior way than in Plato's scheme of a perfect state."[19] A reference to virtuous political associations (*qibbuṣim ḥashuvim*) also appears in the context of the possibility of acquisition of all the intelligibles, where he suggests that this is very improbable; it would require a lifetime of work and the help of many other people, as one might only hope to find in the ideal of a virtuous state. But it is improbable that nature would endow so many people with the strong desire for acquisition of this sort virtue or knowledge.[20] The unattainable possibility of philosophic rule also explains why the political role of the prophet is absent from Gersonides' description of prophecy in *Wars* Book 3. Instead, the role of the prophet is purely to predict the future.

The clearest example of the political action of a prophet in Maimonides' model is the biblical Moses, who challenges the authority of Pharaoh, legislates a law and leads the people out of Egypt and through the desert. Gersonides presents a paradoxical portrait of Moses, as successful in his intellectual endeavors, but highly unsuccessful in striving to combine those intellectual pursuits with his political ones. And, as a result, in Gersonides' view, this leads to a failure in both activities. To be sure, Gersonides is clear about Moses' attempt to combine both pursuits. Moses was devoted to both deep contemplation of God and nature[21] and was considered the King of Israel.[22] Gersonides describes Moses as a "jack of all trades," being a prophet, king, high priest and head of the Sanhedrin.[23] One of his intellectual accomplishments is his legislation of a perfect law, the Torah, in imitation of the Agent Intellect, the rational plan of the universe in the mind of God.[24] A second intellectual accomplishment is his perfect ability to guide the Israelites to victory in war without any loss.[25] While this may appear supernatural or magical, Gersonides seems to suggest that Moses has the prophetic ability to predict the future through his study of nature and thus is capable of being the perfect military strategist. A third success that results from his intellectual contemplation is his bringing good to those he rules, which Gersonides uses to explain why Moses crossed the river to divide the land more perfectly and quickly.[26] All of these are impressive accomplishments.

Yet according to Gersonides, Moses faced distinct challenges in combining this high level of intellectual seclusion with his practical duties as a political leader of the Israelites. One of these challenges was his lack of rhetoric, made apparent in his admission that he is "slow of speech, and of a slow tongue."[27] Gersonides interprets Moses' need of Aaron to communicate with Pharaoh as resulting from the fact that once his intellect was isolated and focused on divine contemplation, he could not use the other faculties of his soul without losing the philosophic connection. He explains that

> [t]he eighteenth lesson is in opinions (*deot*) and this is what we learn from the story: what is unique about Moses' prophecy that comes to him while he is awake is that he has the strength of isolating (*hitbodedut*) his intellect from all the other powers of the soul to be with God constantly. Until the time that he [God] began to speak to him [at Exodus 3], he [Moses] was constantly isolated in contemplating God, according to his ability. He could not separate this isolation [of the mind] in a way that would allow him to complete his *hishtadlut* to organize [practical] matters as is appropriate in speaking with people because he was inundated in constant love [of God]. This is why the prophecy comes to him while awake and whenever he desires, as was explained in *Wars 2*.[28]
>
> The nineteenth lesson is to inform us the reason why Moses, peace be upon him, needed an intermediary between himself and the people when he was speaking with them. And God, may He be exalted, did not [simply] decide through the power of his providence that he [Moses] should have a faculty to present his material appropriately in speaking with people without the need of an intermediary, because Moses withheld himself from it, as we explained in the exegesis to the story.[29]

Moses thus removed himself from the ability to speak to other people by isolating his intellect to such an extreme and needed Aaron as his translator for this purpose.[30] What does it mean that God did not miraculously give Moses a practical faculty on top of his faculties for theoretical knowledge? Gersonides seems to imply that God does not simply change nature on request so that Moses could fully perfect his material intellect and practical intellect at the same time. Hence, the natural outcome according to God's construction of nature of someone isolating their intellect to such an extent is to void the usage of the practical faculties, suggesting that they must make a choice if they desire perfecting their material intellect and practical intellect. Another challenge Moses faced, which arose from the previous one, was the ability to exercise practical judgment. Moses sought to be the sole judge of the people, so that they would come to him to settle any dispute, since he has the perfect knowledge of the divine law and thus with his knowledge he can most justly apply it to individual cases. In fact, Moses' father-in-law Jethro criticizes Moses for taking on this ambitious role advising him instead to appoint other judges. Not only would it take too long for one man to issue judgments to everyone, but also he would lose his intellectual connection to God out of sheer fatigue, if he attempted to be the sole judge of all the people. Gersonides expands on the terse conversation between Moses and Jethro at Exodus 18:14–16:

Jethro did not see why Moses did not appoint other judges [to judge] the people to ease his burden. This is what he [Jethro] said: "why do you sit all alone?"[31] that there is no judge beside you, for this is the reason that the entire people stands before you from morning until evening. And this is because one who comes seeking judgment before you cannot hear your response immediately, but sometimes must wait from morning until evening, to hear the multitude of arguments put before you.

And Moses said to his father-in-law [Jethro]: I cannot appoint another to ease my burden. This is because the people will come to me anyways by necessity, to know through prophecy [the meaning of] what they ask of me...and without a doubt, there is no one among the people who could ease my burden. Also with respect to interpersonal laws, one cannot place before them one who could ease my burden. This is because when they have a dispute between one another—"it comes to me"[32]—to judge between a man and his neighbor and I will judge them according to the necessities of the laws of the Torah and no one else could do this, other than me, because the laws of the Torah came solely to me through prophecy. It was mentioned "the statutes of God and His laws"[33] since it is not possible that a man could know them through wisdom and speculation. Nonetheless, the commandments that the intellect obligates independent [of prophecy], it is possible for man to know their laws without the Torah.

And Moses' father-in-law [Jethro] responded: "what you do is not good."[34] Overwhelming tediousness will overtake you in this matter and all people with you, because you cannot solely judge all the matters of their quarrels. And it will tire should they bring all the matters of their quarrels in a way that you can judge between them, until the extreme fatigue will separate the conjunction between you and God, may He be exalted, in a way that will prevent you from receiving prophecy when you desire it.[35]

Hence, Jethro's advice to Moses is given so as to ensure that he will be able to maintain his intellectual life, since he perceived that combining both roles is impossible for an extended period of time.[36] Moreover, once one is in that level of intellectual focus, it is very difficult to remove oneself from it.[37] The last difficulty Moses faces is the ability to cultivate the proper emotional response after being in a state of contemplation. Following Maimonides here, Gersonides uses the example of Moses hitting the rock as an example,[38] of leaning to the moral extreme of anger as a response to the Israelite's complaint for water.[39] Although Gersonides does not explain the political problem with anger at this point, it is evident through his discussion of a similar incident involving Moses' anger. Gersonides asserts that when Moses angrily smashed the tablets after the Israelites built the golden calf[40] this extreme anger also removed some of his intellectual cleaving to God.[41] Indeed, Moses is caught in a kind of paradox: intellectual seclusion makes one lose focus on the emotions and when one has to return to use the emotions in practical situations, one's responses are erratic. Furthermore, these erratic responses make one lose one's focus on God even more. While Moses successfully reveals the Torah as a perfect law, his failure in leadership is a lesson on the dangers of attempting to combine the intellectual and political lives and the necessity for different practitioners for each.

As a result of this problem, Gersonides reinterprets the command to appoint a king, "thou shalt in any wise set him king over thee, whom the LORD thy God shall choose,"[42] as a limited monarch.[43] Accordingly, the difference between the Israelite model of kingship and a kingship among the rest of the nations is that the gentile model gives their monarch the role of legislating a law that is desired by the king. In contrast, the Israelite kingship is under the law of the Torah and the king cannot legislate another law to replace it; it thus focuses purely on the executive role of fighting wars and ensuring the security of the state. The Israelites' request to Samuel for a king, "make us a king to judge us like all the nations,"[44] is for an all powerful king but God responds by giving them a limited monarch.[45]

While Gersonides critiques the concept of the philosopher-king, as it is exemplified as an ideal in the medieval Islamic and Jewish interpretations of Plato by Al-Farabi, Averroes and Maimonides, he also, most likely unknowingly (since he only had access to Averroes' *Commentary*), gives expression to the skeptical voice of this position that already exists within Plato's *Republic* itself that sees the rule of the philosopher-king as a potentially rare, but highly unlikely possibility. For example, while Averroes in his *Commentary on Plato's Republic*, sees philosophic politics as the political model that Plato is simply advocating in which theoretical perfection guides practical wisdom, this only remains one part the work. As Charles Buttersworth argues,

[t]his manner of interpreting Plato's *Republic* allows Averroes to take as a practical suggestion for statecraft something which Socrates himself characterizes as a paradigm set up in heaven and which his young interlocutor Glaucon understands to be simply a city in speech....He passes over in silence the whole question of the founding of the first city and the doubts expressed by Socrates about whether or not this is the true and healthy city.[46]

Gersonides thus takes Socrates' skepticism even further regarding the viability of a philosopher-king, warning about both the impossibility and the danger of imposing such a solution.

INSTITUTIONAL SEPARATION OF THE KING, PRIEST AND PROPHET AND THE INDIVIDUALISTIC ORIGINS OF THE STATE

Gersonides' solution to what he regarded as the impossibility of having philosophic rulers is not asceticism or simply education, but a separation of roles into different institutions. These political institutions mirror the separate parts of the human soul and their different ethical obligations. One could even view this model as a radicalized Aristotelianism for it is one that creates sharper distinctions than Aristotle does. Plato famously raises the status of wisdom as the guiding principle behind ethics, psychology and politics, and has Socrates argue for philosophers to rule the state; in this scheme, philosophy appears to be the ideal way of living one's life since rationality (*logos*) is viewed as the dominant part of the human soul. At the same time, while presenting this slanted portrait of reason, Plato also admits to the limitations of this portrait of Socrates, who courageously defends reason and philosophy and is then struck down by forces less friendly to philosophy within the state. In contrast, Aristotle presents a different model where different areas of study are set into separate disciplines, creating the independent fields of ethics, political science, physics, metaphysics and psychology.[47] But within each, he also presents the Platonic voice, questioning the separation of each from one another. For example, within the *Nicomachean Ethics*, he describes ethics as belonging to various categories: as part of political science,[48] as dependent on knowledge of the different parts of the soul[49] and as guided toward the study of metaphysics.[50]

Gersonides delineates a sharper distinction between the practical and the theoretical sciences. The psychological implications are such that the functions of the practical intellect and material intellect are more distinct; furthermore, the ethical repercussions are such that the ethics and virtues of self-preservation are not directly related to the altruistic virtues that lead one to contemplation and imitate the divine nature. This separation equally has political ramifications as well, magnifying this distinction on a collective scale, as the practical realm is managed by kings and the theoretical realm is in the hands of priests. As many Latin interpreters of Averroes argued, by separating the different realms, one can pursue each stronger and with full force, as opposed to a synthesis which leads to one ruling the other. Gersonides sees this exemplified in the biblical verse "the rich and the poor meet together—the LORD is the maker of them all,"[51] which he interprets as showing the necessity of society being constructed as a stratified structure with human differences. He assets that if no one was poor, then no one would complete the practical arts. Moreover, if no one was rich, then there would be no one to generate money. The solution is that God makes some rich and some poor to maintain the order of reality.[52] The same idea can be extrapolated for the political divisions within society: the practical intellect needs to be developed on a larger scale by the kings and the theoretical intellect on a greater scale by the priests, for otherwise society would not contain the proper balance. In examining this division, Horwitz raises the possibility that Gersonides may have been influenced by the conflicts over the power of religious authority in Provence, suggesting that

> Ralbag certainly could have absorbed Aristotelian ideas regarding self-sufficiency of the material world, for example even without reading a Hebrew translation of *Politics*. Hence, it need not come as a surprise that in many respects, Ralbag's political philosophy may indeed agree with the "lay" spirit of Latin Christian authors in 14th Century who described Aristotelian philosophy based on Latin translations of *Politics*.[53]

Whether or not Gersonides read Latin, or even read the works of Marsilius of Padua and William of Ockham, it would still be surprising if he was ignorant of their thought while working for the Pope in the 1320s during their rejection by the papacy after they advocated political power that is independent of papal authority.

A significant feature of institutional separation is its origins in the collective agreement of individuals for their own physical and intellectual preservation. Similarly for Gersonides, instead of the Torah being the model of the perfect form of government, legislated by the prophet as philosopher-king, he develops a model of the origin of the state based on an accord among persons.[54] This may sound at first glance to be a form of modern social contract, but in fact it is quite distinct from it, as it does not imply that there is a nonpolitical state of nature that preceded the state and that these political institutions that were created were against nature. On the contrary, the kingship and priesthood are a fulfillment of natural human inclinations.[55] Gersonides in effect developed a more radically individualistic form of Aristotelianism, with respect to both the origin and the goal of the state. Aristotle argues that the state begins with families who unite to form a village and that many villages (which are a larger extension of the family) unite to form a city.[56] In Gersonides' version, political associations fulfill the needs of the individual's physical and intellectual preservation but on a larger scale. The goal of the state is not to determine who should rule and to what end, or whether it is just or not, but whether the leader can achieve the necessary physical and intellectual ends for individuals.[57]

One clear example of this in Gersonides' writings is his redefinition of the terms political philosophy (*ḥokhma medinit* and *filosofiya medinit*) and political association (*qibuṣ medini*). The classical question of political philosophy is the quest for the best and most just form of government, and a political association (or regime) refers to the various structures of governance, such as monarchy, aristocracy, oligarchy and democracy. Those who wrote about medieval Jewish political thought prior to Gersonides mostly answered this question by identifying the best regime with the divine law. Yet when Gersonides discusses political philosophy and political associations in his biblical commentaries, he only refers to the cultivation of individual character and maxims for individuals to achieve their best ends. It thus appears that Gersonides' work in this area signifies a definitive shift in that he redefines political philosophy and the nature of a political association through the necessities of individuals.

Accordingly, Gersonides describes the origins of the first political associations in the first eleven chapters of Genesis, as forming for the sake of ensuring physical survival and basic material needs. Some of these associations were created for mutual well-being, while others for the advantage of the few. For example, after killing Abel, Cain was exiled from the land in which he was under divine providence. Hence, according to Gersonides, Cain was now in danger of being killed by animals and had to wander to search for land to grow plants for food. This suggests that it is only fitting that Cain (or his son) built the first city to ensure the stability that he lacked in wandering.[58] He also points to those who formed associations in order to prey on the weak. For example, the "sons of God" (*benei ha-elohim*)[59] were a group that formed, and due to their largeness and strength,[60] and following the philosophy that might makes right, they were able to kidnap local women. Nimrod also arose after the flood and pursued greater power for himself, becoming king over numerous regions due to his subjugation of others.[61] Gersonides, however, interprets the building of The Tower of Babel as an attempt to create an association for the sake of preservation by forcing individuals to be located in one place. Though ultimately failing, the Tower was intended to prevent individuals from wandering off too far to look for habitable lands.[62]

Gersonides also presents ways that political associations are perfected (*tiqqun qibuṣ ha-medini*). The criterion for political perfection is not justice alone, but ensuring peaceful relations with others and avoiding interpersonal conflict, suggesting that there is no greater threat to one's physical well-being than embroiling oneself in wars and strife. Gersonides provides many biblical examples of those who strive to create strong relations with others. For example, Abraham strove to have many friends and few enemies,[63] fought a war to rescue his brother when taken captive[64] and mourned and cried for Sarah on her death.[65] Similarly, Joseph's brother lied to him to achieve peace[66] and Moses saved an Israelite man who was being beaten and who had no strength to defend himself.[67] Abraham strove to avoid conflict and strife by parting ways with Lot[68] and was not jealous if Lot's shepherds received better grazing land.[69] Shechem and Hamor are also criticized for coveting Jacob's land[70] and the conflict that arose because of it. Thus a state is perfected not through being perfectly just, but through stable and peaceful relations between individuals.

In addition, Gersonides suggests that political associations also form to ensure the preservation of scientific knowledge that has been acquired and to successfully transmit it to the next generation. This is so that they can build on what previous generations have acquired and allow more individuals to attain their immortality. Scientific knowledge is a cumulative process that is not achievable through one generation, but must see itself as part of a larger historical development. Gersonides explores this point further in interpreting the Song of Songs 7:14, "new and old, which I have laid up for thee," citing it as evidence that most knowledge cannot be apprehended by any one individual alone, but is gathered and built on that which has been explored by one's predecessors.[71] He perceived that even with cumulative scientific research over multiple generations, only a minutia of potential knowledge of the universe has been explored, stating that "we have grasped less than an iota of God's creation."[72]

For Gersonides, the institution of the kingship is the political representation of the practical intellect and the ethics of self-preservation. His first glimpse of this is in Genesis where he compares the nature of political leadership to that of the imagination. In characterizing *elohim* in "ye shall be as *elohim*, knowing good and evil,"[73] he interprets them as judges and political leaders who use their imagination in most of their perceptions.[74] Similarly, Eve's eating of the fruit represents the desires of the imagination, which he also delineates as being on the level of judges and political leaders.[75] Two forms of leadership that fall under thus rubric are judges, as described in the Book of Judges, and kings, as appear most prominently in I-II Samuel to I-II Kings, which differ in the fact that judges arise on a case-by-case basis to fight wars, while kingship is a permanent institution dedicated to that purpose. There is much debate in rabbinic literature over which institution is preferable, the spontaneous leadership of the judges, as presented in *Judges*, or the hereditary institution of kingship that is developed in the Book of Samuel and the Book of Kings.[76] One reading, as proposed by Martin Buber, highlights the fact that God is the true king, and the more minimal the position of human leadership, the better, since it is a mere imitation and concession, emphasizing the statement "I will not rule over you myself, nor shall my son rule over you; the Lord alone shall rule over you."[77] The other interpretation focuses on the anarchic tendencies of rotating leaders and the necessity of a permanent chain of command for political stability, highlighting the refrain "in those days there was no king in Israel; every man did that which was right in his own eyes."[78] Gersonides does not present a decisive answer to this question and brings out the strengths and weaknesses of both. The king has more power than the judge and thus the stronger ability to create a stable political order and have continuous power against enemies. But it is also easier for a king to adopt idolatry and usurp power and forget the limited nature of their political role, giving a certain advantage to a rule of temporary judges.

The best compromise solution, according to Gersonides, is to cultivate a limited model of kingship that is responsible purely for executive functions, but not legislative or judicial ones. He sees this as the difference between the Israelite model of monarchy and the model of monarchy advocated by all other nations. As he explains in interpreting "now make us a king to judge us like all the nations,"[79]

[t]hey asked me to give them a king to judge them "like all the nations."[80] This is where they erred, because Israel [does not have a system of law] such that the king judges according to his desire, like kings of other nations that establish for their people laws (*nimusim*) when it suits their fancy. This is why the Torah said that if Israel should ask to give them a king, like all the nations around them, that you cannot give them [one], unless he is one of your brethren [see: Deuteronomy 17:15], that are bound to keep the Torah and will act by its dictates, and will not follow other laws.[81]

It also explains why God commanded the king to write a Torah scroll, and also restricted the number of wives he may have and the amount of horses, gold and silver he may acquire, since each is meant to strengthen his faith in the Law of Torah. Writing a Torah scroll forces him to know the text as the law he is beholden to. Limiting the number of horses prevents his return to Egypt. If he can purchase unlimited horses, he will send people to buy from Egypt and will learn from their behavior. Limiting the number of wives prevents them from taking the king's heart away from God and devoting all his time to them. Similarly, restricting his acquisition of gold and silver prevents an endless addiction to economic growth.[82] Thus when the Israelites requested a king "like all the other nations,"[83] their request was problematic according to Gersonides' interpretation of why Samuel rejected it. This is because their request was for a king who also legislates a new law with his executive authority rather than purely abiding by the Torah's law.[84] This goes against Gersonides' understanding of the Torah as *the* true law which imitates nature's true laws. In other words, to legislate one's own law is not to be guided by the motivation of truth, but by ambition.[85]

The executive role of the king is put into practice through fighting wars and accumulating wealth.[86] Gersonides sharpens the extent to which the king is a model of "political realism" by stressing the purely materialistic aspirations for the king. As Toutati puts it, "cette restriction de Gersonides qu'on ne rencontre ni dans le Talmud, ni chez d'autres auteurs, s'explique par son réalisme politique."[87] While the basic request of the people is to have a king to fight their wars to defend the Torah[88] and acquire wealth for the betterment of the community,[89] the duties of a king in Gersonides' view can be extended to maintaining order and stability within the state as well. A king must also negotiate with the leaders of the nation to prevent rebellion and maintain internal stability. To do so, sometimes a king must appease the leaders before demanding a difficult matter from the populace, or otherwise they may rebel against the king. For example, Joseph avoided nationalizing and dividing up the land of the priests of Egypt, as a form of appeasement, according to Gersonides' interpretation, while doing so for the rest of Egypt.[90] A king also must ensure that his subjects have the proper fear of him, since respect for his authority begins there.[91] This is why, Gersonides argues, it is commanded not to have a king who is a non-Jew or with physical disabilities, not because of anything inherently biological, but because people will not revere him.[92]

Another important quality that distinguishes kingship is that a king must be driven by honor, but not be egotistic or full of pride (*ga'ava*). Aristotle recognizes honor as the goal of the political life and it is the central nameless virtue in Aristotle's list of eleven moral virtues,[93] perhaps suggesting that reliance on honor is at the core of moral virtues.[94] In Gersonides' model, honor is necessary for the king as a means of commanding fear, but too much self-obsession might lead him to prioritize his own interests over the material success of the state overall. One form of honor is the deferential way people are required to speak to the king, advising that it is "appropriate for man to bestow honor upon royalty."[95] For example, Joseph shaved and donned fresh clothes to honor the king to ensure that the Pharaoh listens to his words.[96] Judah also speaks gently to Joseph to assuage his anger and gives honor to him by flattering him.[97] Honoring the ruler even applies if it is one's son, as shown by Jacob struggling to sit upright as he greets Joseph while on his deathbed.[98] Maintaining the honor of a ruler also applies to how a king speaks to others. Gersonides argues that it is inappropriate to show strong bursts of emotion, such as crying or laughing, in front of subjects, as it diminishes their respect and fear for him. For example, Joseph refused to cry in front of his men and commanded that everyone leave the room as he cried.[99] This respect for the king begins with how he presents himself, which must be pleasurable, since it makes others love him and want to work for him.[100] But if the king begins to prioritize honor to the extent that it leads to pride this may have dire consequences such as the removal of the kingdom from the king. Hence it is the intention of the divine law to diminish pride lest it lead to a political disaster.[101]

The only king whom Gersonides describes as truly embodying this model of limited monarchy is David. Gersonides' description of David is very different than the rabbinic portrait. The Talmud has no doubt about David's military prowess, but combines it with a description of him as a high level scholar and judge. It details how "until midnight he would study Torah, from midnight onwards he would sing praises"[102] and by God that "The Holy One, blessed be He, said to him: 'One day of your studying Torah is better than a thousand offerings that your son Solomon is destined to place before me'."[103] Interestingly, this image of David as a scholar and warrior is adopted by Maimonides who interprets David as a form of philosopher-king. For example, David is listed in the Introduction to the *Mishneh Torah* as being part of the chain of transmission of the Torah and in *Laws of Sanhedrin* (in *Book of Judges in Mishneh Torah*), David is described as ordained and ordaining others.[104]

Gersonides too praises David though purely for his accomplishments in the material success of the kingdom. David is described as a "mighty man of valour" (*gibor ḥayil*) and "a man of war" (*'ish milehama*).[105] Gersonides interprets these two phrases as indicating bravery (*'omeṣ*) and the ability to construct stratagems (*taḥbulot*) to defeat enemies and win. He concludes that someone who has these qualities is fit to be king.[106] Also, in commenting on the story of David's impressive victory over the Philistine warrior Goliath, Gersonides argues that David attained the kingship due to his victory over Goliath.[107] Thus, kingship came to David easily because of success in war.[108] However, Gersonides stresses that David used the booty of war—the gold and silver that he acquired—in order to benefit the common good, such as for building the Temple and for fighting wars.[109] In fact, Gersonides views it as a positive trait that David did not fight nations for money, but to raise the stature of the Torah. He took spoil for the sake of the Torah and not to line his own pockets.[110] Unlike the rabbinic commentators who tend to portray David primarily as a scholar and judge, Gersonides focuses on him as a military tactician. He emphasizes David's excellence in cultivating virtues of endeavor (*hishtadlut*) and ingenuity (*hithakmut*) in crafting stratagems (*taḥbulot*). He even notes how David crafted an ingenious stratagem by pretending to be crazy, thus saving him from Ahish king of Gat.[111]

According to Gersonides' analysis, the failure of the Israelite model of limited monarchy led to the destruction of the kingdom and the exile of the people from the Land of Israel. This was not only due to the inability of the kings to succeed both strategically and militarily but it was also due to their failure to recognize the limited power of their position. This is the intention of Gersonides' observation that the rest of the kings of Israel did not rule with the fear of God and as a result, the kingdom did not last long.[112] By "fear of God" he is not referring to pious humility, but a respect for the role and limitations of kingship, as dictated by

God's law. Gersonides perceived that by not following the restrictions on kingship that were delineated by the Torah, they overstepped their goal of physical preservation and extended their reach into other areas. As a result, they did not focus properly on security and self-defense and made military and strategic mistakes, which hurt the long-term safety and security of the nation.

The first example of a king who did not act in a way that is appropriate for a king (*minhag ha-meleḥ*) is Saul. According to Gersonides, Saul did not fight wars with the correct intention. God's objective was to wipe out Amalek and take revenge for what they did to the Israelites, *not* to take spoils and enjoy their possessions. When Saul and Israelites took their belongings, this contradicted the intention of revenge. Taking for one's own benefit is the opposite of divine intention. This is why the Israelites in the time of Mordechai and Esther had to attack the Amalek of their day; they did so in order to take revenge on them, and not to take their property.[113] Gersonides also argues that Saul did not receive the proper honor by the people since he did not act like a king; he cites the verse "Saul came following the oxen out of the field,"[114] implying that Saul failed to behave with authority. As a result, the people did not make sacrifices to honor his leadership.[115] Similarly, he shows that Saul did not act in a kingly way that would inspire fear in the people until he defeated Nachash King of Ammon.[116] Moreover, Saul is shown to have ultimately failed as king because he not only overstepped the boundaries and commands of God's law in the case of Amalek but also disobeyed God in making a sacrifice before Samuel arrived, caving in to the people's demands and their fears.[117]

This failure can equally be found among later Israelite kings. Even Solomon's great wisdom did not stop him from disobeying God's command, for he increased his desire for women beyond God's limitation. His lust for women began an increasingly destructive chain reaction that led him to marry Pharaoh's daughter, and then when that did not satisfy him, he married many more women, including idol-worshippers. This eventually culminated in his worshipping of other gods and the eventual destruction of the kingdom.[118] Similarly, Jeroboam created a god of gold and exiled priests and Levites and Rehoboam married a non-Israelite woman and his son began worshipping other gods.[119] However, Gersonides points out that the final act that led to the destruction of the Temple was the moral miscalculation of King Zedekiah. He derives this inference from Proverbs 28:14, "Happy is the man that feareth always; but he that hardeneth his heart shall fall into evil," which in the Talmud is used to indicate that the destruction of the Temple resulted from the embarrassment of Bar Kamtza caused by a fellow Jew.[120] Interestingly, Gersonides uses the same verse for different purposes: to show how Zedekiah did not exercise the virtue of courage properly. Instead of standing up and challenging the Babylonians when he needed to, Zedekiah hid from them out of fear; according to Gersonides, this is the reason that the Temple was destroyed and Israel was subjugated to foreign powers.[121]

Moreover, in Gersonides' scheme, the institution of the priesthood is the political representation of the material intellect and the ethics of altruistic enlightenment. Indeed, in his description of the priests, he presents them as both philosophers and teachers.[122] Gersonides justifies the identification of priests as philosophers by the fact that Ezra, a descendent of Aaron, was described as a *sofer*, which means a counter (*mone*), referring to the ability to quickly count the evidence behind the different propositions in order to quickly determine which is correct.[123] Since Gersonides regarded the Temple and its rituals as a metaphor for the laws and structure of the universe, he saw the priests who are responsible for these rituals as having a unique understanding of the structure of the cosmos. He explains that

> [t]he lesson that comes out of the priests being a special family of which "no stranger passed among them"[124] [implying that they did not marry non-priests], is apparent according to what is said: and that is, we already introduced that the lesson of the Temple and the worship therein is to guide people to contemplate God, may He be exalted, according to what is possible. Because of the many limitations and the fact it is difficult to achieve this perception, God, may He be exalted, ingeniously planned (*hitehakem*) that there would be one special family whose entire endeavor (*hishtadluta*) is the perfection of the intellect, and they would not have to trouble in acquiring possessions. This family will be persistent in constant study and as a result will be revealed to it many of the secrets of existence, all the more so, since the Torah guided them to this perception in the matters of the Temple and the worship carried out there. Because it would not be possible for all of Israel to be free from work (the arts), it was necessary that this matter be reserved for one special family, and the rest of them [non-priests] will work, and this family would benefit from it. And this family [will benefit] from what will be given to them from the gifts of what the Torah prescribes to them.[125]

In fact, he viewed the priests as the ones who study the philosophical secrets behind the structure of the tabernacle, Temple and sacrificial laws and are able to pass on this knowledge from one generation to the other. This may explain the mysterious death of Aaron's two sons, Nadav and Avihu, who were killed for sacrificing a "foreign fire (*'esh zara*) before the Lord, which he had not commanded them."[126] Gersonides suggests that this strange fire resulted from their having changed the order of the sacrificial ritual,[127] implying that the order is intentionally set up to be a mirror of the cosmos, and changing it is a mistaken interpretation and serious disruption of the set structure of the natural world.

The common goal of the Temple and its sacrificial service, according to Gersonides, is to guide its practitioners toward recognizing that there is one God who is master of all and that they must worship him, since everything comes from him.[128] Each of its laws contributes to this purpose. For example, having only one family (Aaron's) operating the sacrificial ritual serves as a metaphor for Gersonides that there is only one God.[129] Worshipping in one singular location also indicates the oneness of God, since idolaters who worship many deities do so in multiple locations.[130] The stones from which the Temple is built also hint to the nature of God. The stones must be expensive to indicate that they are long-lasting, like God who is everlasting. Similarly, the stones must be complete like God who is perfect with no faults.[131] The two cherubim[132] on the Ark of the Tabernacle refer to the material intellect and Agent Intellect. The wings facing upward suggest that one can strive to go higher and know the truth. The fact that the two tablets are inside[133] signifies that one can receive prophecy through these two cherubim.[134] Yet the gap in space between the Ark of the Tabernacle and between the menorah and table[135] represents the vast difference between the rational part of the soul and the other material parts, with the table representing the vegetative part of the soul and the menorah the sensitive part of the soul.[136] On the table are twelve loaves of bread divided into two,[137] which to Gersonides allude to twelve stars that are divided into six north stars that signify material existence and six south stars that denote material loss.[138]

Furthermore, Gersonides sees the priesthood as constructed according to a specific method to best achieve the knowledge of God and the universe. Belonging to the same family would mean that there is a greater predisposition to grasp the mysteries of worship, for they would all help each other to reach that goal. Aaron's line is specifically chosen over Moses' to inherit the priesthood, since Moses married a Midianite woman and carries a mixed lineage, while Aaron married from within a select Israelite family, from which his offspring will inherit these qualities.[139] The clothing of the priests is also constructed to focus their thoughts and protect them from evil.[140] In fact, all the basic material necessities of priesthood are paid for by the state; they are not required to till the land, but instead can focus their minds on contemplation and attempt to know God to the highest extent possible.[141] Of course, this contemplative role also explains why the priests were not given a specific plot of land by God.[142]

In addition, Gersonides deduces that the priests must use the knowledge they have obtained to teach the rest of society, functioning as a kind of state educational institution. In fact, all priests must participate as educators in teaching God's laws to Israel.[143] Furthermore, in describing God's command to Priests, "so shall they put My name upon the children of Israel, and I will bless them,"[144] Gersonides describes how the priests will impart the secret of God's name to the Israelites in a way that everyone will understand it.[145] However, Gersonides points out that it is important that the priests maintain their responsibility within the realm of education and do not attempt to overstep their role and venture into politics; to be sure, Gersonides' description of the priests is absent of any advocacy of political involvement. The priesthood is thus seen by Gersonides as the training ground for future prophets in the sense that sacrifices serve as mental exercises in helping isolate the mind (*hitbodedut*) from bodily needs.[146]

The prophet also plays a unique role in this scheme as the "moral critic" and as one who prevents corruption of institutions. The separation of kingship from the priesthood *seems* to suggest that the executive and the educational are completely separate, giving the priests the role of education through religious ritual and the kings the arena of political decision making, without any dialogue between them. But it is the prophet who challenges the established opinions in each by discovering new knowledge of "nature" both in its theoretical and practical forms and using that knowledge to correct the priests and kings when they veer away from achieving their appropriate ends. This is in contrast to the portrait of Gersonides' prophet as described by Menachem Kellner who regards the prophet as one who imitates God through further scientific research of the cosmos.[147] But science, for Gersonides, is not just in the theoretical realm, but in the practical realm as well. And while the prophet is not a politician in the sense that he does not get involved in political decision making or assume the role of ruling, he challenges the actions of the king and the priest and proposes methods to reform their behavior. Yet the question still remains, how does the prophetic power to check authority in Gersonides' biblical commentaries connect to his scientific analysis of prophecy in *Wars*? Prophecy is defined by Gersonides as the knowledge concerning future events about human circumstances,[148] and chance events[149] to preserve the human species.[150] Since prophets believe that following God's law will more effectively bring one to the most successful natural ends, be they practical or theoretical, by not following that law one distances oneself from achieving these ends. The prophet strives to bring the king or priest back to more appropriate means by showing him the future outcome if he continues in the current direction.

The prophet recommends particular actions that will allow the practitioner to succeed more effectively; he also predicts what the future entails if that person continues on that path. More specifically, the prophet advises the king how to successfully maximize the "practical intellect" on a societal scale through challenging political leaders who act against God's commands. The prophet thus acts for the material benefit of the people, and if the situation calls for it, as a military strategist.[151] Here Gersonides follows Maimonides in describing courage as the necessary virtue that the prophet must possess in order to criticize political leaders.[152] At the same time, he differs from Maimonides in stressing the need for physical perseverance as the central focus of the critique. Gersonides cites the example of Abraham who courageously challenged Abimelech for instructing his servants to commit acts of theft,[153] Gersonides also looks to the example of Moses who courageously confronted Pharaoh,[154] for not materially rewarding the Israelites for their hard work.[155] Gersonides also cites the example of Samuel who bravely criticized Saul for not listening to God and sparing Agag. Gersonides states that he was "not afraid to speak difficult matters to Saul, even though he was king."[156] In fact, as a result of Saul's sparing of Agag, the Israelites were forced to confront the existential threat of Amalek again in the time of Mordechai and Esther.[157]

The prophet, according to Gersonides, also serves as military strategist to the king before going to battle. One example he uses is the Israelite's confrontation with the Gibeonites in the time of Joshua, focusing on the rebuke that they "asked not counsel at the mouth of the LORD."[158] Gersonides interprets this to mean that the Israelites did not appropriately consult a prophet (in this case Joshua) before signing a peace treaty with the Gibeonites.[159] He similarly argues that the Israelites rushed out to battle with the Philistines without consulting a prophet and as a result much of Israel was killed and the Ark of the Tabernacle was taken captive.[160] Solomon also emphasized the importance of consulting God before declaring war, stating that if they pray to God before war, God will listen; citing this directive, Gersonides adds that consulting with a prophet is one of the major forms of getting access to God before going to war.[161]

Gersonides also points out that the prophet is the one who ensures that the institution of the priesthood successfully follows the path toward maximizing the material intellect.[162] God was the first to condemn the sacrificial method used by the priests through the killing of Aaron's two sons, Nadav and Avihu, who sacrificed a "foreign fire before the Lord, which he had not commanded them."[163] As was discussed earlier, Gersonides suggests that this strange fire resulted from their changing the order of the sacrifice,[164] since the order functions as a kind of mirror of the structure of the cosmos. Therefore priests who diverge from God's order of the sacrifice cannot properly obtain knowledge of God and the natural world. Gersonides also uses the example of God's rebuke of Hophni and Pinheas for their corrupt habits while making sacrifices and his sending Samuel to deliver the message to Eli. It is described that they took extra meat from the sacrifice for their own personal benefit, which Gersonides interprets as being the result of gluttony (*zolelelut*) and uncontrolled desire, leading them to lose their ability to know God. Gersonides explains that God's providing for them was only so that they would not have to work for food, and not so they can take advantage of this gift to satisfy their own personal appetites.[165] Thus, Gersonides shows the need to correct the priestly abuse of power and this is performed by rebuke and relieving priests from their duties.

FAMILY AND FRIENDSHIP

In formulating his political model, Gersonides also looks to the lessons drawn from the bonds of friendship and family. In this respect, he draws on Aristotle who boldly asserts that friendship is a better model for the state to imitate than justice. In Aristotle's introduction to his analysis of friendship in Book 8 of the *Nicomachean Ethics*, he states that "it seems too that friendship holds cities together and that lawgivers are more serious about it than justice...[and] when people are friends they have no need of justice, but when they are just they do need friendship in addition."[166] Friendship is a private relationship that is devoted to a common goal, such as the good, the pleasant or the useful.[167] It manifests itself in the political arena in forms such as good will, concord and beneficence.[168] In contrast, justice is a standard of distributing external goods, such as wealth and honor,[169] according to the standard of fairness in a state. The first method creates a common bond among individuals who have similar aspirations, while the latter distributes the lowest means necessary for survival among individuals. Aristotle's earlier comments argue for the necessity of the state striving for higher goals and not merely ensuring the division of basic necessary goods.[170]

According to Aristotle, the family is a natural basis for a model of friendship as the bonds of family are more natural and powerful than those that unite fellow citizens. As such, friendship must look to the family in cultivating human bonds with the state.[171] The most powerful relationship within the family is especially that of a parent and child. This relationship is based on wishing good for the other, though ultimately it is an unequal friendship,[172] since the parent's love will always be stronger toward the child than a child to its parent due to the origin and length of time of the relationship. First, a parent loves a child as if it is part of itself and a child loves its parents since its being comes from them. Parents see the child as part of their own body, like a tooth or hair. Second, parents love their children from the moment of birth, whereas children begin to love their parents years after birth, when they have gained intelligence or sense.[173] The friendship within the family between a parent and child, which appears to be the most selfless bond is, in fact, according to Aristotle, an attachment to one's own being.[174] The self-interested basis of the family hints toward the natural basis of the highest form of friendship, a philosophic love of the good, which is in fact truly a form of self-love.[175]

Gersonides accepts that both the family (*mishpaḥa* and *qerovav*, literally: relatives) and friendship (*'ohavav*) are private social relationships which are models for material preservation and not as ideals for philosophic love of the good.[176] In Aristotle's terms, friendship for Gersonides is concerned with the useful and not the pleasant or the good.

The first attribute of Gersonides' model of family is that it contains a clear obligation to help one another. The first example of this, in Gersonides' reading, is between Abraham and Lot. He sees the fact that Abraham provided for Lot as fulfilling the obligation to help relatives as he would himself, which would result in Lot helping him in return.[177] This obligation to help other family members includes acts of love, such as marrying one's relatives, as in the case of Jacob and Rachel[178] and also acts of mourning for them.[179] The most common means of fulfilling one's duty to family is through providing food for them. Citing Noah's act of ensuring that the animals in the ark have sufficient food *a fortiori*, Gersonides concludes that one must ensure that members of one's household are similarly nourished properly.[180] Gersonides also establishes the principle that it is inappropriate for a man to provide any less for his sons and members of his household than he possibly can, basing this on Abraham's donation of food for the journey to Hagar and Ishmael after their banishment.[181] He also sees this principle at work when Jacob runs to feed the livestock of Laban and Rachel[182] and in Laban's sheltering of Jacob after his escape from Esau.[183] The obligation to help other members of one's family is also applied by Gersonides to cases of war, citing the case of Abraham declaring war on the four kings in order to rescue his nephew who had been captured.[184]

Another principle Gersonides derives from family relationships is the need to avoid strife and conflict between members of one's family. For example, Abraham practiced this value by dividing up land and separating from Lot in order to not compete over the same land.[185] Abraham also allowed Sarah to exile his maidservant even though it was against his interest (as she was pregnant with Abraham's child). He nonetheless did so to ensure peace with his wife.[186] This also applies to chastising members of one's household without anger, such as how Abraham calmly criticized Sarah for laughing about having a child.[187] Abraham also worked hard to avoid potential conflict over his inheritance after his death by dividing up his belongings according to what he believed was appropriate during his lifetime.[188] Lastly, Joseph's brothers strived to avoid conflict with Joseph after Jacob's death and thus told an untrue story about Jacob's wishes in order to make peace.[189]

Family relationships also require showing honor toward one another. For example, the tradition of levirate marriage (*yibum*) is a process of keeping the memory of one's relatives alive.[190] Gersonides even goes so far as to stress the fact that worldly success, power and business affairs should not divert one from one's responsibility to honor one's family. This explains why even though Joseph was the ruler of Egypt, he still ran out with zeal to welcome his father and honor him.[191]

Friendship in Gersonides' discussions is equally utilitarian and materialistic. He bases this on the verse "the poor is hated even of his own neighbor; but the rich hath many friends"[192] arguing that in giving money or wisdom, one acquires friends. There is also an element of mutual benefit as Gersonides derives from the verse "there is a friend that sticketh closer than a brother"[193] that friends are closer to one another than brothers in times of need. Friendship is also not based on having merely a few close intimate relationships, but the more friends one has the better. Gersonides argues that Abraham was famous for his goal to "endeavor with all strength to have many friends and few enemies for society will benefit through them."[194] Though there are limits even here and one must be careful, as demonstrated by the fact that the Israelites were negatively influenced by their relationship to the mixed multitude, which led them astray.[195]

CONCLUSION

Gersonides' comments on political matters are often found scattered throughout his works, leading many readers to assume that he is uninterested or apathetic about political philosophy. This chapter comes to correct this mistaken assumption and show the significance of Gersonides' political model as an essential component of his philosophy that cannot be separated from his psychology and ethics. In particular, his critique of Moses as both prophet and philosopher-king reveals the limitations of combining these two roles in any one individual; it also demonstrates the necessity for future leaders to divide these roles between the kingship and the priesthood. Furthermore, Gersonides' politics is more individualistic and rooted in biology than that of previous medieval Jewish Aristotelians and as a result he presents the role of the family and friendship as grounded in utility rather than based on striving for the pleasant or the good. Hence, Gersonides should be viewed as a unique political thinker who amalgamates a critique of idealistic politics with a new realistic model based in institutional separation.

NOTES

1. Aviezer Ravitzky uses this approach to interpret the debate within the political thought of medieval Jewish philosophy. See Aviezer Ravitzky, *Religion and State in Jewish Philosophy: Models of Unity, Division, Collision and Subordination* (Jerusalem: Israel Democracy Institute, 2002).
2. Touati, *La Pensée*, 520.
3. Kellner, "Politics and Perfection: Gersonides vs. Maimonides," 49–82.
4. Ibid., 49.
5. Ibid., 71.
6. Harvey, "The Philosopher and Politics: Gersonides and Crescas," 53–65.

7. Ibid., 55.
8. Ibid., 56–57.
9. Eisenmann, "Social and Political Principles in Gersonides' Thought," 319–347.
10. Ibid., 329–332.
11. Ibid., 332–337.
12. Ibid., 328–339.
13. *Guide*, 373–374 (II 37).
14. Gen 28:10–19.
15. *Republic*, 193–198 (Bk 7, 514a–520a) and *Guide*, 41 (I 15).
16. Though Gersonides' references to both Plato's *Republic* and Aristotle's *Nicomachean Ethics* are sparse and thus it is still an open question whether Gersonides actually read Averroes' commentaries in Hebrew translation or merely obtained the ideas second hand. He cites only a few examples from each work. However, it is unclear whether not having a plethora of direct references implies he did not read the work carefully. Either way, Gersonides is responding and reinterpreting some of the central concepts of these works.
17. *Wars*, vol. i, 169 (1.7).
18. *Republic*, 164–169 and 262–264 (485–489, 581–582).
19. *Wars*, vol. ii, 36–37 (2.2); Kreisel, *Prophecy: The History of an Idea in Medieval Jewish Philosophy* (Dordrecht: Springer, 2001), 355; and Eisenmann, "Social and Political Principles in Gersonides' Thought," 322. Gersonides uses this analogy again at *Wars*, vol. iii, 340 (6.1.17), where he used the ruler of perfect state toward the craftsman as analogy for God relation to the heavenly bodies. The *Republic* is also referenced in an unrelated discussion at *Comm Gen*, 76 (on Gen 1:24–31).
20. *Supercomm De Anima*, 151.
21. *Comm Exod*, vol. i, 29 (on Exod 3:14).
22. *Comm Gen*, 438 (on Gen 33:18–37:1) and *Comm Exod*, 304 (Exod 18:6, Ethical Lesson #4).
23. *Comm Exod*, vol. ii, 283–284 (Exod 25–27, Root #3).
24. Ibid., vol. ii, 424 (on Exod 34:6–7) and *Comm Deut*, 351–352 (Deut 33–34, Lesson #18). For an excellent summary of Moses as "super-prophet," see: Feldman, *Gersonides*, 159–165.
25. *Comm Numbers*, 257–259 (on Numb 20:8).
26. *Comm Deut*, 39 (Deut 4, Lesson #10).

27. Exod 4:10.
28. *Comm Exod*, vol. i, 51 (Exod 4:10, Lesson #18).
29. Ibid. (Exod 4:12–16, Lesson #19).
30. Ibid., 44 (on Exod 4:10–16) and 51 (Lesson #18–19).
31. Exod 18:14.
32. Exod 18:16.
33. Ibid.
34. Exod 18:17.
35. *Comm Exod*, vol. i, 297–298 (on Exod 18:14–16).
36. Ibid.
37. *Comm Exod*, 444 (Exod 34:29–30, Lesson #23).
38. Numb 20:8–11.
39. *Comm Numbers*, 257–259 (on Numb 20:8). Compare Maimonides' discussion of this at *Eight Chapters* Ch 4. He does not draw political conclusions from this incident in the setting of his ethical introduction, though perhaps Gersonides' interpretation draws this tension out further.
40. Exod 32:19–21.
41. *Comm Deut*, 79 (Deut 7–11, Lesson #12).
42. Deut 17:15.
43. *Comm Deut*, 147–148 (on Deut 17:15).
44. I Sam 8:5.
45. *Comm Early Proph I*, 172–173 (on I Sam 8:5).
46. Charles Buttersworth, "Philosophy, Ethics, and Virtuous Rule: A Study of Averroes' Commentary on Plato's *Republic*," *Cairo Papers in Social Science* 9, Monograph 1 (1986), 7 and 9.
47. This is confirmed in Al-Farabi's insightful analysis of the difference between Plato and Aristotle. In describing the principle underlying Plato's many dialogues, he argues that the one principle underlying the many different possibilities is "a certain knowledge and a certain way of life." Aristotle, he argues, "sees the perfection as Plato sees it and more. However, because man's perfection is not self-evident or easy to explain by a demonstration leading to certainty, he saw fit to start from a position anterior to that from which Plato had started." See Al-Farabi, *Philosophy or Plato and Aristotle*, trans. Muhsin Mahdi (Cornell: Cornell University Press, 2001), 53, 71.
48. *NE*, 2–6 (1.2–1.4) and 229–235 (10.9).
49. Ibid., 23–25 (1.13).

50. Ibid., 223–226 (10.7).
51. Prov 22:2.
52. *Comm Proverbs*, 103 (on Prov 22:2).
53. Horwitz, *Gersonides' Ethics*, 44.
54. The distinction between regimes though is less common in medieval Jewish political thought. It existed in Samuel Ibn Tibbon's translation of Al-Farabi's *The Political Regime* as *Sefer ha-Hathalot* and Averroes' *Commentary on Plato's Republic*, but neither contribute original thinking on the subject. See Melamed, "The Attitude Towards Democracy in Medieval Jewish Philosophy," *Jewish Political Studies Review* 5, no. 1–2 (1993), 37–41.
55. For a similar critique of Marsilius of Padua, see Gewirth, *Marsilius of Padua and Medieval Political Philosophy*, 89.
56. *Politics*, 37 (1.2).
57. One can find many similarities to Marsilius' approach here as well, whether by intention of coincidence, see Gewirth, *Marsilius of Padua*, 85–91.
58. *Comm Gen*, 128 (on Gen 4:1–26).
59. Gen 6:2.
60. *Comm Gen*, 139 (on Gen 6:2).
61. Ibid., 179 (on Gen 9:18–29).
62. Ibid., 189 (on Gen 11:1–9).
63. Ibid., 194 (Gen 12:3, Ethical Lesson #2).
64. Ibid., 212 (Gen 14:14–17, Ethical Lesson #2).
65. Ibid., 308 (Gen 23:2, Ethical Lesson #1).
66. Ibid., 564 (Gen 50:16–17, Ethical Lesson #12).
67. *Comm Exod*, 21 (Exod 2:11–13, 17, Ethical Lesson #9).
68. *Comm Gen*, 204 (Gen 13:8–9, Ethical Lesson #8).
69. Ibid. (Gen 13:9, Ethical Lesson #9).
70. Ibid., 440 (Gen 34:23–29, Ethical Lesson #7).
71. *Comm Song of Songs*, 86.
72. *Comm Gen*, 69 (on Gen 1:20–23).
73. Gen 3:5.
74. *Comm Gen*, 96 (on Gen 2:4–3:24).
75. Ibid., 108 (on Gen 2:4–3:24).
76. For a good summary of this debate, see *The Jewish Political Tradition*, eds. Michael Walzer, Menachem Lorberbaum and Noam J. Zohar. vol. 1 (New Haven: Yale University Press, 2000),

108–165 and Yair Lorberbaum, *Disempowered King: Monarchy in Classical Jewish Literature* (London: Bloomsbury, 2011), 1–36.

77. Judg 8:23 and Martin Buber, *Kingship of God*, trans. Richard Scheimann (New York: Harper & Row, 1967).

78. Judg 17:6, 18:1, 19:1, 21:25. Interestingly, Samuel Ibn Tibbon adds this verse into his Hebrew translation of Al-Farabi's *Political Regime* in the context of discussing the criticisms of democracy deteriorating into tyranny implying that it is synonymous with the anarchy of the judges. See Melamed, "The Attitude Towards Democracy," 45.

79. I Sam 8:4.

80. Ibid.

81. *Comm Early Proph I*, 172 (on I Sam 8:4).

82. *Comm Deut*, 148 (on Deut 17:16). Eisenmann, "Social and Political Principles in Gersonides' Thought," 336.

83. I Sam 8:5.

84. *Comm Early Proph I*, 172–173 (on I Sam 8:5).

85. This gets around the apparent contradiction between Deuteronomy's command to appoint a king and I Samuel's concession to a king. Rabbinic interpreters noticed this problem and found different ways to harmonize the two. For example, see Sifre on Deut 17 in *Sifre to Deuteronomy*, trans. Louis Finkelstein (New York: Ktav Publishers, 1969), 208 (section 156).

86. Eisenmann, "Social and Political Principles in Gersonides' Thought," 334–335.

87. Touati, *La Pensée*, 522.

88. *Comm Deut* (Deut 16:18–18:8, Lesson #12).

89. Ibid., 148 (on Deut 17:16).

90. *Comm Gen*, 528 (Gen 47:22, Ethical Lesson #8).

91. *Comm Deut*, 149 (on Deut 17:20).

92. Ibid., 158 (Deut 17:15, Lesson #13).

93. *NE*, 6–7 (1.5) and 37 (2.7).

94. George Anastaplo, *The Thinker as Artist: From Homer to Plato & Aristotle* (Ohio: Ohio University Press, 1997), 329.

95. *Comm Gen*, 539 (Gen 48:2, Ethical Lesson #5).

96. Ibid., 481 (Gen 41:14, Ethical Lesson #1).

97. Ibid., 518 (Gen 44:18–34, Ethical Lesson #1).

98. Ibid., 539 (Gen 48:2, Ethical Lesson #5).

99. Ibid., 519 (Gen 45:1, Ethical Lesson #2).

100. *Comm Early Proph I*, 231 (I Sam 12–II Sam 1 Lesson #17).
101. *Comm Deut*, 149 (on Deut 17:20).
102. BT Berachot 3b.
103. BT Shabbat 30a.
104. *MT, Book of Judges, Laws of Kings and their Wars*, 22 (4.7).
105. I Sam 16:18.
106. *Comm Early Proph I*, 198–199 (on I Sam 16:18).
107. I Sam 17:3–7.
108. *Comm Early Proph I*, 232 (I Sam 13–II Sam 1, Lesson #19).
109. *Comm Deut* , 148 (on Deut 17:16).
110. *Comm Early Proph I*, 236 (I Sam 13–II Sam 1, Lesson #37).
111. Ibid., 211 (on I Sam 21:15–16).
112. Ibid., 319 (II Sam 22–24, Lesson #12).
113. Ibid., 192–193 (on I Sam 15:6).
114. I Sam 11:5.
115. *Comm Early Proph I*, 231–232 (I Sam 8–12, Lesson #18).
116. Ibid., 232 (Lesson #22).
117. Ibid., 185–186 (on I Sam 13:3–7, 89, 13–14).
118. *Comm Early Proph II*, 82 (I Kgs 3–11, Lesson #36).
119. Ibid., 120 (I Kgs 12–22, Lesson #6–7).
120. BT Gittin 55b–56a.
121. *Comm Proverbs*, 129 (on Prov 28:14). Thank you to Aryeh Tepper for bringing this to my attention.
122. Touati, *La pensée*, 526–527 and Eisen, *Gersonides on Providence*, 118. My analysis develops theirs further in describing how the priesthood is an institution in competition with the kingship and in relationship with the prophet. It is also demonstrates how the political is a parallel of the ethical and the psychological.
123. *Comm Early Proph II*, 13 (on Ezra 7:6) and Touati, *La Pensée*, 527.
124. Job 15:19.
125. *Comm Exod*, vol. ii, 350 (Exodus 27–30, Lessons).
126. Lev 10:1.
127. *Comm Leviticus*, vol. i, 246 (on Lev 10:1).
128. *Comm Exod*, vol. ii, 289–290 (Exodus 25–27, Lessons).
129. Ibid., 289–290 and 350 (Exodus 25–27, 27–30, Lessons).
130. Ibid.
131. Ibid., 284–285 and 288 (on Exod 25–27, Root #4, 13).
132. Exod 25:18.

133. Deut 10:5.
134. *Comm Exod*, vol. ii, 291–292 (on Exod 25–27).
135. Exod 26:35.
136. *Comm Exod*, vol. ii, 292 (on Exod 25–27).
137. Exod 25:23–24.
138. *Comm Exod*, vol. ii, 295–296 (on Exod 25–27).
139. Ibid., 350 (on Exod 27–30, Lessons).
140. Ibid., 351.
141. Ibid., 290 (on Exod 25–27, Lessons).
142. *Comm Numbers*, 217 (Numb 18:8, Lesson #18).
143. *Comm Leviticus*, vol. i, 39–41 (on Lev 4:3).
144. Numb 6:27.
145. *Comm Numbers*, 55 (on Numb 6:27).
146. Ibid., 361–362 (on Numb 28:1).
147. Kellner, "Politics and Perfection: Gersonides vs. Maimonides," 69–70.
148. *Wars*, vol. ii, 27 (2.1).
149. Ibid.,30–31 (2.2).
150. Ibid., 48 (2.5).
151. Eisenmann, "Social and Political Principles in Gersonides' Thought," 331–332.
152. *Guide*, 376–378 (II 38).
153. *Comm Gen*, 293 (Gen 21:25, Ethical Lesson #10).
154. *Comm Exod*, 120 (Exod 10:9, 25–26; 11:4, 8–10, Intellectual Lesson #2).
155. Ibid., 42 (on Exod 2:23–4:18) and 50 (Exod 3:21–22, Lesson #15).
156. *Comm Early Proph I*, 230–231 (I Sam 13–II Sam 1, Lesson #12–13).
157. Ibid., 192–193 (Comm I Samuel 15:6).
158. Josh 9:14.
159. *Comm Early Proph I*, 39 (on Josh 9:15).
160. Ibid., 137 (on I Sam 4:1).
161. *Comm Early Proph II*, 49–50 (on I Kgs 8:44).
162. One of the challenges here is that many of the prophetic critiques of the priesthood are contained in the later prophets of which Gersonides does not comment on. See Jer 6:20, 7:21–23, Isa 1:11–15, 27:9, 43:23 and Ezek16:18.
163. Lev 10:1.

164. *Comm Leviticus,* 246 (on Lev 10:1).
165. *Comm Early Proph I,* 130 (on I Sam 2:12).
166. *NE,* 164 (8.1).
167. Ibid., 166–167 (8.3).
168. Ibid., 196–200 (9.5–9.7).
169. Ibid., 95–96 (5.3).
170. This is reminiscent of Isaiah Berlin's distinction between positive and negative liberty. Berlin does recognize Aristotle in describing the first category. See Isaiah Berlin, *Four Essays on Liberty: An Introduction* (Oxford: Oxford University Press, 1969), 1–54.
171. Lorraine Pangle, *Aristotle's Philosophy of Friendship* (Cambridge: Cambridge University Press, 2008), 481.
172. *NE,* 174–175 (8.8).
173. Ibid., 175–176 (8.8).
174. Ronna Burger, *Aristotle's Dialogue with Socrates: On the* Nicomachean Ethics (Chicago: University of Chicago Press, 2009), 171.
175. *NE,* 193–196 (9.4) and 200–202 (9.8).
176. It is important to note that in Maimonides' adoption of Aristotle's *Nicomachean Ethics,* in Eight Chapters and Laws of Character Traits in the MT, friendship is absent. Maimonides does find a place to include it in his *Commentary on Pirkei Avot* in commenting on *Avot* 1:4, "appoint for thyself a teacher and acquire for thyself a companion," which follows Aristotle's tripartite model of friendship of the good, the pleasant and the useful.
177. *Comm Gen,* 203 (Gen 13:1, Ethical Lesson #5).
178. Ibid., 393 (Gen 29:11, Ethical Lesson #5).
179. Ibid., 308 (Gen 23:2, Ethical Lesson #1).
180. Ibid., 170 (Gen 6:21, Ethical Lesson #6).
181. Ibid., 292 (Gen 21:14, Ethical Lesson #6).
182. Ibid., 393 (Gen 29:10, Ethical Lesson #4).
183. Ibid. (Gen 29:14, Ethical Lesson #6).
184. Ibid., 212 (Gen 14:8–12, Ethical Lesson #1).
185. Ibid., 204 (Gen 13:8–9, Ethical Lesson #8).
186. Ibid., 234 (Gen 16:6, Ethical Lesson #4).
187. Ibid., 271 (Gen 18:15, Ethical Lesson #12).
188. Ibid., 329 (Gen 25:6, Ethical Lesson #16).
189. Ibid., 564 (Gen 50:16–17, Ethical Lesson #12).
190. Ibid., 462 (Gen 38:8, Ethical Lesson #6).

191. Ibid., 538 (Gen 47:30, Ethical Lesson #2).
192. Prov 14:20.
193. Prov 18:24.
194. *Comm Gen*, 194 (Gen 12:3, Ethical Lesson #1).
195. *Comm Numbers*, 117 (Num 11:4, Lesson #10).

CHAPTER 6

Conclusion

The place of Gersonides' ethics within the history of Jewish thought can be seen as an outcome of great societal controversy over the philosophy of Moses Maimonides that began after his death.[1] One of the central theses of Maimonides' philosophy is that obtaining knowledge of God and the immortality of the intellect is the highest priority. The first command-ment of Maimonides' legal code, the *Mishneh Torah*, is "to know that there is a first Being who brought everything that exists into being."[2] As a result, it was understood by many of his interpreters in Provence, such as Samuel ibn Tibbon and Shem Tov Falaquera, that the goal of life should be detachment from the physical world, and pursuits such as ethics and politics are necessary purely for utilitarian reasons in order that the body can exist so that the intellect can flourish.[3] Furthermore, it appears to make the Torah and *halakha* a means for intellectual contemplation of which the practices are just for the masses, while the true meaning of the Torah is its philosophy. While this is not necessarily the position of Maimonides, who was a serious legal scholar as much as a philosopher, many of his Provencal followers continued his thought in this way. One critical response to this was in the *Commentary of the Torah* of the medieval exegete and mys-tic Moses Naḥmanides, who rejected reading biblical heroes as intellec-tuals and instead advocated characters who prioritized the two primary virtues of belief (*'emuna*) and trust (*biṭaḥon*). In this light, one could say that Gersonides' ethics, of the virtues of endeavor (*hishtadlut*) and diligence (*ḥariṣut*), is a defense of the Aristotelian and Maimonidean approach to reading the Bible against Naḥmanides' critiques of it, not

© The Author(s) 2016
A. Green, *The Virtue Ethics of Levi Gersonides*,
DOI 10.1007/978-3-319-40820-0_6

in rejecting reading biblical characters as perfecting their material intellect, but as adding a special focus on the practical intellect.[4] If one reads
Naḥmanides' *Commentary on the Torah* as a polemic against Maimonides'
biblical interpretation in the *Guide*, Gersonides' *Commentary on the Torah*
can be read as a spirited defense of the Maimonidean approach in light of
Naḥmanides' criticism.[5]

Naḥmanides and Gersonides each possessed different models of the
virtues, arising from their dissimilar understanding of the powers and
limits of nature and the place of miracles within it.[6] While Naḥmanides
famously stated "so it is with all miracles in the Torah or the Prophets:
what can be done by man is done by man and the rest is in the hand of
God,"[7] he differed from Gersonides on the extent to which humanity can
independently achieve its ends and how much is under divine control. At
first glance, Naḥmanides' thought appears to be occasionalist, denying the
existence of the laws of nature and placing all power in the hands of divine
will. He suggests that everything in the world is truly the result of hidden
miracles under the false guise of an apparent natural order (an approach
which Gershom Scholem coined an "optical illusion" in defining the laws
of nature).[8] This is perhaps why Naḥmanides states that "no one can have
a part in the Torah of Moses our teacher unless he believes that all our
words and our events, [as dictated in the Torah], are miraculous in scope
there being no natural or customary way of the world in them"[9] and "one
who believes in the Torah may not believe in the existence of nature at
all."[10] But this perception of Naḥmanides is not correct—he is not antin-
atural, but presents a minimalist conception of nature. Naḥmanides rejects
the self-sufficiency of the Aristotelian model of natural order, whose all-
encompassing nature restricts divine intervention.[11] But he does advocate
rational certainty with regard to the basic moral principles that any community of different individuals must have to survive. He suggests that

> [v]iolence is robbery and oppression…for violence is a sin, as is known and
> universally accepted…the reason is that its prohibition is a rationalist obliga-
> tion (*mitzvah muskelet*), for which there is no need for a prophet to give a
> commandment.[12]

As David Novak argues, these "moral norms evident to reason are those
required by any society to fulfill the basic needs of its members for a
just and stable order."[13] David Berger also makes the argument that for
Naḥmanides, nature without providence operates ninety-eight percent of

the time.[14] But it is the unique reward given to the patriarchs by God that testifies to the existence of public miracles (*nissim mefursamim*) and secret miracles (*nissim nisetarim*) underlying the natural order. To merit this reward, the patriarchs must exemplify the virtues of faith and trust. The distinction between the two was developed in the work *The Book of Faith and Trust* (*'Emuna ve-ha-Biṭaḥon*), which is thought to be written by Naḥmanides or a theologian of his school. Belief is the acceptance of the doctrines of Judaism, and trust is a certitude of God's providence over oneself.[15] God intervenes miraculously at will into the natural order for the sake of the patriarchs by the "merit of the forefathers" (*zekhut avot*) as a reward for their faith and trust.[16]

In contrast to Naḥmanides' minimalist model of nature and maximalist position on miracles, Gersonides presents a more expansive maximalist model of nature and minimalist position on miracles. As discussed earlier, every part of nature is ordered in the plan in God's mind, known as the Agent Intellect (*ha-sekhel ha-po'el*), which is the architectonic plan of the universe.[17] Just as an architect designs every small detail of the house with a function and purpose for the house, so God ensures that every detail of the universe serves a purpose. Hence, Gersonides' unequivocal statement "nature does nothing in vain" (*ha-ṭeva' lo ya'ase davar batel*). Following from this, one must use the patriarchs as exemplars and imitate their cultivation of the virtues of endeavor, diligence and cunning in cultivating stratagems. For Gersonides, miracles do not just come about through faith and trust but one must strive to achieve the end on one's own through the tools that God has given you and only at the last resort when all natural paths have been exhausted will God enter a miracle into the natural realm. This is not to say that a miracle cannot occur in nature, but rather it generates an increased speed in the processes of events that can occur within nature.[18] In conceiving miracles in this way, Gersonides has reinterpreted the talmudic principle that "one cannot rely on a miracle" (*ein somkhin 'al ha-nes*) to fit his interpretation.[19] The *Babylonian Talmud* uses this principle to argue that one should not place oneself in a position of danger and rely on a miracle to be saved. Gersonides in fact employs this principle in describing Jacob's endeavoring to keep his property in departing from Laban[20] and by Gideon, who, aided by God, was confident that he would be victorious over his enemies and thus attempted to find all the reasons to fulfill his goal.[21]

Naḥmanides would fit into this category as someone who adhered to a model of natural law, but one that Gersonides would have been critical of, especially for its ethical implications. One reason that Gersonides may not have referred to Naḥmanides is that he did not usually reference the sources of those he disagreed with in his biblical commentaries; this issue may have been especially charged if there was a competition in Provence between students of Maimonides and students of Naḥmanides to win over followers and influence the community. We know from Menachem Meiri's work *Magen Avot* that Naḥmanides' pupils came to Provence and were attempting to exert their authority there.[22]

This is evident from how Gersonides utilizes two of Naḥmanides' famous critiques of Maimonides, on the sacrifices and on the Land of Israel, and reinterprets Naḥmanides' solution in a philosophic way, incorporating it into an Aristotelian view of the world.[23] Maimonides famously states that the sacrifices were not an essential Jewish ritual, but a ruse intended to wean the Israelites off of Egyptian pagan sacrifices toward an intellectual knowledge of God.[24] In response, Naḥmanides criticizes Maimonides' historicizing of the sacrifices, by presenting the argument that sacrifices preceded idolatry in the Hebrew Bible, and showing examples of how they were employed by Abel and Noah.[25] In fact, he even brings an example from Maimonides' own *Mishneh Torah* of how Adam offered a sacrifice to God.[26] In contrast to Maimonides, Naḥmanides presents two nonhistorical justifications for the sacrifices—one psychological and one mystical. Psychologically, according to Naḥmanides, sacrifices fulfill the human need to be reconciled with God in thought, word and deed. Mystically, the sacrifices represent the secret of the unique name of God, the Tetragrammaton.[27] Whether it is true that Naḥmanides "misrepresents Maimonides' position," as Josef Stern suggests, this method of argumentation is nonetheless useful for Gersonides who uses a similar strategy in *Wars of the Lord* to present a revised Aristotelian position that is not so radically different from that of Maimonides', though openly critical of him.[28]

Indeed, Gersonides also criticizes Maimonides' approach toward sacrifices early in his *Commentary on the Torah* for neglecting to realize that sacrifices pre-date the Israelites' stay in Egypt.[29] Like Naḥmanides, he replaces it with two nonhistorical justifications, a psychological and a metaphysical one.[30] Gersonides asserts that psychologically, the sacrificial ritual helps isolate the intellect from the senses by witnessing the temporality of sensible objects in the death of the animal. To illustrate this, Gersonides describes how Abraham, Isaac and Jacob all made sacrifices before receiving prophecy.[31] He also points out that the structure of worship through sacrifices, such as by means of the tabernacle and Temple, functions as a metaphor for the structure of the cosmos, thus teaching us metaphysical lessons.[32] For example, the table and bread that was always supposed to be upon it in the Temple[33] is a metaphor for the link between the two components of the physical universe, the lower existents and the heavenly bodies suggesting the unity of the created universe.[34] The fact that there are twelve loaves of bread symbolizes twelve stars.[35] Moreover, the strongly scented frankincense candles[36] serve as a metaphor for God who is superior to the heavenly bodies, which all depend on Him for their strength.[37]

Another of Naḥmanides' criticisms of Maimonides' writings was the fact that he failed to designate a specific commandment to live and settle in the Land of Israel.[38] Of course, this may be because for Maimonides, the Land of Israel is viewed mainly as the designated location of the political state, the stability of which is necessary for the sake of attaining intellectual perfection and hence also prophecy.[39] Thus, Maimonides does not appear to hold that there is anything that is essentially different or special about the land other than as the geographical foundation for Jewish intellectual development as well as for free political life which naturally supports the pursuit of intellectual perfection in its prophetic mode.[40] In contrast, for Naḥmanides, the Land of Israel is unique as the location where the forces of nature play a minor role and hidden miracles have more influence.[41] In fact, one detects in Naḥmanides' understanding of the Land of Israel, a mystical adaptation of medieval climatology in which certain lands are considered to be superior due to their climate.[42] Gersonides responds to this critique of Maimonides and the medieval rationalists by reinterpreting their climatological position in a philosophic and astrological vein, asserting that the geographic location of the Land of Israel makes it particularly receptive to "divine overflow" because of the greater positive effect of the stars.[43] Thus, God promised the land to Abraham since divine providence has a more powerful impact in that location.[44]

However, it is interesting to note that the biblical cases that Naḥmanides uses to prove the belief and trust in God's miracles by the biblical patriarchs are many of the same examples that Gersonides uses to prove their endeavor and diligence. The following nine examples illustrate this point.

1. The first example contains one of Naḥmanides' harshest criticisms of a patriarch, reproaching Abraham for an "advertant sin" ('*avon*) in

leaving the Land of Israel and a "great sin" (*ḥeṭ gadol*) though inadvertent one in (*bi-shgaga*) in urging Sara to identify as his sister to the Pharaoh. In both cases, he is criticized for not trusting in God to save him and his wife, with the former having the repercussion of leading Abraham's descendants into exile later.[45] Gersonides though takes the diametrically opposite position, praising Abraham's active virtues of *ḥariṣut* in taking the necessary actions to prioritize their physical and materialistic needs, such as food and possessions, which does not contradict God's command to go to Canaan, but is just a temporary diversion to properly fulfill its ultimate end there.[46]

2. Abraham's success in maintaining his possessions on leaving Egypt provides a second example.[47] Nahmanides raises the possibility that the Egyptians could have accused Abraham of cheating them in trading money for his supposed sister who turned out to be his wife and could have demanded that he return the gifts they gave him. He solves this dilemma by suggesting it is a miracle.[48] To Nahmanides, Abraham's covenant with God is one that is rewarded by special miracles for his success and passed on to his righteous descendants. He states later that "with his saints (*ḥasidav*), he directs conscious attention to them individually, making his care for them continual. His knowledge and mindfulness never departs from them."[49] However, Gersonides interprets Abraham's material success as the result of his own endeavors and not a refusal to simply trust divine promises. Abraham protected his possessions with as much *ḥariṣut* as possible. Even though Abraham was promised material success by God, he used *hishtadlut* to bring along with him all of his possessions from Egypt to Canaan.[50]

3. The third example demonstrating the stark difference between Gersonides and Nahmanides is Abraham's success in chasing the four kings to Damascus.[51] Nahmanides poses the question about how Abraham was able to chase them that great distance, raising the possibility that either he pursued them over many days or it was the result of a great miracle.[52] In contrast, Gersonides praises Abraham on the stratagems he employed in ensuring victory, having pursued them during a night when they were resting confidently with their booty.[53]

4. Abraham's concern over his lack of progeny and his request for a son from God offers a fourth example.[54] Nahmanides debates Rashi on the origin of Abraham's merit of God's blessing. Rashi (based on

Targum Jonathan) posits Abraham's righteousness (*sedaqa*) and belief (*'emuna*) as the source of his merit.[55] In response, Naḥmanides postulates that Abraham was not perfectly righteous, having fought in wars and killed many individuals undeservingly, instead suggesting that Abraham merited children due to God's charity (*sedaqa*).[56] In distinction to both Rashi and Naḥmanides, Gersonides attributes Abraham's merit to his own endeavor to produce offspring to perpetuate the species. Hence, God's charity is in Gersonides' view an outcome of Abraham's active virtue or *hishtadlut*.[57]

5. The fifth example is evident in the disparate approaches of Naḥmanides and Gersonides toward Abraham and Sarah's treatment of Hagar.[58] Naḥmanides is harshly critical of Abraham and Sarah's behavior referring to it as a great sin (*ḥeṭ gadol*) to which, he argues, the Jews are still suffering to this day.[59] Gersonides takes the opposite stance, praising Abraham's behavior for respecting the wishes of his wife. He argues that even though it was in his interest to support the woman he impregnated and is carrying his progeny, peace in the home (*shalom bayit*) takes priority and in this case it requires Abraham to listen to his wife's wishes.[60]

6. The sixth example is evident in how Naḥmanides and Gersonides differ in how they interpret the reason behind God's communication to Abraham to wipe out Sodom following his making a covenant with them and their commitment to do righteousness (*sedaqa*) and justice (*mishpat*).[61] For Naḥmanides, this covenant is simple and straightforward: it entails constant individual attention with continual care.[62] In contrast, Gersonides understands this divine providence in a different light; it entails announcing to Abraham the future evil he will do to Sodom, allowing Abraham to endeavor to guide them to perfection, thus saving them from the evil outcome.[63]

7. The seventh example focuses on the incident of Isaac going to Abimelech, King of the Philistines, because of the famine.[64] Naḥmanides, following Rashi, argues that Isaac was driven by a desire to imitate his father but criticizes this motivation explaining that God stopped him due to the impurity of leaving the Land of Israel.[65] However, Gersonides praises Isaac's forethought in prophesizing famine and planning to go to a land where he can make a living and obtain food.[66]

8. The eighth example concerns the famous story of Jacob's dream about angels ascending and descending on a ladder.[67] In interpreting this narrative, Naḥmanides and Gersonides arrive at opposite conclusions about the nature of providence and ethics. For Naḥmanides, this story is proof that all actions on earth are directed by God and his angel, with the dream teaching Jacob that he would have personal protection directly from God.[68] However, for Gersonides, this dream is a lesson that the nature of divine providence for man is to permanently preserve him by giving him the tools for his protection. Thus one can rely on divine providence or luck for certain times and places, but not every single one, implying the necessity of individual endeavor.[69]

9. The ninth example focuses on the individual responsible for Joseph getting lost in field and redirected by an anonymous man. For Naḥmanides, it was God who was responsible since Joseph's action was fated by divine decree, quoting the maxim "the decree of God is truth, and diligence is falsehood." Thus Naḥmanides argues that God is the ultimate cause of the brothers' descent to Egypt, even though they were the ones who committed the action.[70] Conversely, Gersonides places the blame on Jacob for placing Joseph in a dangerous situation by sending him down to Shechem, which ultimately caused his move to Egypt. Hence, for Gersonides the descent of the Israelites to Egypt was not the result of a divine decree, but of Jacob's tactical error and lack of foresight by failing to pay attention to the dangers of the city due to their inhabitants.[71]

In all these examples, Gersonides' method of countering Naḥmanides is not through direct references and explicit dispute, but through implicit reformulations. Hence, Gersonides contends that his own approach is merely based on looking for the *peshat*, the plain meaning, of the text.[72] In his Introduction to his *Commentary on the Torah*, he presents his method as focusing purely on the *peshat* and not on rabbinical *derashot*.[73] But Gersonides frequently incorporates rabbinical *derashot* into his *peshat* reading of the text![74] David Weiss Halivni argues that defining *peshat* as the literal meaning of the text is a modern construct, very different than both rabbinic and medieval definitions of *peshat*. The Rabbis of the Talmud and Midrash implied that *peshat* was the "meaning in the context of the discourse," which could be metaphorical or allegorical.[75] The medieval model of *peshat*, influenced implicitly by the systematic philosophy of the Islamic and Christian world, understood the text to not simply have a "plain meaning," but only one which is consonant with a systematic worldview.[76]

However, there was often also a need to defend one's position through the appearance of *peshat*, which at times generated a form of polemics. Medieval biblical exegetes were not only striving to articulate a world-view within a commentary, but also to defend that worldview against antagonists. This was especially true between Jews and Christians. Martin Lockshin posits that

> [f]or medieval rabbis, defending the faith against the intellectual onslaughts of Christianity was a crucial task and a sacred duty. Funkenstein has shown that the nature of Christian argumentation against Judaism and the ideological tactics that Christian polemicists employed changed considerably in the twelfth century. This made it more necessary that before for Jews to adopt exegetical positions that would undercut Christian truth claims. It has been suggested that the hesitant movement towards *peshat* at the end of the eleventh century and the more dynamic development of Jewish *peshat* in the twelfth might be a function of rabbis reacting to the religious needs of the Jewish community....A Jew will not convince a Christian by citing the Talmud or *midrash*, nor will a Christian convince a Jew by citing the New Testament or one of the Church Father. The playing field is even and the rules of engagement are reasonable only if discussion centers around *peshat*. So the need to engage in religious polemics may have caused by Jews and Christians to hone their skills as *peshat* exegetes.[77]

In this regard, it is my understanding that Gersonides followed his medi-eval philosophic and exegetical predecessors in carrying out the polemi-cal implications underlying his rhetoric of *peshat*. However, this was not between Jews and Christians, but undertaken by Jewish philosophers defending their reading of the Bible against that of nonphilosophical Jewish traditionalists.[78] Menachem Kellner is the first to suggest such a reading of one of Gersonides' biblical commentaries, proposing that the *Song of Songs* is a polemical work addressed to philosophic amateurs. This would explain why Gersonides cites Aristotle forty-nine times in that commentary and only cites rabbinic texts seven times.[79] His later *Commentary on the Torah* may have a polemical layer as well, but one that is more interested in chal-lenging the interpretations of other quasi-philosophic biblical exegetes.

Was Gersonides successful in this polemic? The history of his recep-tion has had both critics and defenders. Gersonides' biblical commentaries were some of the first printed Hebrew books in the 1470s in Italy. His commentaries on the early prophets were part of the early versions of the rabbinic digest of medieval Jewish bible commentaries, the *Miqr'aot Gedolot*, indicating the popularity of his works at the time.[80] But, around the same time, he was openly attacked by Isaac Abarbanel and Isaac Arama, two important commentators from the same period, in their biblical commentators. This criticism partially stemmed from the general turn against Aristotelian philosophy in the fifteenth and sixteenth centuries.[81] As a result, Gersonides' philosophic approach was characterized disparagingly as "Wars against the Lord," playing on the title of his major work *Wars of the Lord*.[82] Notwithstanding those attacks, he never completely disappeared, having had his constant defenders. One example of such an advocate is Jacob Marcaria in sixteenth-century Italy. He compiled Gersonides ethical lessons into a separate volume that was entitled *To'aliyot ha-Ralbag* containing a small section of the lessons from the Pentateuch and Prophets focusing mainly on the ethical issues and leaving out those related to physics and metaphysics and as well as most of the legal ones.[83] Interestingly, this popularization of Gersonides' thought was mainly as an ethical thinker, whose ethics Marcaria conceived of as directed *against* the ethics of Aristotle, which he criticized.[84] This is perhaps fitting, as during this period, Aristotelian science was in a process of being criticized and rejected, while Gersonides' ethics does share similarities with the "mirror for princes" literature, popular at that time, perhaps most famously, exemplified in Machiavelli's *Prince*. Machiavelli's *Prince* was published in 1513 and Marcaria's *To'aliyot* in 1560 in Italy. While this may be mere coincidence, it is interesting to ask whether Marcaria's adaptation of Gersonides was influenced by the popularity of Machiavelli. Marcaria's *To'aliyot ha-Ralbag* was used for another cultural revival in nineteenth century Warsaw in 1865 by Yeḥi'el ben Shlomo Maharih which he published in order to advocate for the modern Jewish enlightenment, through employing Gersonides as a proponent of the harmonization of Torah and science through his lessons.[85] In other words, Gersonides' exegetical and ethical works have never ceased to play a role in Jewish intellectual history up until fairly recent times, even if not always acknowledged as such.

I hope this work also contributes to what we have witnessed over the last forty years, which is what I would call a "Gersonidean Renaissance." His theological work *Wars of the Lord* was translated into English and a critical edition is in progress; critical editions of his commentaries on the Torah are being published at Yeshivat Maaleh Adumim (comparing all the manuscripts with excellent notes to guide students); and his more technical philosophical commentaries on Aristotle, which Jewish readers have not been reading for hundreds of years, are slowly being edited and published by Israeli scholars. It is a great time to rediscover Gersonides and to rethink the enduring significance of his works. For there is no doubt that Gersonides represents a still-vital position in Jewish religion and intellectual history that continues to nurture as well as to challenge thinkers of all stripes to the present day.

NOTES

1. Joseph Saracheck, *Faith and Reason: The Conflict over the Rationalism of Maimonides* (New York: Hermon Press, 1935); Daniel Jeremy Silver, *Maimonidean Criticism and the Maimonidean Controversy, 1180–1240* (Leiden: Brill, 1965); Gregg Stern, *Philosophy and Rabbinic Culture: Jewish Interpretation and Controversy in Medieval Languedoc* (London: Routledge, 2009).
2. *MT, Book of Knowledge, Laws of the Foundations of the Torah,* 3 (1.1).
3. Ravitzky, "The Political Role of the Philosopher," 347 and Jospe, "Rejecting Moral Virtue," 185–204.
4. It is not clear how carefully Gersonides read Naḥmanides' entire corpus, but he seemed to be familiar enough with his arguments and certain elements of his biblical interpretations. For a study of trust and faith in the Jewish tradition, see R.J.Z. Werblonsky, "Faith, Hope and Trust: A Study in the Concept of *Bittahon,*" in *Papers of the Institute of Jewish Studies,* vol. 1 (Jerusalem: Magnes Press, 1964), 95–139. The difference between these two sets of virtues may also reflect the difference between an Augustinian and Aristotelian perspective of nature. See Shlomo Pines, "Nahmanides on Adam in the Garden of Eden in the Context of Other Interpretations of Genesis, Chapters 2 and 3," in *Exile and Diaspora: Studies in the History of the Jewish People Presented to Haim Beinart,* eds. Aharon Mirsky, Avraham Grossman and Yosef Kaplan (Jerusalem: Ben-Zvi Institute, 1988), 159–164.
5. I argue that Gersonides draws ideas from Naḥmanides, but does not openly cite him. One cannot assume that Gersonides only read what we have listed he owned in his library. For example, the catalogue of his library only lists that he owned Rashi, but he frequently

quotes Abraham Ibn Ezra, Rashbam and Radak. See A.-M. Weil, "Levi ben Gershom et sa bibliothèque privée," in *Gersonide en son temps*, 45–59. It is also a mistake to think that Naḥmanides was Gersonides' father. This was perpetuated in sixteenth century. See Rabbi Abraham, *Sefer Yuḥasin* (1504) quoted in Ben-Meir, *Gersonides Commentary on Ecclesiastes*, 197n47. For the discussion on whether Gersonides was responding to Naḥmanides, see Baruch Braner and Eli Fryman, "Gersonides' Commentary on the Torah," *Maḥanayyim* 4, no. 2 (2002–2003), 231; Cohen, *Legal Exegesis through Peshat*, 44–45n76; and Tzeitkin, *The Characteristics of Biblical Exegesis*, 200–201.

6. Two recent scholars have worked to recover the philosophic and theological (as opposed to mystical or purely hermeneutical) side to Naḥmanides' thought. See David Berger, "Miracles and the Natural Order in Nahmanides," in *Rabbi Moses Nahmanides (Ramban): Explorations in his Religious and Literary Virtuosity*, ed. Isadore Twersky (Cambridge: Cambridge University Press, 1983), 107–128 and David Novak, *The Theology of Nahmanides Systematically Presented* (Atlanta: Brown Judaic Studies, 1992).

7. Moses Naḥmanides, *Commentary on the Torah*, vol. i, trans. Charles B. Chavel (New York: Shilo Publishing House, 1971–1976), 113 (on Gen 6:9). Translation of Novak, *The Theology of Nahmanides*, 70.

8. Berger, "Miracles and the Natural Order," and Gershom Scholem, *ha-Qabbala be-Gerona*, ed. Joseph Ben-Shlomo (Jerusalem: Magnes Press, 1972), 306–307.

9. Naḥmanides, *Commentary on the Torah*, vol. ii, 174 (on Exod 13:16).

10. Ibid., *Sermon on Ecclesiastes*, 192 (translation thanks to Berger, Ibid.).

11. Novak, *The Theology of Nahmanides*, 4.

12. Naḥmanides, *Commentary on the Torah*, vol. i, 109 (on Gen 6:13). Modified translation of Novak, *The Theology of Nahmanides*, 107.

13. Novak, *The Theology of Nahmanides*, 5.

14. Ibid., 6.

15. Ibid., 71.

16. Gersonides has a concept of "merit of the forefathers" that is tied to his model of inherited providence, but the difference is that it is

begun by the initial endeavor and diligence of the forefathers to ensure they were worthy of the covenant. See Eisen, *Gersonides on Providence*, 35–36.

17. *Wars*, vol. i, 146–164 (1.6) and 116–117 (3.4).
18. Ibid., vol. iii, 490–492 (6.2.12).
19. This phrase appears slightly differently in its different talmudic discussions. At *BT* Pesachim 64b: "we do not rely on a miracle" and at *BT* Shabbat 32a: "A man should never stand in a place of danger and say that a miracle will be wrought for him, lest it is not."
20. *Comm Gen*, 399 (Gen 31:18, Ethical Lesson #33).
21. *Comm Early Proph I*, 103 (Judg 6–10, Lesson #11).
22. Menachem Meiri, *Magen Avot* (Jerusalem: Ma'yan ha-Ḥokhmah, 1978). The dedication on the front reads "This book is a defense of the practices and customs of the ancient communities of Provence, France, opposing Spanish traditions introduced by the disciples of Naḥmanides."
23. This is mentioned by both Touati and Eisen, though neither develops this link further. See Touati, *La Pensée*, 503 and Eisen, *Gersonides on Providence*, 219n59–60.
24. *Guide*, 525–531 (III 32).
25. Naḥmanides, *Commentary on the Torah*, vol. iii, 18–20 (on Lev 1:9–2:11). Abel's sacrifice is at Gen 4:3–5, while Noah's sacrifice is at Gen 8:20–21.
26. *MT, The Book of Service, Laws of the Temple*, 11–12 (2:2).
27. Naḥmanides, *Commentary on the Torah*, vol. iii, 21–25 (on Lev 1:9–2:11). Novak, *The Theology of Nahmanides*, 12.
28. Josef Stern, *Problems and Parables of Law: Maimonides and Nahmanides on Reasons for the Commandments* (Albany: State University of New York Press, 1998), 140.
29. *Comm Gen*, 172–174 (on Gen 6:9–9:17).
30. Cf. Israel Drazin, *Maimonides: The Exceptional Mind* (Jerusalem: Gefen Publishing House, 2008), 59–60. Israel Drazin neglects to mention Gersonides' critique of Maimonides with respect to sacrifices and only discusses their similarities. Though Gersonides does come later on to partially agree with Maimonides reasoning at *Guide* III 32 as one of multiple reasons for the sacrifices. See Gersonides, *Comm Leviticus*, 220.
31. Ibid.

32. Eisen, *Gersonides on Providence*, 89–90 and Warren Zev Harvey, "Gersonides on the Sacrificial Cult, Prophecy and Philosophy," in *Wisdom by the Week*, ed. Naftali Rothenberg (New York: Ktav, 2011), 307–316. Nehama Leibowitz pointed out the similar language in the construction of the tabernacle and the creation of the universe and how the former is a human imitation of the latter in the Hebrew Bible. See Nehama Leibowitz, *Studies in Shemot (Exodus)*, trans. Aryeh Newman. vol ii (Jerusalem: World Zionist Organization, 1981), 471–486.

33. Exod 25:23–30.

34. *Comm Exod*, vol. ii, 295–296 (Exod 25–27, Lessons).

35. Ibid.

36. Lev 24:7.

37. *Comm Exod*, vol. ii, 296 (Exod 25–27, Lessons). This appears to be a criticism of Maimonides who at *Guide* III 45 admitted he could not find a reason for this ritual. See Langermann, "Gersonides on Astrology," 512–513.

38. Naḥmanides, *Supplements to Maimonides' Book of Commandments*, In *Sefer ha-Miṣvot im Hasagot ha-Rambam*, ed. Charles Chavel (Jerusalem: Mossad ha-Rav Kook, 1981), Positive Commandment #4.

39. *Guide*, 175 (I 71) and *MT, Book of Judges, Laws of Kings and their Wars*, 412 (11.1) and 419–420 (12.4–5).

40. This issue is more complex, especially with regard to Maimonides' interpretation of rabbinic texts. See Isadore Twersky, "Maimonides on Eretz Yisrael: Halakhic, Philosophic and Historical Perspectives," in *Perspectives on Maimonides: Philosophical and Historical Studies*, ed. Joel L. Kraemer (London: Littman Library of Jewish Civilization, 1996), 257–290.

41. Naḥmanides, *Commentary on the Torah*, vol. iii, 458–463 (on Lev 26:11) and Novak, *The Theology of Nahmanides*, 89.

42. Alexander Altmann, "Judah Halevi's Theory of Climates," *Aleph* 5 (2005), 215–246.

43. *Comm Gen*, 192 (on Gen 12:2–3).

44. Ibid. (on Gen 15:8) and Eisen, *Gersonides on Providence*, 43–44. Eisen suggests that Halevi had a strong influence on Gersonides here, though Manekin's review of the book challenges the influence of Halevi on Gersonides. See Charles Manekin, "Review of Robert Eisen, *Gersonides on Covenant, Providence, and the Chosen*

People," *Jewish Quarterly Review* 88 (1998), 332–336. Halevi's description of the Land of Israel definitely influenced Naḥmanides.
45. Naḥmanides, *Commentary on the Torah*, vol. i, 173 (on Gen 12:9–10).
46. *Comm Gen*, 202–203 (Gen 12:10–13, Ethical lessons #1–3); Novak, *The Theology of Nahmanides*, 95 and Horwitz, *Gersonides' Ethics*, 234–235.
47. Gen 13:1.
48. Naḥmanides, *Commentary on the Torah*, vol. i, 177 (on Gen 13:1).
49. Ibid., 241–242 (Comm Genesis 18:19) Translation from Novak, *The Theology of Nahmanides*, 64.
50. *Comm Gen*, 203 (Gen 13:1–3, Ethical Lesson #6).
51. Gen 14:15.
52. Naḥmanides, *Commentary on the Torah*, vol. i, 188 (on Gen 14:15).
53. *Comm Gen*, 209 (on Gen 14:15).
54. Gen 15:2.
55. Rashi, *Commentary on the Torah*, Gen 15:6.
56. Naḥmanides, *Commentary on the Torah*, vol. i, 197–198 (on Gen 15:6) and Novak, *The Theology of Nahmanides*, 42.
57. *Comm Gen*, 227 (Gen 15:2–3, Ethical Lesson #2).
58. Gen 16:6.
59. Naḥmanides, *Commentary on the Torah*, vol. i, 213 (on Gen 16:6). David Berger point out how Naḥmanides refers to the patriarchs as committing a "great sin" is in only three places. See David Berger, "On the Morality of the Patriarchs in Jewish Polemics and Exegesis," in *Modern Scholarship in the Study of Torah: Contributions and Limitations*, ed. Shalom Carmy (London: Jason Aronson, 1991), 236. Rabbi David Kimchi also took a similar position to Naḥmanides.
60. *Comm Gen*, 234 (Gen 16:6, Ethical Lesson #4).
61. Gen 18:19.
62. Naḥmanides, *Commentary on the Torah*, vol. i, 241–242 (on Gen 18:19) and Novak, *The Theology of Nahmanides*, 64.
63. *Comm Gen*, 272 (Gen 18:19, 23–32, Intellectual Lesson #14).
64. Gen 26:1.
65. Naḥmanides, *Commentary on the Torah*, vol. i, 325–326 (on Gen 26:1).
66. *Comm Gen*, 343 (Gen 26:1, Ethical Lesson #1).

67. Gen 28:12.
68. Naḥmanides, *Commentary on the Torah*, vol. i, 349–350 (on Gen 28:12) and Novak, *The Theology of Nahmanides*, 66.
69. *Comm Gen*, 365 (Gen 28:15, Intellectual Lesson #7).
70. Naḥmanides, *Commentary on the Torah*, vol. i, 455–456 (on Gen 37:15).
71. *Comm Gen*, 455 (Gen 37:12, Ethical Lesson #12) and Horwitz, *Gersonides' Ethics*, 269–270.
72. Cf. Seymour Feldman, "Gersonides and Biblical Exegesis," in *Wars*, vol ii, 214–215.
73. *Comm Gen*, 4 (Intro).
74. Harvey, "Quelques Réflexions."
75. David Weiss Halivni, *Peshat and Derash: Plain and Applied Meaning in Rabbinic Exegesis* (Oxford: Oxford University Press, 1998), xvi.
76. Bernard Septimus, "'Open Rebuke and Concealed Love': Nahmanides and the Andalusian Tradition," in *Rabbi Moses Nahmanides*, 18 and Amos Funkenstein, *Theology and the Scientific Imagination* (Princeton: Princeton University Press, 1988), 215.
77. Martin Lockshin, "Introductory Essay: *Peshat* and *Derash* in Northern France," in *Rashbam's Commentary on Deuteronomy: An Annotated Translation* (Providence: Brown Judaica Series, 2004), 19–20. Though Lockshin criticizes the method of deriving a polemical purpose in every reference to *peshat*.
78. This is also reflective of Gersonides' personal biography. As far as we know, his interactions with Christians were mostly positive and professional. He did not have to assume the role of defending the Jewish faith publicly, as far as we know. For a description of Gersonides' biography, see Yosef Shatzmiller, "Gersonides and the Jewish Community of Orange in his Day," in *Studies in the History of the Jewish People and the Land of Israel*, eds. B. Oded, U. Rappaport, A. Schochat, Y. Schatzmiller, vol. 2 (Haifa: University of Haifa, 1972), 111–26.
79. Menachem Kellner, "Introduction," in *Comm Song of Songs*, xxx and xxii.
80. They appear in the second edition of Daniel Bomberg's second edition of the *Miqr'aot Gedolot* in 1524–26.
81. Menachem Kellner, "Gersonides and his Cultured Despisers: Arama and Abravanel," in *Torah in the Observatory: Gersonides,*

Maimonides and Song of Songs (Brighton, MA: Academic Studies Press, 2009), 305–332.

82. Shem Tov ibn Shem Tov, *Sefer ha-Emunot* (Ferrara, 1556), Part 4, Chapter 19, 45b.
83. Kellner, "Gersonides' To'aliyyot," 285–286.
84. Ibid., 295. Marcaria refers to Aristotle's ethics through the technical term, *ṭumʿa*, ritual impurity.
85. Ibid., 287–288, 295.

Erratum to: The Virtue Ethics of Levi Gersonides

Alexander Green

DOI 10.1007/978-3-319-40820-0_7

The original version of this book contained errors which have been corrected.

The page numbers have been corrected as below for the Index entries war and *Wars of the Lord*.

war
20, 33, 43-45, 76, 108-112, 114, 120n114, 121n117, 127, 130, 134-136, 138-139, 143-144, 146, 163

Gersonides, Levi,
Wars of the Lord- 6, 8-11, 14n23, 15n29, 16n36, 16n44, 23-26, 29, 41, 50n7-10, 50n15, 52n29, 52n31, 53n34, 53n36, 53n39, 54n50, 54n57, 54n59-60, 55n65, 55n88, 57n103, 59n163, 60n187, 73-74, 85n40, 86n47, 87n54, 87n56 -57, 87n61, 87n63, 87n67, 87n73, 88n74, 88n76, 88n79, 88n82, 89n100, 95, 115n12-13, 116n21, 126-128, 143, 148n17, 148n19, 153n148, 160, 166, 169n17, 170n39, 172n72

The updated online version of the original book can be found at http://dx.doi.org/10.1007/978-3-319-40820-0

© The Author(s) 2017
A. Green, *The Virtue Ethics of Levi Gersonides*,
DOI 10.1007/978-3-319-40820-0_7

E1

BIBLIOGRAPHY

PRIMARY SOURCES

Al-Farabi, Abu Nasr. *Philosophy of Plato and Aristotle*, trans. Muhsin Mahdi. Cornell: Cornell University Press, 2001.

Aquinas, Thomas. *Commentary on Aristotle's Nicomachean Ethics*, trans. C. I. Litzinger. Chicago: Henry Regnery Company, 1964.

Aquinas, Thomas. *Summa Theologicae*, trans. Fathers of the English Dominican Province. New York: Benziger Bros., 1947–1948.

Aristotle. *De Anima*, trans. Robert Drew Hicks. New York: Barnes and Nobles Library, 2006.

Aristotle. *Generation of Animals* and *Parts of Animals*, trans. D. M. Balme. Oxford: Oxford University Press, 1972.

Aristotle. *Metaphysics*, trans. Hippocrates G. Apostle. Bloomington: Indiana University Press, 1966.

Aristotle. *Nicomachean Ethics*, trans. Robert C. Bartlett and Susan D. Collins. Chicago: University of Chicago Press, 2011.

Aristotle. *Politics*, trans. Carnes Lord. Chicago: University of Chicago Press, 1984.

Averroes. *Epitome on Aristotle's De Anima*, trans. Deborah Black. Toronto, 2009. http://individual.utoronto.ca/dlblack/WebTranslations/AVEREPAN.pdf

Averroes. *Middle Commentary on Aristotle's Nicomachean Ethics in the Hebrew Version of Samuel Ben Judah*, trans. and ed. Lawrence V. Berman. Jerusalem: Israel Academy of Science and Humanities, 1999.

Babylonian Talmud, ed. Isidore Epstein. London: Soncino Press, 1961.

Buridan, John. "Jean Buridan, Questions on Book X of the *Ethics*," ed. and trans. John Kilcullen, in *The Cambridge Translations of Medieval Philosophical Texts. Volume II: Ethics and Political Philosophy*, ed. Arthur Stephen McGrade, John

© The Author(s) 2016
A. Green, *The Virtue Ethics of Levi Gersonides*,
DOI 10.1007/978-3-319-40820-0

Kilcullen, and Matthew Kempshall. Cambridge: Cambridge University Press, 2001: 498–586.

Buridan, John. *Quaestiones super decem libros Ethicorum Aristotelis ad Nicomachum*. Paris, 1513. Reprint. 1968, as *Super decem libros Ethicorum*, Frankfurt a. M.: Minerva.

Cohen, Hermann. "Charakteristik der Ethik Maimunis," in *Jüdische Schriften*, vol. 3, ed. Bruno Strauss. Berlin: C. A. Schwetschke & Sohn, 1924: 221–289.

Esther Rabbah I: An Analytical Translation, trans. and ed. Jacob Neusner. Atlanta: Scholars Press, 1989.

Gaon, Saadya. *Book of Beliefs and Opinions*, trans. Samuel Rosenblatt. New Haven: Yale University Press, 1989.

Gaon, Saadya. *The Book of Theodicy: Translation and Commentary on the Book of Job*, trans. Lenn Evan Goodman. New Haven: Yale University Press, 1988.

Gersonides, Levi. *Commentary on Song of Songs*, trans. Menachem Kellner. New Haven: Yale University Press, 1998.

Gersonides, Levi. *Wars of the Lord*, trans. Seymour Feldman. Philadelphia: Jewish Publication Society, 1984.

Gersonides, Levi. *Perush 'al ha-Megillot (Commentary on the Five Scrolls)*, ed. Jacob Leib Levi. Jerusalem: Mossad ha-Rav Kook, 2003.

Gersonides, Levi. *Perush 'al ha-Neviim (Commentary on Joshua, Judges and Samuel)*, ed. Jacob Leib Levi. Jerusalem: Mossad ha-Rav Kook, 2008.

Gersonides, Levi. *Perush 'al ha-Neviim (Commentary on Kings, Chronicles, Ezra and Nehemiah)*, ed. Jacob Leib Levi. Jerusalem: Mossad ha-Rav Kook, 2008.

Gersonides, Levi. *Perush 'al ha-Torah (Commentary on the Pentateuch)*, vol. i–vi, eds. Baruch Brenner and Eli Fraiman. Maale Adumim: Maaliot, 1992–2008.

Gersonides, Levi. *Perush 'al ha-Torah (Commentary on the Pentateuch)*, vol. v: Deuteronomy, ed. Jacob Leib Levi. Jerusalem: Mossad ha-Rav Kook, 2000.

Gersonides, Levi. *Perush 'al Mishlei (Commentary on Proverbs)*, ed. Jacob Leib Levi. Jerusalem: Mossad ha-Rav Kook, 2015.

Gersonides, Levi. *Supercommentary on Averroes' Commentary on De Anima*, ed. and trans. Stephen Jesse Mashbaum. In Stephen Jesse Mashbaum, *Chapters 9–12 of Gersonides' Super-commentary on Averroes' Epitome of the De Anima: The Internal Senses*. PhD Diss., Brandeis University, 1981: 1–184.

Gersonides, Levi. *Supercommentary on Averroes' Commentary on De Animalibus*, ed. Ahuva Gaziel. In Ahuva Gaziel, *The Biology of Levi Ben Gershom (Gersonides)*. PhD Diss., Bar-Ilan University, 2008: 91–266.

Halevi, Judah. *The Kuzari*, trans. Henry Slonimsky. New York: Schocken Books, 1974.

Ibn Shem Tov, Shem Tov. *Sefer ha-Emunot*. Ferrara, 1556.

Ibn Tibbon, Samuel. "Preface to Translation of Maimonides, Commentary on *Avot*," trans. and ed. Menachem Kellner in Menaham Kellner, "Maimonides and Samuel Ibn Tibbon on Jeremiah 9:22–23 and Human Perfection," in *Studies in Halakhah and Jewish Thought Presented to Rabbi Professor Menahem Emanuel Rackman on His Eightieth Birthday*, ed. Moshe Beer. Ramat-Gan: Bar-Ilan University Press, 1994: 49–57.

Kant, Immanuel. *Groundwork of the Metaphysic of Morals*, trans. Herbert James Paton. New York: Harper and Row, 1964.

Kant, Immanuel. "On a Supposed Right to Tell Lies from Benevolent Motives," in *Kant's Critique of Practical Reason and Other Works on the Theory of Ethics*, trans. Thomas Kingsmill Abbott. London: Longmans, Green and Co., 1889.

Kant, Immanuel. "Toward Lasting Peace: A Philosophical Sketch," in *Kant's Political Writings*, ed. Hans Reiss. Cambridge: Cambridge University Press, 1991: 93–130.

Kaspi, Joseph Ibn. *Yoreh De'ah*, ed. and trans. Israel Abrahams in *Hebrew Ethical Wills*. Philadelphia: Jewish Publication Society, 1926: 127–161.

Maimonides, Moses. *Commentary on the Mishnah: Tractate Sanhedrin*, trans. and ed. Fred Rosner. New York : Sepher-Hermon Press, 1981.

Maimonides, Moses. "Eight Chapters," in *Ethical Writings of Maimonides*, eds. Raymond L. Weiss and Charles E. Buttersworth. New York: New York University Press, 1975: 59–104.

Maimonides, Moses. "Laws Concerning Character Traits," in *Ethical Writings of Maimonides*, eds. Raymond L. Weiss and Charles E. Buttersworth. New York: New York University Press, 1975: 28–58.

Maimonides, Moses. *Mishneh Torah*. Jerusalem: Mossad ha-Rav Kook, 1956–1968.

Maimonides, Moses. *The Guide of the Perplexed*, trans. Shlomo Pines. Chicago: University of Chicago Press, 1963.

Marsilius of Padua. *The Defender of the Peace (The Defensor Pacis)*, trans. Alan Gewirth. New York: Columbia University Press, 1956.

Nahmanides, Moses. *Commentary on the Torah*, vol. i–v, trans. Charles B. Chavel. New York: Shilo Publishing House, 1971–1976.

Nahmanides, Moses. "Sermon on Ecclesiastes," in *Writings of Nachmanides*, vol 1. Jerusalem: Mossad ha-Rav Kook, 1962.

Nahmanides, Moses. *Supplements to Maimonides' Book of Commandments*. In *Sefer ha-Miṣvot im Hasagot ha-Rambam*, ed. Charles Chavel. Jerusalem: Mossad ha-Rav Kook, 1981.

Ockham, William of. *Philosophical Writings: A Selection*. New York: Bobbs Merrill Company, 1964.

Plato. *Phaedo*, trans. Benjamin Jowett. Waltham: Golden Cockerel Press, 1930.

Plato. *Republic*, trans. Allan Bloom. New York: Basic Books, 1991.

Sifre to Deutoronomy, ed. Louis Finkelstein. New York: Ktav Publishers, 1969.

SECONDARY SOURCES

Allan, Donald James. *The Philosophy of Aristotle*. Oxford: Oxford University Press, 1970.

Allen, Judson Boyce. *The Ethical Poetic of Later Middle Ages*. Toronto: University of Toronto Press, 1982.

Altmann, Alexander. "Judah Halevi's Theory of Climates," *Aleph* 5 (2005): 215–246.

Altmann, Alexander. "Maimonides' 'Four Perfections'," in *Essays in Jewish Intellectual History*. Hanover: University Press of New England, 1981: 65–76.

Anastaplo, George. *The Thinker as Artist: From Homer to Plato & Aristotle*. Athens: Ohio University Press, 1997.

Annas, Julia. "Plato and Aristotle on Friendship and Altruism," *Mind* 86, no. 344 (1977): 532–544.

Anscombe, Elizabeth. "Modern Moral Philosophy," *Philosophy* 33 (1958): 1–19.

Ben-Meir, Ruth. *Gersonides Commentary on Ecclesiastes: Commentary and Text*. PhD Diss., Hebrew University of Jerusalem, 1993.

Ben-Or, Assael. *Commandments and Philosophy in Gersonides' Thought*. PhD Diss., Bar-Ilan University, 2000.

Benor, Ehud. "Meaning and Reference in Maimonides' Negative Theology," *Harvard Theological Review* 88, no. 3 (1995): 339–360.

Berger, David. "Miracles and the Natural Order in Nahmanides," in *Rabbi Moses Nahmanides (Ramban): Explorations in his Religious and Literary Virtuosity*, ed. Isadore Twersky. Cambridge: Harvard University Press, 1983: 107–128.

Berger, David. "On the Morality of the Patriarchs in Jewish Polemics and Exegesis," in *Modern Scholarship in the Study of Torah: Contributions and Limitations*, ed. Shalom Carmy. London: Jason Aronson Inc., 1991: 131–146.

Berman, Lawrence V. "A Manuscript Entitled *Shoshan Limudim* and the Group of *Me'aynim* in Provence," in *Kiryat Sefer* 53 (1978): 368–372.

Berlin, Isaiah. *Four Essays on Liberty: An Introduction*. Oxford: Oxford University Press, 1969.

Berman, Lawrence V. "Greek into Hebrew: Samuel ben Judah of Marseilles: Fourteenth Century Philosopher and Translator" in *Jewish Medieval and Renaissance Studies*, ed. Alexander Altmann. Cambridge: Harvard University Press, 1967: 289–320.

Berman, Lawrence V. "Review of Averroes Commentary on Plato's *Republic* by E. I. J. Rosenthal," *Oriens* 21 (1968–1969): 436–439.

Berman, Lawrence V. "The Political Interpretation of the Maxim: The Purpose of Philosophy is the Imitation of God," *Studia Islamica* 15 (1961): 53–61.

Braner, Baruch and Eli Fryman, "Gersonides' Commentary on the Torah," *Mahanayyim* 4, no. 2 (2002–2003): 224–241.

Buber, Martin. *Kingship of God*, trans. Richard Scheimann. New York: Harper and Row, 1967.

Burger, Ronna. *Aristotle's Dialogue with Socrates: On the* Nicomachean Ethics. Chicago: University of Chicago Press, 2009.

Buttersworth, Charles. "Philosophy, Ethics, and Virtuous Rule: A Study of Averroes' Commentary on Plato's *Republic*," *Cairo Papers in Social Science* 9, Monograph 1. Cairo: American University in Cairo Press, 1986.

Buttersworth, Charles. "What Is Political Averroism?" in *Averroismus im Mittelalter und in der Renaissance*, eds. Friedrich Niewöhner and Loris Sturlese. Zurich: Spur, 1994: 239–250.

Cates, Diana Fritz. "Conceiving Emotions: Martha Nussbaum's *Upheavals of Thought*," *The Journal of Religious Ethics* 31, no. 2 (2003): 325–341.

Cohen, Carmiel. "Human Endeavor and Trust of God in Gersonides' Biblical Commentaries," *Megadim* 45 (2007): 109–123.

Cohen, Carmiel. *Legal Exegesis Through Peshat in Gersonides' Commentary on the Torah*. PhD Diss., Hebrew University of Jerusalem, 2007.

Dan, Joseph. *Jewish Mysticism and Jewish Ethics*. Seattle: University of Washington Press, 1986.

Davidson, Herbert. "Maimonides' Secret Position on Creation," in *Studies in Medieval Jewish History and Literature*, ed. Isadore Twersky. Cambridge: Harvard University Press, 1979: 16–40.

Davidson, Herbert. "Maimonides' *Shemonah Peraqim* and Alfarabi's *Fusūl al-Madani*," *Proceedings of American Academy for Jewish Research* 31 (1963): 33–50.

Davidson, Herbert. "The Middle Way in Maimonides' Ethics," *Proceedings— American Academy for Jewish Research* 54 (1987): 31–72.

Diamond, James. "Maimonides on Leprosy: Illness as Contemplative Metaphor," *Jewish Quarterly Review* 96, no. 1 (2006): 95–122.

Dobbs-Weinstein, Idit. "Gersonides' Radically Modern Understanding of the Agent Intellect," in *Meeting of the Minds: The Relations Between Medieval and Classical Modern European Philosophy*, ed. Stephen F. Brown. Belgium: Brepols, 1998: 191–213.

Dougherty, M. V. *Moral Dilemmas in Medieval Thought: From Gratian to Aquinas*. Cambridge: Cambridge University Press, 2011.

Drazin, Israel. *Maimonides: The Exceptional Mind*. Jerusalem: Geffen Publishing House, 2008.

Dupre, Louis. *Passage to Modernity: An Essay on the Hermeneutics of Nature and Culture*. New Haven: Yale University Press, 1995.

Eisen, Robert. *Gersonides on Providence, Covenant, and the Chosen People: A Study in Medieval Jewish Philosophy and Biblical Commentary*. Albany: State University of New York Press, 1995.

Eisen, Robert. *The Peace and Violence of Judaism: From the Bible to Modern Zionism*. Oxford: Oxford University Press, 2011.

Eisenmann, Esti. "Social and Political Principles in Gersonides' Thought" in *Religion and Politics in Jewish Thought: Essays in Honor of Aviezer Ravitzky*, eds.

Brown Benjamin, Menachem Lorberbaum, Avinoam Rosenak and Yedidia Z. Stern. Jerusalem: Israel Democracy Institute, 2012: 319–347.

Feldman, Noah. "War and Reason in Maimonides and Averroes," in *The Ethics of War: Shared Problems in Different Traditions*, eds. Richard Sorabji and David Rodin. United Kingdom: Ashgate Publishing, 2006: 92–107.

Feldman, Seymour. "Gersonides and Biblical Exegesis," in Levi Gersonides, *Wars of the Lord*, vol ii, trans. Seymour Feldman. Philadelphia: Jewish Publication Society, 1984: 213–247.

Feldman, Seymour. "Gersonides on the Possibility of Conjunction with the Agent Intellect," *AJS Review* 3 (1978): 99–120.

Feldman, Seymour. *Gersonides: Judaism Within the Limits of Reason*. Oxford: Littman Library, 2010.

Feldman, Seymour. "Introduction," in Levi Gersonides, *Wars of the Lord*, vol. i, trans. Seymour Feldman. Philadelphia: Jewish Publication Society, 1984: 3–67.

Feldman, Seymour. "Synopsis of the *Wars of the Lord*: Book One: Immortality of the Soul," in Levi Gersonides, *Wars of the Lord*, vol. i, trans. Seymour Feldman. Philadelphia: Jewish Publication Society, 1984: 71–84.

Finnis, John. *Natural Law and Natural Rights*. New York: Oxford University Press, 1980.

Fox, Marvin. "The Doctrine of the Mean in Aristotle and Maimonides: A Comparative Study," in *Interpreting Maimonides: Studies in Methodology, Metaphysics, and Moral Philosophy*. Chicago: University of Chicago Press, 1995: 93–123.

Frank, Daniel. "Anger as a Vice: A Maimonidean Critique of Aristotle's *Ethics*," *History of Philosophy Quarterly* 7, no. 3 (1990): 269–281.

Frank, Daniel. "The End of the Guide: Maimonides on the Best Life for Man," *Judaism* 34 (1985): 485–495.

Freudenthal, Gad. "Cosmogonie et physique chez Gersonide," *Revue des études juives* 145 (1986): 295–314.

Freudenthal, Gad. "Gersonide, Génie Solitaire", in *Les Méthodes de Travail de Gersonide et le Maniement du Savoir chez les Scolastiques*, eds. Colette Sirat, Sara Klein-Braslavy et Olga Weijers. Paris: Librairie philosophique J. Vrin, 2003: 291–317.

Freudenthal, Gad. "Human Felicity and Astronomy: Gersonides' War Against Ptolemy," *Da'at* 22 (1989): 55–72.

Frydman-Kohl, Baruch. *Faith, Felicity and Fidelity in the Thought of Yishaq Arama*. PhD Diss., Jewish Theological Seminary of America, 2004.

Funkenstein, Amos. "Gersonides's Biblical Commentary: Science, History, and Providence (or: The Importance of Being Boring)," in *Studies on Gersonides*, ed. Gad Freudenthal. Netherlands: Brill, 1993: 305–15.

Funkenstein, Amos. *Theology and the Scientific Imagination*. Princeton: Princeton University Press, 1988.

Gaziel, Ahuva. "Gersonides' Naturalistic Account of Providence in Light of the *Book of Animals*," *Aleph* 12, no. 2 (2012): 243–271.

Gaziel, Ahuva. *The Biology of Levi Ben Gershom (Gersonides)*. PhD Diss., Bar-Ilan University, 2008.

Gewirth, Alan. *Marsilius of Padua and Medieval Political Philosophy*. New York: Columbia University Press, 1951.

Gewirth, Alan. "Philosophy and Political Thought in the Fourteenth Century," in *The Forward Movement of the Fourteenth Century*, ed. Francis Lee Utley. Columbus: Ohio State University Press, 1961: 125–164.

Gillespie, Michael. *The Theological Origins of Modernity*. Chicago: University of Chicago Press, 2008.

Glasner, Ruth. "The Evolution of the Genre of the Commentary in Gersonides," *Da'at* 74–75: 185–196.

Glasner, Ruth. *Gersonides: A Portrait of a Fourteenth-Century Philosopher-Scientist*. Oxford: Oxford University Press, 2015.

Glasner, Ruth. "Gersonides' Lost Commentary on the Metaphysics," *Medieval Encounters* 4 (1988): 130–157.

Goodman, Lenn. *On Justice: An Essay in Jewish Philosophy*. New Haven: Yale University Press, 1991.

Greenberg, Moshe (ed.). *Jewish Bible Exegesis: An Introduction*. Jerusalem: Mossad Bialik, 1983.

Grisez, Germain, "The First Principle of Practical Reason," in *Aquinas*, ed. Anthony Kenny. New York: Anchor Books, 1969: 340–382.

Guttmann, Julius. *Philosophies of Judaism*, trans. David Silverman. New York: Schocken Books, 1964.

Halivni, David Weiss. *Peshat and Derash: Plain and Applied Meaning in Rabbinic Exegesis*. Oxford: Oxford University Press, 1998.

Hardie, W. F. R. *Aristotle's Ethical Theory*. Oxford: Oxford University Press, 1980.

Harvey, Steven. "Did Gersonides Believe in the Absolute Generation of First Matter?" *Jerusalem Studies in Jewish Thought* 7 (1988): 307–318.

Harvey, Steven. "The Nature and Importance of Averroes' *Middle Commentary* on the *Ethics* and the Extent of Its Influence on Medieval Jewish Philosophy," in *Averroes et les Averroïsmes Juif et Latin*, ed. J.-B. Brenet. Turnhout, Belgium: Brepols, 2007: 257–273.

Harvey, Steven. "The Sources of the Quotations from Aristotle's *Ethics* in the *Guide of the Perplexed* and the *Guide to the Guide*," [Hebrew] *Jerusalem Studies in Jewish Thought* 14 (1998): 100–101.

Harvey, Warren Zev. "Gersonides and Spinoza on Conatus," *Aleph* 12, no. 2 (2012): 273–297.

Harvey, Warren Zev. "Gersonides, Odonis, and the Heart Analogy," in *Studies in the History of Culture and Science: A Tribute to G. Freudenthal*, eds. Resianne Fontaine, Ruth Glasner, Reimund Leicht, and Giuseppe Veltri. Leiden: Brill 2011: 356–359.

Harvey, Warren Zev. "Gersonides on the Sacrificial Cult, Prophecy and Philosophy," in *Wisdom by the Week*, ed. Naftali Rothenberg. New York: Yeshiva University Press, 2011: 307–316.

Harvey, Warren Zev. "Grace or Loving-Kindness," in *Contemporary Jewish Religious Thought: Original Essays on Critical Concepts, and Beliefs*, eds. Arthur Cohen and Paul Mendes-Flohr. The Free Press, NY, 1988: 300–302.

Harvey, Warren Zev. "Love: The Beginning and the End of the Torah," *Tradition* 15, no. 4 (1976): 5–22.

Harvey, Warren Zev. "Maimonides' First Commandment, Physics and Doubt," in *Hazon Nahum: Studies in Jewish Law, Thought and History*, eds. Yaakov Elman and Jeffrey Gurock. New York: Yeshiva University Press, 1997: 149–162.

Harvey, Warren Zev. "Maimonides on Human Perfection, Awe and Politics," in *The Thought of Moses Maimonides: Philosophical and Legal Studies*, eds. Ira Robinson, Lawrence Kaplan, and Julien Bauer. Lewiston, New York: Edwin Mellon Press, 1990: 1–15.

Harvey, Warren Zev. "The Philosopher and Politics: Gersonides and Crescas," in *Scholars and Scholarship: The Interaction Between Judaism and Other Cultures*, ed. Leo Landman. New York: Yeshiva University Press, 1990: 53-65.

Heller-Wilensky, Sarah. *The Philosophy of Isaac 'Arama in the Framework of Philonic Philosophy*. Jerusalem, 1956.

Horwitz, David. *Gersonides' Ethics: The To'alot be-Middot in Ralbag's Biblical Commentaries*. PhD Diss., Yeshiva University, 2006.

Horwitz, David. "*Ha-Haritzut Emet*: Ralbag's View of a Central Pragmatic/ Ethical Characteristic of Abraham," in *Hazon Nahum: Studies in Jewish Law, Thought, and History Presented to Dr. Norman Lamm*, ed. Yaakov Elman and Jeffrey S. Gurock. Hoboken, NJ: Ktav, 1997: 265–309.

Husik, Isaac. *A History of Mediaeval Jewish Philosophy*. New York: Harper and Row, 1966.

Jacobs, Jonathan. "Aristotle and Maimonides: The Ethics of Perfection and the Perfection of Ethics," in *American Catholic Philosophical Quarterly* 76, no. 1 (2002): 145–163.

Jospe, Rafael. "Rejecting Moral Virtue as the Ultimate Human End," in *Studies in Islamic and Judaic Traditions*, ed. William Brinner and Stephen Ricks. Atlanta: Scholars Press, 1986: 185–204.

Kahn, Charles. "Aristotle and Altruism," *Mind* 90, no. 357 (1981): 20–40.

Kaye, Joel. *Economy and Nature in the Fourteenth Century: Money, Market Exchange and the Emergence of Scientific Thought*. Cambridge: Cambridge University Press, 1998.

Kellner, Menachem. "Chosenness, Not Chauvinism: Maimonides on the Chosen People," in *A People Apart: Chosenness and Ritual in Jewish Philosophical Thought*, ed. Daniel Frank. Albany: State University of New York Press, 1993: 51–76, 85–89.

Kellner, Menachem. "*Farteitcht Un Farbessert* (On 'Correcting' Maimonides)," *Meorot* 6, no. 2 (5768): 2–13.

Kellner, Menachem. "Gersonides and His Cultured Despisers: Arama and Abravanel," in *Torah in the Observatory: Gersonides, Maimonides and Song of Songs*. Brighton, MA: Academic Studies Press, 2009: 305–332.

Kellner, Menachem. "Gersonides, Providence and the Rabbinic Tradition," *Journal of the American Academy of Religion* 42, no. 4 (1974): 673–685.

Kellner, Menachem. "Gersonides' To'aliyyot: Sixteenth Century Italy Versus Nineteenth Century Spain," in *As a Perennial Spring: A Festschrift Honoring Rabbi Dr. Norman Lamm*, ed. Bentsi Cohen. New York: Downhill Publishing LLC, 2013: 281–304.

Kellner, Menachem. "Introduction," in Levi Gersonides, *Commentary on Song of Songs*, trans. Menachem Kellner. New Haven: Yale University Press, 1998: xv–xxxi.

Kellner, Menachem. "Maimonides and Gersonides on Astronomy and Metaphysics," in *Torah in the Observatory: Gersonides, Maimonides and Song of Songs*. Brighton, MA: Academic Studies Press, 2009: 149–157.

Kellner, Menachem. "Maimonides and Gersonides on Mosaic Prophecy," *Speculum* 52, no. 1 (1977): 62–79.

Kellner, Menachem. "Philosophical Misogyny in Medieval Jewish Thought: Gersonides vs. Maimonides," in *Y. Sermonetta Memorial Volume*, ed. Aviezer Ravitzky. Jerusalem: Magnes Press, 1998: 113–28.

Kellner, Menachem. "Politics and Perfection: Gersonides vs. Maimonides," *Jewish Political Studies Review* 6 (1994): 49–82.

Kellner, Menachem. "Translator's Introduction," in Levi Gersonides, *Commentary on Song of Songs*, trans. Menachem Kellner. New Haven: Yale University Press, 1998: xv–xxxi.

Klatzkin, Jacob. *Oṣar ha-Munaḥim ha-Filosofiyyim*. Reprint. New York: Feldheim, 1968.

Klein-Braslavy, Sara. "Aristotle's Concept of Chance as an Investigative Tool in Gersonides' *Wars of the Lord*," *Aleph* 12.1 (2012): 65–100.

Klein-Braslavy, Sara. "Determinism, Contingency, Free Choice, and Foreknowledge in Gersonides," in *"Without any Doubt": Gersonides on Method and Knowledge*, trans. Lenn J. Schramm. Leiden: Brill, 2011: 221–296.

Kraut, Richard. *Aristotle on the Human Good*. Princeton: Princeton University Press, 1989.

Kreisel, Howard. *Maimonides' Political Thought: Studies in Ethics, Law, and the Human Ideal*. Albany: State University of New York Press, 1999.

Kreisel, Howard. *Prophecy: The History of an Idea in Medieval Jewish Philosophy*. Dordrecht: Kluwer Academic Publishers, 2001.

Langermann, Tzvi. "Gersonides on Astrology," in Levi Gersonides, *Wars of the Lord*, vol. iii, trans. Seymour Feldman. Philadelphia: Jewish Publication Society, 1999: 506–519.

Langermann, Tzvi. "Gersonides on the Magnet and the Heat of the Sun," in *Studies on Gersonides*, ed. Gad Freudenthal. Leiden: E.J. Brill, 1992: 267–284.

Leibowitz, Nehama. *Studies in Shemot (Exodus)*, trans. Aryeh Newman. vol ii. Jerusalem: World Zionist Organization, 1981.

Lennox, James G. "Aristotle on the Biological Roots of Virtue: The Natural History of Natural Virtue," in *Biology and the Foundation of Ethics* ed. Jane Maienschein and Michael Ruse (Cambridge, 1999): 10–31.

Lockshin, Martin. "Introductory Essay: *Peshat* and *Derash* in Northern France," in *Rashbam's Commentary on Deuteronomy: An Annotated Translation*. Providence: Brown University Press, 2004: 1–25.

Lorberbaum, Menachem. "Maimonides' Concept of Tikkun Olam and the Teleology of Halakha," *Tarbiz* 64 (1994): 64–82.

Lorberbaum, Yair. *Disempowered King: Monarchy in Classical Jewish Literature*. London: Continuum, 2011.

Lutz, Christopher. *Tradition in the Ethics of Alasdair MacIntyre: Relativism, Thomism and Philosophy*. Oxford: Lexington Books, 2004.

MacIntyre, Alasdair. *A Short History of Ethics: A History of Moral Philosophy from the Homeric Age to the Twentieth Century*. 2nd edition. Notre Dame: University of Notre Dame Press, 1988.

MacIntyre, Alasdair. *After Virtue*. 2nd edition. Notre Dame: University of Notre Dame Press, 1984.

MacIntyre, Alasdair. *Three Rival Versions of Moral Enquiry: Encyclopaedia, Genealogy, and Tradition*. Notre Dame: University of Notre Dame Press, 1991.

MacIntyre, Alasdair. *Whose Justice? Which Rationality?* Notre Dame: University of Notre Dame Press, 1988.

Mancha, J. L. "Levi ben Gerson's Astronomical Work: Chronology and Christian Context," *Science in Context* 10, no. 3 (1997): 471–493.

Manekin, Charles. "Conservative Tendencies in Gersonides' Religious Philosophy," in *The Cambridge Companion to Medieval Jewish Thought*, eds. Daniel Frank and Oliver Leaman. Cambridge: Cambridge University Press, 2003: 301–345.

Manekin, Charles. "Freedom Within Reason?: Gersonides on Human Choice," in *Freedom and Moral Responsibility: General and Jewish Perspectives*. College Park: University Press of Maryland, 1997.

Manekin, Charles. "Review of Robert Eisen, *Gersonides on Covenant, Providence, and the Chosen People*," *Jewish Quarterly Review* 88 (1998): 332–336.

Melamed, Abraham. "Maimonides on Women: Formless Matter or Potential Prophet?" in *Perspectives on Jewish Thought and Mysticism*, ed. Alfred Ivry, Elliot Wolfson and Allan Arkush. Amsterdam: Harwood Academic Publishers, 1998: 99–134.

Melamed, Abraham. "The Attitude Towards Democracy in Medieval Jewish Philosophy," *Jewish Political Studies Review* 5, no. 1–2 (1993): 33–56.

Mittleman, Alan. *A Short History of Jewish Ethics: Conduct and Character in the Context of Covenant*. West Sussex: Wiley-Blackwell, 2012.

Moody, Ernest. "Empiricism and Metaphysics in Medieval Philosophy," *Philosophical Review* 67 (1958): 145–163.

Nadler, Steven. "Virtue, Reason, and Moral Luck: Maimonides, Gersonides, Spinoza" in *Spinoza and Medieval Jewish Philosophy*, ed. Steven Nadler. Cambridge: Cambridge University Press, 2014: 152–176.

Nelkin, Dov. *Recovering Jewish Virtue Ethics*. PhD Diss., University of Virginia, 2003.

Nelkin, Dov. "Virtue," in *The Cambridge History of Jewish Philosophy*, eds. Martin Kavka, Zachary Braiterman and David Novak. New York: Cambridge University Press, 2012: 739–758.

Novak, David. *Jewish-Christian Dialogue: A Jewish Justification*. Oxford: Oxford University Press, 1992.

Novak, David. "Maimonides' Concept of Practical Reason," *Rashi* (1993): 615–629.

Novak, David. *The Theology of Nahmanides Systematically Presented*. Atlanta: Brown Judaic Studies, 1992.

Nuriel, Avraham. "The Divine Will in *More Nevukhim*," *Tarbiz* 39, no. 1 (1969): 39–61.

Nussbaum, Martha. "Virtue Ethics: A Misleading Category?" *The Journal of Ethics* 3, no. 3 (1999): 163–201.

O'Connor, David K. "The Aetiology of Justice," in *Essays on the Foundations of Aristotelian Political Science*, eds. Carnes Lord and David O'Connor. Berkley: University of California Press, 1991: 136–164.

Parens, Joshua. "Prudence, Imagination and Determination of Law in Alfarabi and Maimonides," in *Enlightening Revolutions: Essays in Honor of Ralph Lerner*, eds. Svetozar Minkov and Stephane Douard. Oxford: Lexington Books, 2006: 31–56.

Pines, Shlomo. "Naḥmanides on Adam in the Garden of Eden in the Context of Other Interpretations of Genesis, Chapters 2 and 3," in *Exile and Diaspora: Studies in the History of the Jewish People Presented to Haim Beinart*, eds. Aharon Mirsky, Avraham Grossman and Yosef Kaplan. Jerusalem: Ben Zvi Institute, 1988: 159–164.

Pines, Shlomo. "Several Topics in Isaac Pollegar's *'Ezer Ha-Dat* and Their Parallels in Spinoza's Writings," in *Studies in Jewish Mysticism, Philosophy and Ethical Literature—Presented to Isaiah Tishby on His 75th Birthday*. Jerusalem: Magnes Press, 1986: 395–457.

Pines, Shlomo. "Scholasticism After Thomas Aquinas and the Teachings of Hasdai Crescas and His Predecessors," in *Studies in the History of Jewish Thought*, eds. Warren Zev Harvey and Moshe Idel. Jerusalem: Magnes Press, 1997: 489–589.

Pines, Shlomo. "The Limitations of Human Knowledge According to al-Farabi, ibn Bajja, and Maimonides," in *Studies in Medieval Jewish History and Literature*, ed. Isadore Twersky. Cambridge, 1979: 82–109.

Pines, Shlomo. "The Philosophic Sources of *The Guide of the Perplexed*," in Moses Maimonides, *The Guide of the Perplexed*. Chicago: University of Chicago Press, 1963: lvii–cxxxiv.

Pines, Shlomo. "Truth and Falsehood Versus Good and Evil. A Study in Jewish and General Philosophy in Connection with the *Guide of the Perplexed*, I, 2," in *Studies in Maimonides*, ed. Isadore Twersky. Cambridge: Harvard University Press, 1990: 95–157.

Rawls, John. *A Theory of Justice*. Cambridge: Harvard University Press, 1971.

Ravitzky, Aviezer. *Religion and State in Jewish Philosophy: Models of Unity, Division, Collision and Subordination*. Jerusalem: Israel Democracy Institute, 2002.

Ravitzky, Aviezer. "The Political Role of the Philosopher: Samuel Ibn Tibbon Versus Maimonides," in *Maimonidean Studies*, vol. 5, eds. Arthur Hyman and Alfred Ivry. New York: Yeshiva University, 2008: 345–374.

Ross, David. *Aristotle*. London: Methuen, 1923.

Samuelson, Norbert. *The Wars of the Lord. Treatise Three: On God's Knowledge*, trans. Norbert Samuelson. Toronto: The Pontifical Institute for Medieval Studies, 1977.

Samuelson, Norbert. *Judaism and the Doctrine of Creation*. Cambridge: Cambridge University Press, 2007.

Saracheck, Joseph. *Faith and Reason: The Conflict over the Rationalism of Maimonides*. New York: Hermon Press, 1935.

Scholem, Gershom. *ha-Qabbalah be-Gerona*, ed. Joseph Ben Shlomo. Jerusalem: Akademon, 1972.

Schwarzschild, Steven. "Moral Radicalism and 'Middlingness,'" in the Ethics of Maimonides" in *The Pursuit of the Ideal: Jewish Writings of Steven Schwarzschild*, ed. Menachem Kellner. Albany: State University of New York Press, 2009: 137–160.

Schweid, Eliezer. *The Classic Jewish Philosophers: From Saadia Through the Renaissance*, trans. Leonard Levin. Leiden: Brill, 2008.

Seeskin, Kenneth. "Maimonides' Appropriation of Aristotle's Ethics," in *The Reception of Aristotle's Ethics*, ed. Jon Miller. Cambridge: Cambridge University Press, 2013: 107–112.

Septimus, Bernard. "Isaac Arama and the Ethics," in *Jews and Conversos as the Time of the Expulsion*, eds. Yom Tov Assis and Yoseph Kaplan. Jerusalem: The Zalman Shazar Centre for Jewish History, 1999: 1–24.

Septimus, Bernard. "'Open Rebuke and Concealed Love': Nahmanides and the Andalusian Tradition," in *Rabbi Moses Nahmanides (Ramban): Explorations in His Religious and Literary Virtuosity*, ed. Isadore Twersky. Cambridge: Harvard University Press, 1983: 11–34.

Septimus, Bernard. "What Did Maimonides Mean by 'madda'?" in *Meah She'arim: Studies in Medieval Jewish Spiritual Life, in Memory of Isadore Twersky*, eds. Gerald Blidstein, Ezra Fleischer and Bernard Septimus. Jerusalem: Magnes Press, 2001: 96–102.

Shatz, David. "Maimonides' Moral Theory," in *The Cambridge Companion to Maimonides*, ed. Kenneth Seeskin. Cambridge: Cambridge University Press, 2005: 167–192.

Shatzmiller, Yosef. "Gersonides and the Jewish Community of Orange in His Day," in *Studies in the History of the Jewish People and the Land of Israel*, eds. B. Oded, et al. vol. 2. Haifa, 1972: 111–26.

Silver, Daniel Jeremy. *Maimonidean Criticism and the Maimonidean Controversy, 1180–1240*. Leiden: Brill, 1965.

Sirat, Collette. *A History of Jewish Philosophy in the Middle Ages*. Cambridge: Cambridge University Press, 1990.

Sirat, Collette. "Gersonide, la scholastique et le commentaire biblique," 2012. Unpublished.

Sorabji, Richard. "The Role of Intellect in Virtue," in *Essays on Aristotle's Ethics*, ed. Amélie Rorty. California: University of California Press, 1980: 201–219.

Statman, Daniel. "Introduction to Virtue Ethics," in *Virtue Ethics: A Critical Reader*. Edinburgh: Edinburgh University Press, 1997: 1–41.

Staub, Jacob. *The Creation of the World According to Gersonides*. California: Scholars Press, 1982.

Stern, Gregg. *Philosophy and Rabbinic Culture: Jewish Interpretation and Controversy in Medieval Languedoc*. London: Routledge, 2009.

Stern, Robert. "MacIntyre and Historicism," in *After MacIntyre: Critical Perspectives on the World of Alasdair MacIntyre*, eds. John Horton and Susan Mendus. Cambridge: Polity Press, 1994: 146–160.

Stern, Josef. *Problems and Parables of Law: Maimonides and Nahmanides on Reasons for the Commandments (taamei ha-mitzvot)*. Albany: State University of New York Press, 1998.

Strauss, Leo. *Philosophy and Law: Contributions to the Understanding of Maimonides and His Predecessors*. Albany: State University of New York Press, 1995.

Taylor, Charles. "The Politics of Recognition" in *Multiculturalism: Examining the Politics of Recognition*, ed. Amy Gutmann. Princeton: Princeton University Press, 1994: 25–74.

The Jewish Political Tradition, vol. 1, eds. Michael Walzer, Menachem Lorberbaum and Noam J. Zohar. New Haven: Yale University Press, 2000.

Tirosh-Samuelson, Hava. *Happiness in Pre-modern Judaism: Virtue, Knowledge and Well-Being*. Cincinnati: Hebrew Union College Press, 2003.

Touati, Charles. *La Pensée Philosophique et Théologique de Gersonide*. Paris: Les Éditions de Minuit, 1973.

Twersky, Isadore. "Maimonides on Eretz Yisrael: Halakhic, Philosophic and Historical Perspectives," in *Perspectives on Maimonides: Philosophical and Historical Studies*, ed. Joel L. Kraemer. London: Littman Library of Jewish Civilization, 1996: 257–290.

Tzeitkin, Yechiel. *The Characteristics of Biblical Exegesis in the Works of Peshat Commentators of the Maimonidean School of Provence in the 13th and 14th Centuries.* PhD Diss., Bar-Ilan University, 2011.

Tzeitkin, Yechiel. "'The Straight Path Our Forefathers Followed': To'alot Interpretation of Biblical Narratives in Provençal Exegesis," *Jewish Studies (Ma'adei ha-Yahadut)* 49 (2013): 103–130.

Uyl, Douglas J. Den. *The Virtue of Prudence.* New York: Peter Lang Publishing, 1991.

Walsh, James J. "Nominalism and the Ethics: Some Remarks About Buridan's Commentary," *Journal of the History of Philosophy* 4, no. 1 (1966): 1–13.

Walsh, James J. "Some Relationships Between Gerald Odo's and John Buridan's Commentaries on Aristotle's *Ethics*," *Franciscan Studies* 35: 237–275.

Weil, A.-M. "Levi ben Gershom et sa bibliothèque privée," in *Gersonide en son temps*, ed. G. Dahan. Louvain: Peeters, 1991: 45–59.

Weinrib, Ernest. "Aristotle's Forms of Justice," *Ratio Juris* 2, no. 3 (1989): 211–26.

Weiss, Raymond. *Maimonides' Ethics: The Encounter of Philosophic and Religious Morality.* Chicago: University of Chicago Press, 1991.

Weiss, Roslyn. "Natural Order or Divine Will: Maimonides on Cosmogony and Prophecy," *Journal of Jewish Thought and Philosophy* 15 no. 1 (2007): 1–26.

Werblonsky, R. J. Z. "Faith, Hope and Trust: A Study in the Concept of *Bittahon*," in *Papers of the Institute of Jewish Studies*, vol. 1. London, 1964: 95–139.

Wieland, George. "The Reception and Interpretation of Aristotle's Ethics," in *The Cambridge History of Later Medieval Philosophy*, eds. Norman Kretzmann, Anthony Kenny, Jan Pinborg and Eleonore Stump. Cambridge: Cambridge University Press, 1982: 657–672.

Wolfson, Harry. *Crescas' Critique of Aristotle: Problems of Aristotle's Physics in Jewish and Arabic Philosophy.* Cambridge: Harvard University Press, 1971.

Wolfson, Harry. "Maimonides and Gersonides on Divine Attributes as Ambiguous Terms," in *Mordecai M. Kaplan Jubilee Volume, on the Occasion of His Seventieth Birthday*, English Section. New York: Jewish Theological Seminary of America, 1953: 515–530.

INDEX

A

Aaron, 44, 128, 140, 141, 144

Abarbanel, Isaac, 166

Abel, 30, 31, 49, 94, 95, 133, 160, 169n25

Abimelech, 33, 110, 111, 143, 163

Abraham, 13, 33, 35–8, 40–3, 45, 51n17, 56n96, 59n170, 61n230, 78–82, 102–4, 106–11, 134, 143, 145–7, 160–3, 168n5

Absalom, 44, 77

Account of the Chariot, 70, 86n48

Adam, 21, 29, 50n17, 69, 99, 160, 167n4

Agent Intellect, 23, 24, 33, 50n15, 69–74, 87n70, 93, 121n130, 126, 127, 141, 159

Ahasuerus, 76, 79, 81, 82, 101, 102

Alexander of Aphrodisias, 50n15

Al-Farabi, Abu Nasr, 11n2, 52n30, 67, 93, 125, 130, 149n47, 150n54, 151n78

Altmann, Alexander, 14n26, 67, 85n32, 85n34, 170n42

altruism, 2, 3, 49, 63–91, 125

Amalek, 44, 76, 139, 143

Amnon, 44

anger, 4, 11n1, 49, 101, 102, 130, 137, 146

Aquinas, Thomas, 51n21, 93, 115n8, 119n74

synderesis, 51n21

'Arama, Isaac, 166, 172n81

Aristotle

De Anima, 27, 57n106

Metaphysics, 5, 8, 11n1, 63, 94

Nicomachean Ethics, 5, 7, 11n2, 21, 22, 27, 51n22, 52n24, 64, 96, 100, 111, 118n56, 121n115, 144, 148n16, 154n174, 154n176

Organon, 10

Politics, 85n37, 123

Topics, 8

art, 12n7, 21, 26, 28–31, 53n37, 64, 95

Note: Page numbers with "n" denote notes.

© The Author(s) 2016

A. Green, *The Virtue Ethics of Levi Gersonides*, DOI 10.1007/978-3-319-40820-0

astrology, 8, 9, 23, 25, 26, 52n27,
    86n46, 170n37
astronomy, 8, 9, 13n14, 16n34,
    16n40, 25, 55n88, 69–73,
    86n46, 86n50
Averroes (Ibn Rushd)
    De Anima, 8, 10, 27, 54n48, 78
    De Animalibus, 6, 8, 10, 78
    De Caelo, 8, 10
    De Generatione et Corruptione, 8, 10
    Meteorology, 8, 10
    Organon, 10
    Physics, 8, 10
    Porphyry's Isagoge, 10
    Republic, 4, 7, 95, 111, 112,
        121n116, 121n117, 125, 126,
        130, 149n46, 150n54

B
Balaam, 44
Barak, 38
belief (*'emuna*), 157, 159, 163
beneficence (*haṭava*), 3, 63, 73, 77
Berger, David, 158, 168n6, 168n8,
    168n10, 171n59
Boaz, 75–7
Buber, Martin, 135, 151n77
Buridan, John, 97, 98, 116n37,
    117–18n53
Buttersworth, Charles, 15n32, 130,
    149n46

C
Cain, 30, 31, 49, 94, 95, 133
celestial spheres, 9, 71
chance, 23–6, 33, 41, 46, 47,
    52n25–7, 79, 143
character, 2, 5, 9, 12n5, 12n7, 19, 27,
    31–3, 35, 49, 55n67, 60n187, 72,
    78, 79, 81, 97, 102, 112, 115n4,
    120n105, 133, 154n176, 157, 158

choice, 4, 12n5, 52n28, 56n96, 64,
    65, 95–104, 106, 107, 114,
    119n84, 119n88, 128
circumcision, 47
Cohen, Hermann, 67, 85n29
conflict, 3, 40, 65, 91, 92, 104–14,
    121n118, 132, 134, 146, 167n1
consideration, 67, 100
consultation, 100, 101, 118n56
contentedness, 32, 33
Cordovero, Moses, ix
courage, 2, 32, 33, 44, 140, 143
creation, biblical account, 8, 10
cunning (*hithakmut*), 2, 19, 33, 43

D
David, 34, 44–6, 75–7, 97, 115, 137,
    138, 158, 164
death, 24, 36, 37, 76, 109, 110, 113,
    134, 141, 146, 157, 160
deliberation, 12n5, 22, 27, 91,
    98–105, 114, 118n56, 119n84
diligence (*ḥariṣut*), 2, 19, 33, 42, 43,
    106
Dinah, 113
divine overflow, 43, 106, 161
divine providence, 74, 133, 161, 163,
    164
divine will, 55n77, 158
Dobbs-Weinstein, Idit, 114, 121n130

E
Egypt, 12n2, 37, 38, 40–2, 44, 76,
    95, 96, 102–4, 106, 107, 127,
    136, 137, 146, 160, 162, 164
Ehud ben Gera, 46
Eisenmann, Esti, 10, 17n48, 17n49,
    60n184, 125, 148n9, 148n19,
    151n82, 151n86, 153n151
Eisen, Robert, 10, 17n48, 61n230, 72,
    88n77, 120n99, 152n122, 170n44

Eliezer, 16n43, 36, 38, 43
endeavor *(hishtadlut)*, 2, 19, 33–9, 42, 75, 76, 79, 138, 140, 157, 162, 163
Enoch, 31, 69
Esau, 37, 38, 40, 41, 44, 78, 82, 102, 146
Esther, 6, 9, 10, 35, 38, 39, 41, 58n140, 58n143, 58n144, 59n159, 59n165, 59n167, 79, 81, 90n131, 100, 101, 107, 117n50, 118n63, 118n64, 118n73, 121n119–23, 139, 143
Eve, 21, 29, 50n17
Ezra, 10, 12n6, 140, 152n123, 165n5

F
family, 35–7, 40, 46, 91, 96, 97, 104, 109, 133, 140, 141, 144–7
firmament, 71
food, 20, 21, 24, 27, 30, 31, 35, 42, 43, 47, 80–5, 95–7, 99, 102, 103, 106–8, 121n118, 133, 144–6, 162, 163
'foolish pietist,' 107, 108, 119n93
friendship, 39, 40, 64–6, 84n11, 96, 144–7, 154n171, 154n176
Funkenstein, Amos, 10, 17n47, 165, 172n76

G
Gabirol, Joseph ibn, ix
Galen, 6, 32
Garden of Eden, 21, 28, 71, 99, 167n4
Gerald Odonis, 7, 97
Gersonides, Levi
    Commentaries on Averroes; *De Anima*, 8, 10, 27, 33, 42; *De Animalibus*, 6, 8, 10, 33, 78; *De Caelo*, 8, 10; *De Generatione et Corruptione*, 8, 10; *Meteorology*, 8, 10; *Physics*, 8, 10, 33

Commentaries on Bible; *Chronicles*, 10, 102; *Daniel*, 10; *Deuteronomy*, 125, 136; *Ecclesiastes*, 8, 10, 99; *Esther*, 6, 9, 10, 35, 58n140, 59n165, 59n167, 121n119; *Exodus*, 43, 44, 89n101, 128, 129, 152n125, 152n128, 152n129; *Ezra and Nehemiah*, 10; *Genesis*, 9, 29, 33, 40, 49, 53n32, 54n63, 58n129, 59n170, 70, 71, 80, 87n60, 99, 102, 107, 110, 118n56, 171n49; *Joshua*, 119n95; *Judges*, 135, 138, 152n104; *Kings*, 24, 33, 120n97, 135, 152n104, 170n39; *Leviticus*, 52n27, 61n217, 61n219, 61n222, 90n146, 116n15, 152n127, 153n143, 153n164, 169n30; *Numbers*, 58n139, 59n164, 59n174, 60n191, 88n81, 116n19, 119n95, 148n25, 149n39, 153n142, 153n145, 155n195; *Proverbs*, 5, 10, 14n19, 43, 45, 60n87, 60n180, 60n182, 60n202, 79, 80, 89n99, 89n112, 89n114, 89n119, 89n121, 89n123, 89n125, 89n128, 90n133–5, 116n21, 118n58, 118n60, 118n62, 118n66, 118n68, 119n80, 120n110, 139, 150n52, 152n121; *Ruth*, 10, 59n179, 89n95, 89n96; *Samuel*, 24, 53n32, 88n89, 89n97, 153n157; *Song of Songs*, 10, 28, 35, 50n12–14, 54n56, 56n88, 57n108, 86n50, 86n51, 87n70, 88n76, 115n12, 134, 150n71
Wars of the Lord, 6, 8–11, 14n23, 15n29, 16n36, 16n44, 23–26, 29, 41, 50n7–10, 50n15,

Gersonides, Levi (*cont.*)
  52n29, 52n31, 53n34, 53n36,
  53n39, 54n50, 54n57,
  54n59–60, 55n65, 55n88,
  57n103, 59n163, 60n187,
  73–74, 85n40, 86n47, 87n54,
  87n56–57, 87n61, 87n63,
  87n67, 87n73, 88n74, 88n76,
  88n79, 88n82, 89n100, 95,
  115n12–13, 116n21, 126–128,
  143, 148n17, 148n19,
  153n148, 160, 166, 169n17,
  170n39, 172n72
God
  altruistic, 3, 63, 66, 67, 69, 72, 73
  intellect, 23, 29–32, 50n15, 63, 67,
    69, 70, 72, 73, 104, 127–9,
    132, 140, 141, 143, 144, 157,
    159
  thirteen attributes, 77
  unmoved mover, 63
golden calf, 44, 130
Goliath, 138
grace (*ḥanina*), 3, 63, 73, 74, 77

H
Hagar, 35, 36, 38, 104, 109,
  120n105, 146, 163
Haman, 38, 39, 41, 101, 112, 113
ḥanina. See grace
ḥariṣut. See diligence
Harvey, Warren Zev, 14n27, 16n45,
  35, 57n102, 57n104, 57n106,
  88n78, 89n101, 124, 170n32
heavenly bodies, 24–6, 33, 70, 71,
  73–5, 126, 127, 148n19, 161
ḥesed. See loving-kindness
hishtadlut. See endeavor
hitḥakmut. See cunning
honor, 17n48, 22, 37, 39, 52n24,
  54n63, 79, 81, 137, 139, 145, 146

Horwitz, David, 10, 13n14, 15n33,
  17n48, 17n49, 56n96, 59n168,
  72, 88n75, 132, 150n53,
  171n46, 171n71

I
Ibn Tibbon, Samuel, 13n13, 69,
  86n42, 86n44, 150n54, 151n78,
  157
Isaac, 16n43, 36–8, 59n170, 78, 160,
  163, 166
Ishmael, 120n105, 146, 169

J
Jabal, 31
Jacob, 36–8, 40, 41, 46, 56n96, 70,
  78, 80, 82, 101, 102, 108, 113,
  114, 126, 134, 137, 145, 146,
  159, 160, 164, 166
Jacobs, Jonathan, 99, 117n46
Jacob's ladder, 126
'Jacob's Staff,' 70
Jeremiah, 67, 69, 85n28,
  86n44, 103
Jeroboam, 139
Jethro, 75, 76, 97, 129
Joab, 44
Jochebed, 36
Jonathan, 45, 76, 97, 99, 117n46,
  163
Joseph, 37–41, 45, 80, 95–7, 102,
  103, 113, 114, 134, 137, 146,
  164, 167n1
Joshua, 45, 109, 110, 119n95,
  143
Judah, 7, 14n26, 15n30, 37, 40,
  52n24, 56n102, 95, 118n56,
  126, 137, 170n42
justice, 43, 65, 67–9, 73, 75, 84n16,
  91–121, 134, 144, 163

K

Kant, Immanuel, 67, 90n132, 120n96
Kaspi, Joseph ibn
  Terumat Kesef, 7, 14n28
  Yoreh De'ah, 7, 13n12, 14n28
Kellner, Menachem, 11, 13n18,
  16n45, 51n17, 55n88, 85n30,
  85n40, 85n51, 86n44, 94, 124,
  142, 147n3, 153n147, 165,
  172n79, 172n81, 173n83
kingship, 3, 123, 124, 130, 133, 135,
  137–9, 142, 147, 151n77,
  152n122
kisharon ha-ma'ase, 99, 100, 117n47,
  117n48
Klein-Braslavy, Sara, 14n20, 23–5,
  52n25–8, 53n33
Kreisel, Howard, 99

L

Laban, 36, 40, 80, 82, 108,
  146, 159
Land of Canaan. *See also* Land
  of Israel
  Gersonides, 36, 106
  Maimonides, 108
  Naḥmanides, 162
Land of Israel, 43, 138, 160–3,
  171n44, 172n78
Lockshin, Martin, 165, 172n77
Lot, 33, 36, 40, 59n170, 104, 108,
  134, 145, 146
loving-kindness (*ḥesed*), 3, 63, 66–8,
  73–7
Luck. *See* chance
Luzzato, Moses Hayyim, ix

M

MacIntyre, Alasdair, ix, viii, x
  tradition, ix, viii, x

magnificence, 32
Maharih, Yeḥi'el ben Shlomo,
  13n18, 166
Maimonides, Moses
  Book of Knowledge, 1, 12n6
  Eight Chapters, 1, 11n2, 32,
    149n39, 154n176
  Guide of the Perplexed, 12n2, 46,
    50n17, 99
  Land of Israel (*see* Land of
    Canaan)
  Laws of Character Traits, 1,
    154n176
  Mishneh Torah, 1, 2, 12n2, 108,
    138, 157, 160
  prophet, 3, 51n17, 68, 73, 93,
    123–7, 130, 138, 143, 147
  sacrifices (*see* sacrifices)
Marcaria, Jacob, 166, 173n84
Marsilius of Padua, 7, 15n33,
  51–2n22, 97, 116n34, 132,
  150n55, 150n57
material intellect, 21, 50n15, 71,
  72, 126, 128, 132, 140,
  144, 158
'measure for measure,' 94, 116n20
'merit of the forefathers,' 159,
  168n16
messiah, 108
milk and meat, 46, 82
miracle, 24, 29, 53n32, 158, 159,
  161, 162, 168n6, 168n8, 169n19
  public *vs.* secret miracles
    (*see* Naḥmanides)
Miriam, 37, 38
Mordechai, 75, 76, 79, 80, 82, 100,
  112–14, 139, 143
Moses, 1, 13n13, 36–8, 40, 44,
  57n103, 66, 68, 75, 76, 95, 97,
  126–30, 134, 141, 143, 147,
  148n24, 157, 158, 168n6,
  168n7, 172n76

N
Naḥmanides, Moses
  Land of Israel (*see* Land of Canaan)
  public *vs.* secret miracles, 159
negative theology, 68, 72, 85n38
Nehemiah, 10, 82
New year, 48
Nimrod, 134
Noah, 31, 49, 69, 121n114, 145, 160,
  169n25
Novak, David, 83n3, 158, 168n6,
  168n7, 168n11–13, 169n27,
  170n41, 171n46, 171n49,
  171n56, 171n62, 172n68

P
Paquda, Bahya ibn, ix
Passover, 48
peace, 3, 7, 40, 75–7, 82, 91, 97,
  104–14, 116n34, 120n96,
  120n99, 120n105, 120n114,
  121n118, 125, 128, 134, 143,
  146, 163
peshat, 17n48, 164, 165, 168n5,
  172n75, 172n77
Pharaoh, 36, 39, 40, 95–7, 107, 127,
  128, 137, 139, 143, 162
philosopher-king. *See* prophecy
physical preservation, 3, 19–61, 104,
  123, 125, 139
Pinchas, 38
Pines, Shlomo, 50n17, 52n30,
  60n186, 67, 85n31, 117n41,
  167n4
Plato
  Laws, 92
  Phaedo, 6, 14n24
  Republic, 112, 121n116, 121n117,
    125, 126, 130, 131, 148n16,
    149n46, 150n54

practical intellect, 8, 19–23, 25–7,
  29–33, 35, 51n21, 128, 132,
  135, 143, 158
practical wisdom, 2, 3, 12n5, 21, 22,
  27, 32, 51n21, 51n22, 91–121,
  130
pride, 137
priesthood, 3, 123–5, 133,
  140–2, 144, 147, 152n122,
  153n162
property, 42, 66, 91, 104–14, 139,
  159
prophecy, 24, 26, 53n36, 55n77, 71,
  85n40, 102, 126–9, 141, 143,
  148n19, 160, 161, 170n32
purity, 47

Q
Quran, 111, 120n114

R
Rahab, 45
Ravitzky, Aviezer, 17n48, 51n17, 69,
  86n42, 86n44, 86n45, 147n1,
  167n3
Rebecca, 37, 43
Rehoboam, 139
Reuben, 41
ruse ('*orma*). *See* cunning (*hithakmut*)
Ruth, 10, 14n25, 14n27, 15n34,
  16n37, 43, 59n179, 76, 86n48,
  89n95, 89n96

S
Saadya Gaon, 66, 84n25
sacrifices
  Maimonides, 160, 169n30
  Nachmanides, 160, 169n25

Samuel, 7, 13n13, 14n26, 15n30, 24,
    52n24, 53n32, 69, 83n3, 84n25,
    86n42, 86n44, 88n89, 89n97,
    95, 118n56, 126, 130, 135, 136,
    139, 143, 144, 150n54, 151n78,
    153n157, 157
Samuel ben Judah of Marseille, 7,
    14n26, 15n30, 52n24, 95, 126
Sarah, 35–8, 41, 59n170, 103, 104,
    109, 111, 120n105, 134, 146,
    163n5
Saul, 24, 44, 75, 76, 139, 143
Scholem, Gershom, 158, 168n7
Schwartzchild, Steven, 67
separate intellects, 70
shame, 29, 30, 55n67, 82
Shechem, 113, 134, 164
Simeon, 113
Sirat, Colette, 4, 13n13, 14n20,
    16n41, 16n43
Socrates, 6, 131, 154n174
soul
    appetitive faculty, 20, 22, 23, 104
    imaginative faculty, 20, 42
    nutritive faculty, 1
    rational faculty, 21
    sentient faculty, 20
Stern, Josef, 160, 169n28
stratagems (taḥbulot), 2, 19, 33, 43–5,
    138
synderesis. See Aquinas, Thomas

T
taḥbulot. See stratagems
Taylor, Charles, xiin1
Temple, 103, 138–41, 161, 169n26

Theimistius, 50n15
Touati, Charles, 17n46,
    115n12, 117n53, 123–4,
    147n2, 151n87, 152n122,
    152n123, 169n23
Tower of Babel, 31, 134
trust (biṭaḥon), 157
Tubal-Cain, 31
Tzelafchad, 42

V
virtue
    intellectual virtue, 21, 43, 72, 123
    mean, 2, 33, 49
    moral virtue, 2, 3, 5, 15n31, 21, 32,
        33, 44, 49, 56n92, 64, 65, 67,
        68, 92, 93, 97, 137, 167n3
    virtue of altruism, 2, 63–90
    virtue of physical preservation,
        26–46

W
war, 20, 33, 43–45, 76, 108–112,
    114, 120n114, 121n117, 127,
    130, 134–136, 138–139,
    143–144, 146, 163
wealth, 42, 43, 52n24, 98,
    136, 144
Weiss Halivni, David, 164, 172n75
Weiss, Raymond, 11n1, 99
William of Ockham, 7, 97, 132

Z
Zedekiah, 103, 139, 140